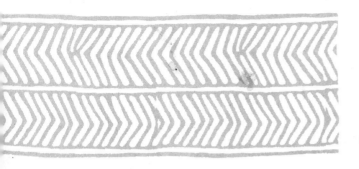

La c
de la
frontera

La cocína de la frontera

MEXICAN-AMERICAN COOKING FROM THE SOUTHWEST

JAMES W. PEYTON

SANTA FE

RED CRANE BOOKS

FIRST EDITION

Manufactured in the United States of America

Book design by Jos. Trautwein

Photography by James W. Peyton

Drawings by Andrea Peyton

Cover painting by Diana Bryer

Designs and art applications are from
Precolumbian Mexico (1971) and *Ancient Mexico* (1953),
both by Jorge Enciso, published by Dover Publications, Inc.

Library of Congress Cataloging-in-Publication Data

Peyton, James W.
    La cocina de la frontera:Mexican-American cooking
from the Southwest / James W. Peyton. — 1st ed.
        p.   cm.
    Includes bibliographical references and index.
    ISBN 1-878610-34-1
    1. Cookery, American—Southwestern style.
2. Cookery, Mexican.   I. Title.
TX715.2.S69P48
641.5979—dc20   93-33788
                                                      CIP

Red Crane Books
826 Camino de Monte Rey
Santa Fe, New Mexico 87505

To the Mexican-American people, who, by sharing their cuisine, have given all Americans one more thing for which to be thankful.

ACKNOWLEDGMENTS

I would like to thank the many friends and acquaintances who helped with this project. Unfortunately, over the many years when I had no idea that I would someday write a book, I did not keep a record of the names of those who were of assistance. Therefore, I ask for the indulgence of those whose names may have been omitted. In any case, many thanks to the following who helped in one important way or another.

Ray Salcido, Katy Meek, Elena Hannon, Catalina Gonzáles, Truman Smith, Judy England, Lillian Guitierrez, Susan and Bill Yanda, Lucinda Hutson, Andrea Schneider, Al Regensburg, José Ortega, Creighton Robinson, Orlando Casados, Bo and Kenny Beanland and Kenny's parents Mary and Kenneth Beanland, Carlotta Dunn Flores, John Thomas, Vernon Price, Joe Haynes, Carlos García, Orlando Romero, Mary Lou Mendoza, Rudy Lira, Elsie Timoskevich, and Edmundo Flores; Ann Mason, who edited this book, and Jos. Trautwein, who designed it; the fantastic staff of Red Crane Books, and most especially Carol Caruthers, Jim Mafchir, Winnie Culp, Marguerite Culp, and Marianne and Michael O'Shaughnessy.

A special thanks to Murrae Haynes and Michael O'Shaughnessy, without whose technical and artistic expertise the photographs would not have attained the level of professionalism which they did.

And, most importantly, thanks to my mother, Georgina Peyton, for years of encouragement, and to my wife, Andrea, for the fine drawings and more than there is space to mention.

CONTENTS

*"La primera pareja humana—
segun el Popol Vuh—fue modela-
da por Dioses con maíz, y no con
barro como en la tradición cris-
tiana occidental. Olmecas, mayas,
nahuas, y sus descendientes en
Mesoamerica fueron, entonces,
hombres y mujeres de maíz e
hicieron de ése grano su base ali-
menticia."*

"The first human couple—according to Popol Vuh [the Mayan story
of the creation]—was formed by
the Gods from corn, and not with
clay as in the Western Christian
tradition. Olmecs, Mayas, Nahuas,
and their descendants in Middle
America were, therefore, men and
women of corn and they made this
grain their sustenance."

(From the preface to Teresa Castelló Yturbide's book
Presencia de la comida prehispanica *written by*
Fernando Gamboa.)

e love it, often to the point of addiction. We used to search for it in hole-in-the-wall cafés but now often find it in colorful, upscale restaurants. It is prepared in different ways in various parts of the country, and we are fiercely loyal to our favorite version. It is America's most popular ethnic cooking style. We call it "Mexican" food.

Our appreciation is appropriate, but our definition is not accurate. The cuisine in question is not really "Mexican," except in the sense that most of its forms originated in Mexico. Actually, the cooking is Mexican-American. It was derived from several regional styles of native Mexican cooking and transformed to its present state on this side of the border. Like people from nearby but different regions these styles have both similarities and distinctions. However, when linked by their common origins and the collective events that nurtured their development, they form a cuisine that is uniquely Mexican-American.

Brought to us originally through restaurants founded by immigrants, Mexican-American cooking has engendered a wider interest in the cuisines of Mexico's interior, as evidenced by the large number of books on the subject of Mexican cooking now in print. Amazingly, Mexican-American cooking itself, which was responsible for this popularity in the first place, has been left almost entirely out of the cookbook boom.

La Cocina de la Frontera: Mexican-American Cooking from the Southwest for the first time presents a comprehensive overview of Mexican-American cooking from both a historical and culinary perspective: where it came from; how it evolved; how it relates to other aspects of Mexican cooking; regional variations of the cuisine in the southwestern United States; and, most importantly, how to prepare the dishes that have made it so popular.

Focusing on the styles found in California, Arizona, New Mexico, and Texas, the book explores the regional diversity of the cuisine. The relationship between the cooking in each of these areas and that from the part of Mexico from which most of its immigrants came is explained. Further, in order to put the history of Mexican-American cooking in proper perspective, there are also chapters containing some of the finest pre-Hispanic and post-Hispanic recipes from Mexico's interior. Included is the most complete collection of Mexican-American recipes to date, many of them from the best Mexican-American cooks in homes and restaurants.

The recipes in the book represent the culmination of more than eighteen years of research on Mexican-American cooking. In collecting the recipes for this book as I did for my previous book, *El Norte: The Cuisine of Northern Mexico*, I traveled widely throughout the southwestern United States and Mexico, gleaning favorite recipes from cooks in homes and restaurants. In addition to such firsthand sources, for this book I also researched out-of-print cookbooks, some from around the turn of the century. Before including the most interesting of these recipes, I checked with acquaintances in various regions to determine whether they were still part of the cuisine and then tested the modern versions against the originals to determine whether they merited inclusion. The recipes I decided to include were the best interpretations of the recipes I researched and sometimes resulted from a combination of aspects of several different recipes. The primary criteria I used for the collection were whether the dish was an important part of the cuisine and whether it had universal appeal. (I did deviate from these criteria in a few instances, such as the section on "Variety Dishes," where the dishes were of historical importance to the cuisine even though they might lack universal appeal.) All recipes in this collection were kitchen-tested, and my personal adjust-

Preparing tortillas near the Tampico branch of the Mexican railroad.

Courtesy of The Library of the Daughters of the Republic of Texas at the Alamo, 71–217.

ments were made where I felt it to be necessary. With today's health-conscious individuals in mind, in numerous sections I have included "nutrition hints" that indicate ways in which the recipes can be adapted to low-fat or low-cholesterol diets. The book also contains an entire chapter on the red chile "master" sauces which are responsible for much of this style of cooking's uniqueness and popularity.

Although most of the ingredients necessary to prepare the recipes in this book are widely available in United States supermarkets, a list of mail-order sources is included in the Appendix, enabling cooks, no matter where they live, to prepare the cuisine's most popular dishes in all their variations.

It is my hope that in addition to offering cooks of many regions a comprehensive collection of extraordinary recipes, this book will also provide the reader with a new understanding of the Mexican-American people, who, by sharing their cooking, have given us one more thing for which to be thankful.

introduction

When I was growing up during the 1950s in southern California, just north of San Diego, my family often went to a "Mexican" restaurant called Tony's. In those days not many Anglos were familiar with this kind of cooking. But a family friend, Ray Salcido, was also a friend of Tony's, and took us there the first time and many times afterwards.

Situated in what was euphemistically called Eden Gardens, a tiny Mexican-American community just north of Del Mar, Tony's was a place of adventure and new tastes to a young person—the first evidence that eating could be infinitely more than just something one was ordered to do. It was a place where even a youngster, with a youthful appetite unencumbered by worries of weight gain, could barely finish the combination plate. As the years went by Tony's became a tradition, a place to go for family celebrations and reunions, not to mention an inexpensive spot to take a date.

When I was at college in San Antonio, places like Mi Tierra, La Fonda, and the hole-in-the-wall Taco Land served essentially the same purposes. Later, in Dallas for graduate school, Casa Dominguez became a locale I frequented regularly. When I traveled to and from California, I never failed to stop at La Posta in Mesilla, New Mexico, while El Pinto and La Placita were never missed on trips to Albuquerque to visit friends.

All these restaurants were places where I felt comfortable; they were homes away from home, locales where stress disappeared and all was right with the world. These were places you needed to be—at least once a week. Just approaching the buildings and getting the first whiff of simmering chile sauce and steaming corn tortillas ordered the taste buds to full alert. And even though you often had to wait for a table, it did not matter because you knew that within seconds of being seated you would be served a large basket of hot tortilla chips, accompanied by a bowl of salsa.

Without realizing it Mexican food had gradually become an important part of my culture, as it has become for so many other Anglos.

A few years later while spending a year and a half abroad, where Mexican food was unavailable, the importance of this food to me became very evident as I experienced acute withdrawal-like symptoms. Some experts believe that the near narcotic effect on some people of food spiced with chile, especially Mexican food, is due to the fact that chiles release endorphins in the brain, chemical substances which resemble morphine. All I can say is that although East Indian curries, fiery Thai food, and the chile-infused offerings of Hunan and Sichuan cuisines helped alleviate my symptoms of "withdrawal," they never were quite

Chile stand in San Antonio's Military Plaza, circa 1937.

Courtesy of The Institute of Texan Cultures, San Antonio, Texas, 83–477.

The original Tony's Jacal, circa 1949.

Courtesy of Catalina Gonzáles.

enough. Perhaps it is the *combination* of chile, corn, and cheese found in most Mexican-American dishes that enhances the effect.

Later, I had a similar experience during the first of five years I spent in Hawaii, where decent "Mexican" food was just as unobtainable. In frustration I bought every cookbook on the subject only to be disappointed. Nowhere were instructions for cooking anything resembling the dishes from my favorite restaurants; instead, the recipes in these books were either for unfamiliar dishes from Mexico's interior or they were too "gringoized."

Fortunately, I was able to take a five-week break on the mainland each year and spent a good part of that time traveling in the southwestern United States and Mexico, collecting recipes. It was from this experience that my first book, *El Norte: The Cuisine of Northern Mexico*, grew.

During these trips not only did I notice that the cooking changed as one moved from northern to southern Mexico, but also that there was a distinct difference between the food on one side of the border and that found on the other side. A comparison of the dishes served in border towns such as Douglas, Arizona, across from Agua Prieta; El Paso, Texas, across from Ciudad Juárez; and Del Rio, Texas, across from Ciudad Acuña, demonstrated this fact clearly and consistently. It became evident that while the "Mexican" cooking on the United States side did not have the variety of traditional entrée dishes found in Mexico, it compensated with a far greater selection of *antojitos mexicanos*, the traditional corn- and tortilla-based Mexican specialties. Cheddar cheese and ground meat were almost unknown in Mexico, while the white *asadero* cheese and boiled shredded beef so popular in Mexico were rare in the United States, except in the better restaurants in Arizona and California. There were also other differences, including the way enchiladas were prepared in Mexico, without the same large quantity of sauce and the final heating done in the United States.

Just as evident as the changes in the cuisine from one side of the border to the other were the differences as one traveled from east to west within the United States. While the "Mexican" cooking within specific states was quite similar, there were significant differences between the "Mexican" cooking of one state and another. It became clear that not only did the "Mexican" cooking found on the United States side of the border consistently differ from that found in Mexico, but also that there were equally distinct variations between the cooking of one area and another.

For example, while the cooking in Phoenix and Tucson was quite similar, nowhere else did I find the *machaca* or enchilada-style *chimichangas* found in these cities. Equally distinctive was the *carne guisada* and thick Tex-Mex chile gravy served on enchiladas and combination plates in San Antonio, Austin, and Dallas; or the traditional red and green chile sauces and *sopaipillas* that are ubiquitous in Las Cruces, Albuquerque, and Santa Fe, New Mexico; or the turkey tamales and seafood tacos of California. All these specialties and many more just seemed to stop at state lines.

These early impressions of the regional differences in Mexican-American cooking came almost entirely from restaurant fare. However, my experience of the last eighteen years, five of them spent in Arizona and the rest in Texas, has confirmed the accuracy of these early observations. Such distinctions can still be made, in spite of the fact that each year the lines become more blurred so that now *chimichangas* are widely found in New Mexico, crab enchiladas in Arizona, and a few attempts at *sopaipillas* are being made in Texas.

In addition to numerous regional differences in Mexican-American cooking, I also discovered that there are some significant variations between the food found in Mexican-American homes and that found in popular restaurants. First, many of the garnishes and combinations found in Mexican-American restaurants are eschewed in home use. Mexican-Americans are not much different from other Americans in their eating habits, and to think that they sit down each evening to the Number 1 combination plate would be erroneous. Instead, they frequently partake of the standard American fare, including the food of other ethnic cuisines, as well as dishes traditional in their own culture.

Second, there are many home-style dishes served by Mexican-American families which one cannot find in restaurants. For example, while the use of recipes based on variety meats seems to be declining, such recipes are still fairly common in Mexican-American homes. However, except for *Barbacoa*, these dishes are almost never found on menus, particularly in restaurants frequented by Anglos. In Mexican-American culture, as in many other cultures, the original objective of many home-style dishes was to provide nourishment at minimum cost. Because of this the recipes for such dishes often rely on what today would be considered an inordinate amount of lard or oil. Consequently, with today's health consciousness in mind, for this book I selected typical home-style dishes whose fat content could be reduced to a more acceptable level without seriously undermining their integrity. Although I have included enough of these recipes to provide a feeling for the genre, the majority of this collection of recipes consists of the more familiar dishes that have made all Americans fall in love with Mexican-American cooking.

These issues, while important, are but additions to the main objectives of the book—to provide the most comprehensive collection of Mexican-American recipes to date and to instruct the reader in their preparation. The instructions and techniques provided will enable even the novice cook to prepare recipes as fine as those served in any Mexican-American home or restaurant.

In addition, in order to foster a better understanding of Mexican-Americans and their cuisine, I have included background material on the origins of Mexican cooking and the historical forces which influenced its development in each area of the Southwest. Besides the fact that Mexican-American cooking is so delicious it is essential that these people, who are playing an ever more important role in the lives of all Americans, be more fully understood. And attempting to understand their cooking, the merit of which most Americans agree upon, is a fine place to start. As Joe S. Graham said in his article "Mexican-American Traditional Foodways at La Junta De Los Rios": "To have something so fundamental as foods not only be accepted but liked, sometimes passionately, is to have one's culture validated. It is a small but important victory over Anglo culture, which is often quite hostile to other aspects of Mexican-American culture (p. 1)." It is my hope that this book will contribute to the appreciation and recognition of Mexican-American cuisine, which continues to achieve ever greater heights of popularity.

ORigins

MEXICAN COOKING

*t*o understand Mexican-American cooking fully, we must first look into Mexican cooking from its inception among the pre-Columbian Indians to its current forms. The development of contemporary Mexico, including its cooking, commenced on Good Friday in 1519 when Hernán Cortés landed at present-day Veracruz, Mexico. It was then that the Spanish and Indian cultures began to merge, eventually creating the culture we know today as Mexican.

The Spaniards came to the New World as conquerors, representing their country and their church, which to many of them were one and the same. Their goal was to obtain treasure for the Crown as well as personal wealth. And if they could simultaneously convert some of the "heathen," so much the better. Because the conquistadors were on a mission of conquest and had brought few women with them, they needed cooks and enlisted local Indian women as household servants. It was in this way that the Spaniards were introduced to the native cuisine. As time went on, marriage and less formal liaisons brought the two cultures even closer together.

Descriptions of the Indians of the era (usually the Aztecs, who played a dominant role in south-central Mexico at the time) often imply that they were a homogeneous collection of peoples sharing similar characteristics. However, if this were entirely true Mexican culture, including its cuisine, would be much more uniform (and less interesting) than it is. To me, a great deal of Mexico's charm is its diversity, due, in large part, to the influence of numerous tribes of Indians, including the Mayas of the

Yucatán, the Zapotecs and Mixtecs of Oaxaca, the Terrascas of Michoacán, and the Tarahumaras, Yaquis, Seris, and Huicholes of northern Mexico.

The Spanish found south-central Mexico with a well-developed if somewhat violent culture, including a cuisine that was surprisingly sophisticated. The famous historian and Franciscan Friar Bernardino Sahagún, in his work *Historia General de las Cosas de Nueva España*, describes the food and related customs in detail, including more than seven kinds of tortillas, such as hot, white, folded tortillas; thick, white, large tortillas; and little, oblong breads about the size of the palm of a hand. He tells of more than six types of tamales with various fillings, some unfilled, and some that were decorated with "shells" made of beans; as well as grilled hens and quail; *empanadas* filled with chicken and yellow chiles; and dishes of hen with tomatoes and ground squash seeds. Another dish of frog with green chile is described, as are dishes, perhaps less appetizing to us, such as tadpoles, winged ants, and worms from the maguey cactus (pp. 305–08).

More to our liking would be the dish of lobster that Sahagún describes as a *"muy sabrosa comida"* ("very delicious food"), as well as the one of little white fish, yellow chiles, tomatoes, and unripened plums. There were several *atoles* (corn-based gruel) flavored with chiles and honey. And he tells of the many chocolate drinks, some flavored with honey and various herbs, poured from ornate jugs and stirred with spoons made of turtle shell.

Numerous early chronicles portray the sophistication of the Indian cultures and cuisines of the era. Hernán Cortés, in his second letter to the emperor Charles V, included in *Hernán Cortés: Letters from Mexico*, describes Tlaxcala as follows:

> The . . . city is much larger than Granada and very much stronger, with as good buildings and many more people than Granada had when it was taken, and very much better supplied with the produce of the land, namely, bread, fowl and game and fresh-water fish and vegetables and other things they eat which are very good. There is in this city a market where each and every day upward of thirty thousand people come to buy and sell, without counting the other trade which goes on elsewhere in the city (p. 67).

After describing the vast array of items available at the market, including "jewelry of gold and silver," "pottery of many sorts," and "firewood and charcoal and medicinal and cooking herbs," Cortés goes on to portray the sumptuous daily meals at Montezuma's palace:

> When they brought food to Mutezuma [*sic*] they also provided for all those chiefs to each according to his rank; and their servants and followers were also given to eat. The pantry and the wine stores were left open each day for those who wished to eat and drink. Three or four hundred boys came bringing the dishes, which were without number, for each time he lunched or dined, he was brought every kind of food: meat, fish, fruit and vegetables. And because the climate is cold, beneath each plate and bowl they brought a brazier with hot coals so that the food should not go cold. They placed all these dishes together in a great room where he ate, which was almost always full. . . . While he ate, there were five or six old men, who sat apart from him; to them he gave a portion of all he was eating. One of the servants

Shaping masa, *San Antonio, Texas.*

Courtesy of The Institute of Texan Cultures, The San Antonio Light Collection, 1759-AA.

set down and removed the plates of food and called to others who were farther away for all that was required. Before and after the meal they gave water for his hands and a towel which once used was never used again, and likewise with the plates and bowls, for when they brought more food they always used new ones, and the same with the braziers (pp. 111–12).

It is clear that when the Spaniards arrived in America the Aztecs were not just scrounging a few ears of corn and killing a squirrel now and then. Instead, they had a highly developed cuisine and related traditions. Frederick A. Peterson sums up the extensive development of their culture in his book *Ancient Mexico*:

The Spaniards found in America an advanced agriculture lacking only plough animals, and a well-organized economic system. The Indians had discovered the uses and properties of hundreds of plants and animals. They were already cultivating plants from which they obtained food, spices, flavourings, medicines, poisons, fibres, gums, dyes and paints, and we owe to their intelligent observation our present knowledge of at least forty foods which have improved world living conditions (p. 166).

Peterson goes on to state that the "American Indian raised over fifty species of beans (ibid.)" and mentions that the spices used by pre-Columbian Indians included chile, oregano, coriander, and sage. These were used to flavor innumerable stews of vegetables, meat, fish, and fowl, which included quail, dove, pigeon, duck, and turkey. Peterson concludes that, "The great variety of Indian products suggests that Mexico gained less economically from contact with the Old World than it gave (p. 170)."

This thesis has been expanded more recently by Jack Weatherford in *Indian Givers*, who declares that:

In America the importance of Indian foods continued without interruption by the European invasion. Even though the Europeans did bring bread, dairy products, and new meats with them these only supplemented but did not replace the American diet. Instead, the Europeans learned to eat American-style. This is nowhere more obvious than in Mexico, where beans and corn continued as the staples of the cuisine (p. 107).

This is not to say that the Spanish contributions to the cuisine of beef, pork, lamb, rice, wheat, milk, cheese, butter, lard, cinnamon, and sugar were not significant; certainly the use of meat from domestic animals was viewed as easier and more acceptable than catching and butchering armadillos, iguanas, rabbits, and deer. But a tamale or taco was (and is) still a tamale or taco whether made with traditional Indian game or Iberian-bred pork.

It is important to include a comment on the use of fat by the pre-Hispanic Indians. The fact that lard was introduced by the Spanish is often taken to mean that the original Indian menu was nearly fat free. The truth is that while prior to the introduction of lard, fat for cooking was more difficult to obtain and was probably used in much less quantity, it was certainly part of most dishes in the Indian diet. In her fascinating book *Cocina prehispanica*, Ana M. de Benitez states: "Beyond a doubt, the ancient inhabitants of Mexico knew how to cook with fats and vegetable oils. They used the fats of the wild boar, the turkey and the armadillo. . . . Vegetable oils were obtained from peanuts and pumpkin seeds (p. 43)."

The importance of Spanish contributions to the cuisine of Mexico undoubtedly varied according to climate and natural resources. For example, the Spanish contributions were of relatively less importance in south-central Mexico than in the north and west. In the south the Indians had the advantages of a temperate climate, ample rainfall, and an abundance of fruits, wild fowl, and other animals. However, tribes in the north and west experienced little of the variety or sophistication of the cooking of the south. To them the ingredients introduced by the Spanish were much more significant.

It is possible to get a sense of the limited variety of food available to the northern Indians compared to the abundance that covered the Aztec table by looking at the diet of the Tarahumara Indians who still live in the deep, wild canyons of the state of Chihuahua. As I have observed during many visits over the last ten years, the traditional, basic diet of corn, beans, squash, and chiles still prevails with not a great deal of variety for those still living in the old way. It follows that newly conscripted Indian cooks in northern or western Mexico of the early colonial era were surely a great deal more affected by the new Spanish comestibles than their southern counterparts. In addition, the introduction of cattle, sheep, goats, and wheat had a tremendous impact in the more arid climates.

Where natural resources were favorable, the Indians' food culture developed to a much greater degree than in regions where life was more arduous. In addition to the degree of development, styles of cooking varied based on the differences in the resources which provided the basic ingredients. About the only constants throughout the land were the staples of corn, beans, and squash, for even the types of chiles varied from one area to another, giving regional dishes different characters.

Thus many factors contributed to the evolution of the different styles of cooking that developed among the early Indians—climate and resources as well as the influence of Spanish ingredients to various degrees. From this viewpoint it would surely be surprising if Mexican cooking were as homogeneous as is often inferred.

Although there are many ways Mexican cuisine could be categorized, dividing it into three basic types of dishes is the one I prefer. (It is important to note that I do not mean to imply that all Mexican dishes fall into one of these categories. Mexican cooking is far too complex and unstructured for that to be possible. In reality, many dishes in one category share characteristics with dishes in others. Nevertheless, generalizations such as the following can be made and are useful in understanding the cuisine.) The first category includes entrée dishes of meat, fish, and poultry which came substantially from the Spanish table. These are the dishes found in upper-class homes and restaurants, and with which most gringos are probably least acquainted. *Biftec á la plancha*, grilled or fried fish in garlic sauce, and *Arroz con pollo* (p. 290) are typical of this category. However, even these dishes which most reflect Spanish origins are usually served with beans, tortillas, and a chile salsa.

The second category of Mexican cooking includes the famous stews and soups of southern Mexico. These range in complexity from the simple dishes, still close to their pre-Hispanic roots, such as the more basic *pipiánes*, to the haute cuisine dishes such as *Chiles en nogada* (p. 36) and the more elaborate *moles*. Examples of the former are found in the section on "Pre-Hispanic Recipes" and the latter, most of which resulted from the collaboration between the Spanish sisters and Indian cooks, are in the section on "Post-Hispanic Mexican Recipes."

The third category of Mexican cooking is what in Mexico is called *antojitos mexicanos*. This classification usually refers to snacks or light meals, particularly among the wealthy. However, for the poor, this aspect of the cuisine often constitutes the principal diet. Included in this category are the corn- and tortilla-based specialties such as tacos, tamales, and enchiladas. These are the direct descendants of original Indian dishes. While Spanish-introduced ingredients, particularly lard, cheese, beef, and pork, are used extensively in these recipes, their basic form and much of their content are Indian in origin. This is also the branch of Mexican cooking most familiar to us in the United States, since it is the *antojitos* that make up the majority of dishes on the menus of Mexican-American restaurants.

The preceding discussion and everything else I have learned about Mexican food causes me to question the usual description of it as a melting pot of Spanish and Indian cooking. To me it is more an absorption by the Indian cuisine of the Spanish ingredients. And it is the *antojitos*, overwhelmingly the most important category of Mexican-American cooking, that most reflect the Indian heritage of Mexican cuisine.

As the famous Mexican journalist and gastronome Salvador Novo said so poetically in his seminal book *Cocina Mexicana*: "*Pero advirtamos, complacidos, que en esta larga, lenta, venturosa gestación, los cromosomas culinarios de los mexicas prevalecieron sobre los genes de los españoles. Estos acabarán por comer chile. Exclamarán, reconocerán*

> '*que el pipián es célebre comida,*
> *que al sabor dél, os comeréis las manos (p. 32).*' "

Loosely translated this means: "But, let us point out, happily, that in this long, slow, successful gestation, the culinary chromosomes of the *mexicas* prevailed over the genes of the Spaniards. They will end up eating chile. They will exclaim, they will acknowledge:

'that the *pipián* is a renowned food,

that upon tasting it, you will lick your fingers.'"

Sebastián Verti substantiates this in his *Tradiciones mexicanas*: "*El Mole tiene una larga carrera histórica y con ella sigue el destino de su pueblo: si los pueblos indígenas habían de mezclarse con el español, los platillos de su mesa harían lo mismo. Puede aseverarse del mole, que este monumento gastronómico es producto no de las imaginación de una monjita, sino del devenir de la historia (p. 292).*" Again, loosely translated this means: "*Mole* has a long historical career which follows the destiny of its people. If the indigenous people had to mix with the Spanish, the dishes of their table did the same thing. But you can assert about the *mole* that this gastronomical monument is a product, not of the imagination of a nun, but evolved from history."

PRE-HISPANIC AND MEXICAN HAUTE CUISINE RECIPES

In order to provide a feel for the elements that make up Mexican cooking and a contrast to the aspects of the cuisine with which we are most familiar, I have included the following recipes. They are representative of both the pre-Hispanic and the more complex haute cuisine cooking that was developed to a high art by the Spanish sisters following the conquest.

The pre-Hispanic Indian recipes were selected both for their appeal to the North American palate and to illustrate the fact that pre-Hispanic cuisine, while certainly more basic than current Mexican cooking, was

Baking in a horno, *Chamita, New Mexico.*

Courtesy of Museum of New Mexico, Neg. No. 146094.

not something that would be considered crude subsistence fare. Interestingly, you will find that these recipes are right in line with today's emphasis on a low-fat diet and the use of fresh ingredients.

Sources of the pre-Hispanic recipes are the writings of Bernardino Sahagún and other primary sources, as well as three excellent books on the subject, including *Presencia de la comida prehispanica* by Teresa Castelló Yturbide, *Cocina prehispanica mexicana* by Heriberto García Rivas, and *Cocina prehispanica* by Ana M. de Benitez.

The modern Mexican recipes come entirely from recent explorations, during which I spent considerable time with some of Puebla's and Oaxaca's best cooks. These recipes are included to illustrate the differences between current "high" Mexican cooking and pre-Hispanic cooking on the one hand, and the Mexican-American recipes that follow on the other. The second and possibly most important reason I included these recipes is that they are simply some of the best I have ever found. *¡Buen provecho!*

PRE-HISPANIC RECIPES

GUACAMOLE

2 large avocados, peeled
   and seeded
1 tomato, chopped
2 serrano chiles, seeded and
   minced
   Juice from 1 lime
½ teaspoon salt, or to taste

Yes, the Indians invented this famous dish!

As *Presencia de la comida prehispanica* by Teresa Castelló Yturbide points out, because of the shape of the fruit, the Aztecs called the avocado tree *árbol de testículos,* or testicle tree.

Grind all the ingredients together in a *molcajete* and serve. *Serves 4 as an appetizer or a garnish for tacos.*

ENSALADA DE CAMARONES

Shrimp Salad

1 pound small shrimp,
   peeled and deveined
2 tomatoes, chopped
¼ cup onion, minced
2–4 serrano chiles, seeded and
   minced
2 avocados, peeled, seeded,
   and chopped
¼ cup toasted pumpkin
   seeds, ground in a
   molcajete
¼ cup lime juice
2 tablespoons orange juice
1 tablespoon cooking oil
½ teaspoon salt, or to taste

Place the shrimp in boiling water, remove the pot from the heat, and allow to cook for 1 minute. Drain the shrimp and allow them to come to room temperature.

Combine the shrimp with the tomatoes, onion, chiles, avocados, and pumpkin seeds.

Combine the lime juice, orange juice, oil, and salt and toss the mixture with the other ingredients. *Serves 4.*

SOPA DE PESCADO

Fish Soup

Combine the *pulque* or beer and water and bring to a boil.

Add the remaining broth ingredients and simmer, covered, for ½ hour; then strain the broth into a bowl and discard the other ingredients.

Return the broth to a boil, add the squash, and simmer for 10 minutes. Add the fish and simmer for 3 minutes or until the fish is just cooked.

Serve the soup in bowls, accompanied by the lime wedges. *Serves 4.*

FOR THE BROTH:

1 *cup* **pulque** *or flat beer*
1 *quart water*
1 *pound of fish heads, skin, tails, and bones*
½ *onion, chopped*
2 *tomatoes, chopped*
1 *poblano,* **Anaheim,** *or* **New Mexico** *chile, seeded and chopped*
½ *teaspoon salt, or to taste*
1 *teaspoon oregano*

FOR THE SOUP:

2 *cups squash, chopped*
1 *pound white fish filets (catfish is fine)*
2 *limes, cut into wedges*

SOPA DE PAPAS

Potato Soup

Boil the potatoes in water to cover until they are just tender.

Instead of grinding the remaining ingredients in a *molcajete* as the Indians did, place them in a blender and blend for 1 minute.

Pour the mixture from the blender into a large pot and add enough water to make a total of 4 cups. Bring the liquid to a boil, add the potatoes, and simmer for 10 minutes. *Serves 4.*

1 *quart very small red potatoes, with or without peels*
3 *pounds tomatoes, peeled, seeded, and chopped*
1 *tablespoon* **pequín** *chiles*
½ *teaspoon salt, or to taste*
Water

POLLO PIBIL

Pit-cooked Chicken

FOR THE MARINADE:

1 *tablespoon powdered* **achiote** *or annatto seeds*

½ *tablespoon oregano*

3 *cloves garlic, minced*

1½ *tablespoons onion, minced*

1 *teaspoon salt*

3 *tablespoons orange juice*

1 *tablespoon lime juice*

1 *tablespoon cider vinegar*

2 serrano *or* jalapeño *chiles, seeded and minced*

FOR THE CHICKEN:

2 *large, skinned chicken breasts, cut into 2 pieces each, or a total of 4 pieces*

Banana leaves or foil

1 *tomato, sliced*

1 *small onion, peeled and sliced into thin rounds*

If you have seen pictures of prepared ants, grasshoppers, and worms in pre-Hispanic cookbooks and they evoked a feeling of repugnance, try this delectable Mayan dish instead. In fact, to impress guests serve it with a complete pre-Columbian meal, including *Ensalada de camarones* (p. 28) and *Sopa de pescado* (p. 29).

Today, *Pollo pibil* is cooked very much as it was by the Mayans before Cortés's arrival, except that instead of being prepared in the classic *pib*, or pit, it is usually baked in an oven.

The best way to simulate the pit-cooking method is to use a water smoker. If you do not care to do this, wrap the chicken in foil instead of banana leaves and cook it directly on the coals for 20 minutes. You will lose some of the steamy, smoky taste and texture, but the flavor will be excellent and the time required for cooking much shorter. (You may even prefer this method since the banana leaves add a strong flavor to the dish.)

Annatto seed (whole or ground) and banana leaves (frozen or fresh) can be found in stores specializing in South American and Caribbean food products.

To make the marinade blend all the ingredients into a paste. If you are using whole annatto seeds instead of the powdered variety, either grind them in a spice or coffee grinder or simmer them in water for 5 minutes, leave them in the water overnight, and then grind them together with the other ingredients in a blender.

Coat the chicken with the marinade and leave, covered, overnight in your refrigerator. Before the final preparation allow the chicken to come to room temperature.

Cut the banana leaves into pieces large enough to wrap 1 breast, and simmer them in water to cover for 15 minutes to make them pliable. Banana leaves are frustrating to work with since they tear easily. Do not attempt to tear them. Instead, use a knife or scissors.

When the leaves have cooled enough to handle, place a breast on each of them. Top the breasts with the sliced tomato and a layer of large pieces of sliced onion, then fold and tie the leaves to make 4 packages.

If you are cooking with a water smoker, cook for about 1½ hours.

If you are using the alternate method of cooking, wrap the ingredients in 2 layers of regular weight aluminum foil cut in pieces measuring 12 inches square. Heat the coals until nearly grey; then place the packages, bone side down, directly on the coals. Cook for 5 minutes, then turn the packages and cook another 5 minutes. Repeat the process for a total of 20 minutes and serve. *Serves 4.*

However you cook the chicken serve it with pickled onion rings, the recipe for which follows.

PICKLED ONION RINGS

Mix all the ingredients except the onions together in a saucepan and bring to a boil. Simmer for 5 minutes and pour into a nonreactive bowl over the onions. Cover and allow to steep for 1 hour. *Serves 4.*

1 *cup vinegar*
⅔ *cup water*
6 *tablespoons orange juice*
1 *teaspoon oregano*
2 *cloves garlic, crushed*
2 serrano *or* jalapeño *chiles, minced*
½ *teaspoon salt, or to taste*
2 *onions, cut into separated rings*

Pato en Pipián Verde

Duck in Green Pipián

FOR THE SAUCE:

- **1 pound** tomatillos
- **½ cup** pumpkin seeds
- **2** poblano *chiles, peeled, seeded, and chopped*
- **⅓ cup** peanuts
- **½ cup** onion, chopped
- **2** cloves garlic
- **½ tablespoon** cider vinegar
- **1 tablespoon** honey
- **½ teaspoon** salt, or to taste

FOR THE DUCK:

- **1 or 2** ducks or Cornish game hens, cut into serving pieces
- **1 tablespoon** cooking oil

Pipiáns are the forerunners of the *moles*. They are basically stews that are thickened by their own ingredients, such as pumpkin seed and ground tortillas, instead of with flour or cornstarch.

As duck is not always available I find that Cornish game hens make a decent (and less expensive) substitute. Also, since our domestic, farm-raised birds have far more fat than the wild ducks caught by the Aztecs, you should remove at least ¾ of the skin.

Cover the *tomatillos* with water and simmer until they are tender, 5 to 10 minutes; then place them in a blender.

Meanwhile, heat a skillet over medium heat and "toast" the pumpkin seeds, stirring often. They will pop and dance around like popcorn as they are roasted. Do not allow them to burn. Add the toasted seeds and the remaining sauce ingredients to the blender and blend, adding enough water to make a total of 4 cups.

To make the duck, heat a pot over medium heat, add the oil, then brown the duck pieces.

Add the sauce to the pot, bring to a boil, and simmer until the duck is cooked, about 20 to 30 minutes.

Serve this dish with steamed squash and fresh, hot corn tortillas. *Serves 4.*

POST-HISPANIC MEXICAN RECIPES

ENCHILADAS CON CREMA

This recipe is my rendition of the enchiladas served at the Café de Tacuba, my favorite restaurant in Mexico City, where they are called *Enchiladas especiales Tacuba*. Among its other claims to fame the Café de Tacuba is said to be the restaurant where Señor Sánchez in Oscar Lewis's *Children of Sánchez* worked.

This dish is simple, delicious, and a perfect example of French influence on Mexican cooking. Serve one or two of these enchiladas with a thin piece of tenderloin and you have the equally famous *Filete Tacuba*.

FOR THE SAUCE:

2 *tablespoons* poblano *chile, peeled, seeded, and minced*

2 *tablespoons spinach, washed and minced*

2 *cups whipping cream*

3 *tablespoons butter*

Place the chile, spinach, and half the cream in a blender and blend for 15 seconds or until the vegetables are pureed.

Melt the butter over medium heat and stir in the puree. Add the remaining cream, stirring constantly. Simmer the sauce until it is slightly thickened, about 5 minutes.

Preheat your oven to 350 degrees.

Soften the tortillas in hot oil according to the instructions in the section on enchiladas (see p. 205).

Moisten the Shredded Chicken with a little of the sauce, then roll about 2 tablespoons of the mixture in each tortilla and place on ovenproof dinner plates.

Cover the enchiladas with the sauce, top with the cheese, and bake for 10 minutes, or until the cheese begins to brown. *Serves 4.*

FOR THE ENCHILADAS:

12 *corn tortillas*

1 *recipe Shredded Chicken (p. 158)*

4 *ounces Swiss cheese, shredded*

MOLE POBLANO

Puebla-style Mole

1½ *quarts homemade chicken or turkey broth*
Cooking oil

SPICE MIXTURE:

1 *tomato, broiled until well charred*

¼ *cup* tomatillos, *chopped*

½ *teaspoon coriander seeds*

½ *teaspoon chile seeds*

3 *tablespoons sesame seeds*

¼ *teaspoon anise seeds*

2 *cloves*

½ *-inch piece stick cinnamon*

¼ *teaspoon black peppercorns*

3 *tablespoons pumpkin seeds*

2 *tablespoons roasted peanuts*

2 *tablespoons almonds*

2 *tablespoons raisins*

3 *tablespoons dried prunes, chopped*

3 *-inch piece of plantain, or substitute banana*

½ *corn tortilla*

½ *piece white bread*

Although most accounts, legendary and otherwise, credit the sisters of the convent of Santa Rosa in Puebla with inventing *Mole poblano*, this is probably not the entire story. Nearly all the important ingredients for this recipe—turkey, chiles, tortillas, chocolate, and squash seeds—were being used by the Aztecs long before the Spanish arrived; and numerous similar dishes are described by historians of pre-Hispanic Indian culture. Nevertheless, although the Indians provided the basic structure and ingredients for *Mole poblano* and many similar recipes, according to all the written accounts, these dishes achieved their current forms in the convents. The sisters' responsibilities included supervising the cooking, particularly the feasts that were prepared for visiting dignitaries. They added ingredients like sesame seeds, lard, and cinnamon to the basic Aztec recipes, tinkering with them endlessly, desiring to honor and impress their important guests.

This is my favorite version of this classic dish.

Place the broiled tomato in the container of a blender.

Fry the *tomatillos* in a little oil until just soft (about 5 minutes), drain, and add to the blender.

Heat a medium-size heavy skillet over low heat and toast the coriander seeds, chile seeds, sesame seeds, anise seeds, cloves, cinnamon, and peppercorns, stirring constantly until the sesame seeds just begin to brown (3 to 5 minutes). Add the toasted seeds and spices to the blender. (For a smoother texture, grind these items in a coffee or spice grinder before placing them in the blender.)

Fry the pumpkin seeds in a little oil until they puff up. Be careful since they will pop and spatter oil in the process. Drain and add to the blender.

Fry the peanuts, almonds, raisins, and prunes in a little oil for about 2 minutes or until the raisins are puffed but not browned. Drain and add to the blender.

Fry the plantain in some oil until it just begins to brown; drain it and add it to the blender.

Fry the tortilla and bread in a little oil. Drain them, chop coarsely, and add them to the blender.

Blend the spice mixture, adding just enough chicken broth to make a thick paste. Remove the paste to a bowl.

CHILE PASTE:

Traditionally, at this point the chiles are fried in a little oil until they just begin to darken and become fragrant. Alternately, you can toast the chiles by placing them in a 275-degree oven for 5 to 10 minutes or until they become fragrant; but do not allow them to scorch.

After either frying or toasting the chiles, place them in a bowl, cover them with hot water, and soak them for 20 minutes. Next, remove the stems, seeds, and veins, and place the chiles in the blender. Add just enough of the soaking liquid to blend the chiles to a paste. Strain the paste using a food mill.

FINAL ASSEMBLY:

Heat the oil over medium-high heat in a large heavy skillet and quickly brown the chicken breasts; then remove and reserve them.

Heat the lard over low heat in a saucepan large enough to hold the spice and chile mixtures. Add the chile mixture and cook, barely at a simmer, for 5 minutes. Add the spice mixture and continue simmering for another 5 minutes. Then add enough broth to produce a sauce about as thick as a thin milk shake. It should just coat a spoon. Then add the sugar and chocolate and stir to incorporate.

CHILES:

8 mulato *chiles*
4 ancho *chiles*
4 pasilla *chiles*
1 chipotle *chile*

FINAL ASSEMBLY:

2 *tablespoons cooking oil*
3–4 *boneless, skinless chicken breasts, cut in half*
¼ *cup lard*
Chile paste
Spice mixture
1–2 *cups chicken broth*
1 *tablespoon sugar*
1 *ounce Mexican or semisweet chocolate*
2–3 *tablespoons sesame seeds for garnish*

Add the chicken breasts and simmer, uncovered, for 5 to 10 minutes or until just cooked through.

Serve the dish garnished with the sesame seeds.

To prepare *Mole enchiladas*, simply wrap the shredded chicken in corn tortillas which have been softened in hot oil, top with the sauce, garnish with sesame seeds, and heat at 350 degrees for 10 minutes. For more detailed instructions on making enchiladas, see p. 204. *Serves 4.*

CHILES EN NOGADA
Chiles with Walnut Cream Sauce

THE CHILES:

8 poblano *chiles*

THE FILLING:

3 *tablespoons cooking oil*

⅔ *cup onion, minced*

2 *cloves garlic, minced*

1½ *pounds lean ground pork*

6 *tablespoons raisins*

6 *tablespoons blanched,
   slivered almonds*

1½ *pounds tomatoes, peeled,
   seeded, and chopped*

1 *cup peaches, chopped*

1 *cup pears, chopped, or
   substitute apples*

This is the classic dish that was invented to celebrate the defeat of the French at Puebla on the holiday that is now called Cinco de Mayo. Ironically, the use of cream shows a strong French influence, but nevertheless this is one of Mexico's premier gastronomic accomplishments. It makes a fantastic luncheon dish or first course, one that is surprisingly easy to prepare. In fact, virtually the entire preparation can be done a day ahead of serving. (This dish is often served *capeado*, or deep-fried with an egg batter, but I find this version too rich.)

To prepare the chiles for stuffing, first remove the skins: either roast the chiles over an open flame until the skins are well charred or deep-fry them until the skins turn white. (If you choose the latter method, be careful of spattering oil. Drain the chiles on paper towels.) After preparing them using one of these two methods, place the chiles in a plastic bag and leave them for 20 minutes.

Then peel off the chile skins, make a slit in one side of each chile, and carefully remove the seeds.

To make the filling, heat the oil in a heavy skillet over medium heat. Add the onion and garlic and cook until just soft, but not browned.

Add and brown the pork, pour off the excess oil (to keep the dish from being greasy), and add the remaining filling ingredients except for the sherry.

Turn the heat to low and simmer the sauce, stirring frequently, until most of the liquid has evaporated, about 15 minutes. Stir in the sherry and continue cooking for 5 minutes.

Fill each chile with about ¼ cup of the filling, and place 2 on each of 4 serving plates.

Cover the walnuts with boiling water and leave for 5 minutes. Drain the nuts, and when they are cool enough to handle, remove their skins.

Meanwhile, place the bread in ¼ cup of the milk to soak, reserving the remaining ½ cup milk.

Place the nuts, bread, cream, cheeses, cinnamon, and sugar in a blender. Blend the mixture until smooth, adding just enough of the reserved milk to make a thick sauce (about the consistency of a thick milk shake).

Cover the stuffed chiles completely with the sauce and garnish with the pomegranate seeds and parsley. Serve at room temperature. *Serves 4.*

¼ *teaspoon ground cinnamon*

1 *teaspoon salt*

½ *teaspoon ground black pepper*

¼ *cup dry sherry*

THE SAUCE:

⅓ *pound walnuts, shelled*

1 *piece bread, crust removed*

¾ *cup milk*

1 *cup whipping cream*

⅓ *pound Monterey Jack cheese, grated*

2 *tablespoons cream cheese, softened*

½ *teaspoon ground cinnamon*

2 *teaspoons sugar*

THE GARNISH:

Seeds from 1 pomegranate

2 *tablespoons parsley, minced*

ESTOFADO DE POLLO

Chicken Stew

5	*tablespoons lard or olive oil*
2	*small onions, chopped*
10	*small cloves garlic, peeled and chopped*
3¼	*pounds tomatoes, chopped*
1	*8–10-ounce jar pitted green olives*
¼	*pound raisins*
2	*tablespoons sugar*
1½	*tablespoons dried thyme*
2–2½	*tablespoons loosely packed, broken cinnamon sticks*
	Salt to taste
¼	*pound whole almonds*
2½–3	*pounds chicken, cut into serving pieces, with ⅔ skins removed*
	Garlic salt
½	*of 7-ounce can of* pickled *serrano* chiles *(105 grams net weight)*
¼	*cup parsley, minced*

Chicken stew? Doesn't sound like much? It didn't to me either. But my interest was somewhat pricked when Carmen Solis, with whom I was studying cooking in Oaxaca, informed me that it is one of the seven famous *moles*. What a surprise as I watched the dish begin to unfold and could see something special was happening.

Estofado de pollo is one of those dishes that appeals to nearly everyone. The heat level, which is not intense in the first place, is easily adjusted. It is also very easy to prepare and can be made a day or two in advance; in fact, it's much better that way.

The whole, cut-up chicken is cooked with the stew. If you are careful, there will be lots of sauce left over. Simply refrigerate it, then use it to simmer boneless, skinless chicken breast for 5 minutes or so, or until it is done, and you will have several other meals in no more time than that.

Heat 2½ tablespoons lard or olive oil in a large pot over medium heat. Add the onions and garlic and cook until just soft, but not browned. Then add the tomatoes.

Chop half the olives and raisins (reserving the remaining portions), add them to the pot, and continue to cook for 2 minutes. Add the sugar, thyme, cinnamon sticks, and salt and cook 5 minutes.

Meanwhile, boil the almonds for 5 to 10 minutes, allow them to cool, and then remove the skins.

Place the cooked sauce mixture and half the almonds in a blender and blend for 1 minute. You may have to do this in 2 batches.

Sprinkle the chicken pieces with garlic salt; then fry them in the remaining 2½ tablespoons lard or olive oil over medium to medium-high heat in a large pot or Dutch oven until well browned.

Strain the blended sauce into the pot with the chicken. Add the reserved whole olives and raisins, the almonds, the ½ can of chiles with its juice, and the parsley to the pot and simmer, covered, for 20 minutes.

Serve with white Oaxaca-style rice, which is made as follows: fry 1½ cups long grain rice in 2 tablespoons of oil for 3 minutes over medium heat. Add ¼ cup minced onion and 1 clove minced garlic and continue cooking 1 minute. Add 3 cups water and 1 teaspoon salt, bring the water to a boil, turn the heat to low, and steam the rice, covered, for 20 minutes. *Serves 4 with lots of sauce left over, which can be used on poached chicken breast.*

Cooking oil

¼ pound whole almonds

2 French-style dinner rolls, cut into strips 1 inch wide

1 large plantain (about 1 foot long), peeled and sliced in 1-inch pieces

¼ pound sesame seeds

1 onion, chopped

12 cloves garlic, peeled

¼ pound raisins

2 tablespoons thyme

3–3½ tablespoons loosely packed broken cinnamon sticks

4½ pounds tomatoes, chopped

3 heaping tablespoons sugar

1½ teaspoons salt

½ pound pasilla chiles, stems, veins, and seeds removed, but seeds reserved

3½ ounces chilhuacle chiles, stems, veins, and seeds removed, but seeds reserved

2½–3-pound chicken cut into serving pieces, or an equal amount of bone-in breast

1 onion, quartered

12 cloves garlic, peeled

Additional sugar

¼ pound Mexican chocolate, or substitute semisweet chocolate

MOLE NEGRO DE OAXACA

Oaxacan Black Mole

When one thinks of *mole*, one usually thinks of *Mole poblano*, Puebla's famous specialty. But I must confess that after studying cooking in both Puebla and Oaxaca, my vote goes unequivocally to the Oaxaca version, although I am probably in the minority. However, the inky blackness and mysterious complexity of *mole negro* evokes so many sensations in me, all of them pleasant, that I cannot help the prejudice.

This version of *mole negro*, a recipe I learned from Carmen Solis, with whom I studied cooking in Oaxaca, is the best I have had. It is not quite as black or as sweet as some of those made from preground pastes, but it has the earthiness combined with sophistication that the dish should possess.

Much of the flavor of *mole negro* is due to the combination of chiles and most particularly to the *chilhuacle* chile. This medium-size, brown, dried chile may be the most expensive in the world at its current price in Oaxaca's markets of $25 a pound. It is unfortunate that this chile is almost impossible to find outside of Oaxaca, even in Mexico City. The closest substitute is the *mulato* chile that is the basis of *Mole poblano*.

Heat a skillet over medium heat, add a little oil, and fry the almonds until just browned. Remove the almonds to drain.

Add a little more oil and fry the bread pieces until they are well browned but not burned; then remove them to drain.

Fry the plantain until well browned, then remove to drain.

In a small saucepan fry the sesame seeds in just enough oil to coat them until just browned and add the onion and garlic. Continue to cook until the onion is soft, but not burned; then add the raisins, thyme, and cinnamon sticks and fry 1 or 2 more minutes.

Place the fried almonds, bread, and plantain in a bowl with the sesame seed mixture and reserve.

Place the tomatoes in a large pot over medium heat, bring to a boil, and simmer for 5 minutes. Add 3 heaping tablespoons sugar and the salt and continue to cook until the tomatoes begin to turn into a sauce, but are still watery, 10 to 15 minutes. Blend and strain the mixture.

Toast the chiles. This is the most difficult part of the recipe since the chiles must be toasted much more than in most recipes but not completely burned. Heat a *comal* or iron griddle over medium heat and toast the chiles until they are blackened, but not too burned. The blackening process is important to both the color and taste of the sauce. When I asked Carmen why her sauce was not quite as black as other sauces, she told me the commercial pastes overburn the chiles and make up for the bitter taste by adding too much sugar. I found her method results in a much more subtle taste.

I suggest you experiment with 1 chile at a time until you get the feel of it. The chiles are properly done when they become very dry and brittle and are easily crumbled. The problem is that if you wait for this stage to occur, they may be too burned. The reason for this is that after you remove the chiles from the *comal*, they continue to cook. So begin by toasting 1 chile until it is just blackened, then remove it from the heat. Wait 1 or 2 minutes and if it is not quite brittle and easy to crumble, cook the next one a while longer. You will soon get the timing down.

Toast the reserved seeds (there should be about 1 cup) on the *comal* or griddle until they are a blackish brown.

At this point most Oaxaca cooks take the sesame seed-spice mixture to one of the many mills in the central markets and have them ground with the chiles and finally with the tomato mixture, which is added during the process to "lubricate" the grinding machinery. Since you probably will not have access to this equipment, you must try to imitate the fine grind. Use a blender, adding just a little

of the sesame mixture with just enough of the tomato mixture to allow the blades to operate. As the mixture is pureed, put it through a food mill using the finest blade that will work. The process is tedious and messy, but it is necessary to obtain a properly smooth sauce. Reserve any tomato sauce not blended into the mixture.

Meanwhile, simmer the chicken with the onion and garlic for about 20 minutes. Remove the chicken and strain and reserve the broth, discarding the garlic and onion.

Cook the pureed spice and chile mixture in ⅓ cup lard or cooking oil. At this point you will need to add additional sugar to taste. Add the sugar, little by little, until the taste is no longer bitter but not too sweet. Continue cooking the paste until it releases its fat and stops sticking to the pan, about 15 minutes.

Add the reserved tomatoes, with any tomato juice that has accumulated, and cook for 5 minutes. Then add the chocolate and stir until well mixed.

Taste the sauce again and add more sugar, if necessary; then add enough of the broth in which the chicken was cooked to make about 3 cups of sauce. It should be thick enough to stick to a spoon but not too thick.

Cook the sauce until the fat begins to render, about 5 minutes; then add the cooked chicken and heat through.

You can serve the chicken immediately with Oaxaca-style white rice (p. 39), or better yet, leave the chicken in the sauce, refrigerated overnight, to absorb the flavors, then reheat and serve. *Serves 4.*

FILETE ESPECIAL

Special Filet

This steak recipe is found, in one form or another, in better restaurants in many parts of Mexico. It is one of my favorite recipes and is always a hit at dinner parties.

Sauté the onion and garlic in 2 tablespoons olive oil over medium heat until they are medium brown in color.

Add the *tomatillos* and water to the pan and simmer, covered, until the *tomatillos* are soft, 5 to 10 minutes.

Place the *tomatillo* mixture in a blender with both types of chiles and blend for 1 minute. Strain the sauce and return it to the blender. Then add the cilantro to the blender and blend until it is just minced.

Heat the remaining 2 tablespoons of olive oil in a saucepan over medium heat; add the sauce from the blender, then add the reduced broth, thyme, and tomato sauce. Bring to a boil and simmer the sauce, gently, until the fat renders, about 35 minutes.

To prepare the steak, heat a skillet over medium-high heat, add the butter, and sauté the steaks 1 or 2 minutes on each side to brown them. Turn the heat to medium low, add the sauce, and continue simmering the steaks until they are cooked as you like them. These steaks are often garnished with a piece of white cheese, like Monterey Jack, and passed under a broiler until it is melted.

Serve the steaks with rice and hot corn tortillas. *Serves 4.*

THE SAUCE:

- 2 *tablespoons olive oil*
- 1 *cup onion, chopped*
- 2 *cloves garlic, minced*
- 12 *tomatillos, husks removed*
- 1½ *cups water*
- 1 *large or 1½ small canned* chipotle *chiles*
- ¾ *large or 1 small* ancho *chile, soaked in hot water for 15 minutes*
- ¼ *cup cilantro*
- 2 *tablespoons olive oil*
- ¾ *cup beef broth, reduced to ½ cup*
- ¾ *teaspoon thyme*
- ¼ *cup tomato sauce*

THE STEAK:

- 2 *tablespoons butter*
- 4 *6–8 ounce tenderloin steaks*
- ¼ *pound Monterey Jack cheese, sliced very thin or grated (optional)*

TACOS DE FLOR DE CALABAZA

Squash Blossom Tacos

THE FILLING:

¼ *cup cooking oil*

¼ *cup onion, minced*

1 *clove garlic, minced*

1 poblano *chile, peeled, seeded, and minced*

3 *cups squash blossoms*

¼ *cup heavy cream*

½ *teaspoon thyme*

½ *teaspoon ground pepper*

½ *teaspoon salt, or to taste*

¼ *cup Monterey Jack cheese, grated*

THE TACOS:

Oil for frying the tortillas

12 *corn tortillas*

Tomatillo Sauce *(p. 116)*

You will probably not be able to make this recipe unless you have a garden with a substantial amount of squash planted in it. Even if squash blossoms were universally available in markets, the results of this dish would probably not be ideal because the optimal results are obtained when the dish is cooked soon after picking the flowers. However, it is a very interesting dish and well worth the effort, particularly as a meal for special guests. Diana Kennedy, the best-known authority on the cooking of interior Mexico, suggests that the best blossoms are the male variety and that they are at their maximum freshness in the morning.

To make the filling, heat a skillet over medium heat, add the oil, and cook the onion, garlic, and chile until they are soft but not browned. Turn the heat to low, add and mix in the squash blossoms, and cook, covered, for about 8 minutes or until the flowers are just becoming soft.

Add just enough of the cream to bind the ingredients and contribute a little flavor; then add the thyme, pepper, and salt and cook 1 or 2 minutes more. Then sprinkle the cheese over the cooked blossoms and remove the pan from the heat. This should allow the cheese to melt into the other ingredients.

To make the tacos, heat about 1 inch of oil in a skillet until very hot but not smoking. Using kitchen tongs immerse a tortilla in the oil and immediately fold it in half. Fry just until the tortilla begins to stiffen, turn, and fry on the other side. The tortilla shells should be firm but still pliable, not crisp. Make the remaining tortilla shells in the same manner.

Stuff the shells with the filling and serve with the sauce. *Serves 4.*

MEXICAN-AMERICAN FOOD IN THE SOUTHWEST

When I began to research this book, I knew that Spaniards and Mexicans had been living in the Southwest since before the United States declared independence. Therefore, I reasoned that Mexican cooking would have been significant in the area's culture from the very beginning. However, I was astonished to discover that, except in the case of New Mexico, whose cuisine has been based on chiles and corn from the beginning, it was not until the last thirty-five years or so that this occurred. Mexican food really began to attain meaningful popularity in the broader southwestern culture during the 1950s. The answer to why it took so long for Mexican cooking to reach its current status in Arizona, California, and Texas, and why it was more rapidly accepted in New Mexico tells a great deal about both the cuisine and its development.

In the relatively short period between 1519 and 1542, Spanish explorers discovered present-day New Mexico, Arizona, Texas, and California. While settlements were established in New Mexico as early as 1598, it was not until 1682, 1700, and 1769, respectively, that even preliminary Hispanic settlements were founded in Texas, Arizona, and California. So while only twenty-three years separated the discovery of the regions of the present-day southwestern states, New Mexico was settled 84 to 171 years before the other southwestern states, giving New Mexico a formidable head start.

The following outlines of historical events in New Mexico, Arizona, Texas, and California will help illuminate the factors that influenced the development of Mexican-style cooking within their borders. They also contain descriptions of the territory's early and more recent cooking.

New Mexico

In 1598, Juan de Oñate established the first settlement in New Mexico, and in 1609 the king of Spain formally assumed responsibility for the territory. However, it was not until Mexico's independence from Spain in 1821 that trade restrictions which had been imposed by the Spanish were eliminated and outsiders began to influence the area. And twenty-five more years passed before the United States took possession of New Mexico in 1846, at the beginning of the Mexican War.

Thus, 223 years elapsed between the founding of New Mexico's first colony and the arrival of significant outside influence—time enough to establish a unique indigenous culture, including a remarkable cuisine. During this period the Spaniards built presidios and missions as they had in Mexico. They also dealt with the local Indians in familiar fashion: employing, converting, marrying, and, if all else failed, fighting with them. The result was the same as it had been in Mexico: the cultures mixed. However, the Pueblo Indians, dominant in New Mexico at the time, were quite different from the Aztecs and most of the other Indians. Also different were the climate and the natural resources.

The Pueblo Indians lived in an arid, high-altitude desert where winters brought hard freezes and snow, so that food preservation, usually through drying, was of utmost importance. The Pueblos grew the distinctive blue corn, seldom found elsewhere, and learned to dry, roast, and prepare it in unique ways. In fact, according to William Hardwick in *Authentic Indian-Mexican Recipes*, "The blue corn was held to be of divine origin (p. 2)." The following Taos Pueblo corn grinding song, quoted from Marcia Keegan's *Southwest Indian Cookbook*, indicates the depth of the Indians' feelings about corn:

> From the corn we gather the pollen. The pollen that is
> like gold, reminds us of the color of anointment of the
> ancient ones. Grinding the corn it reminds us of heaven and

it reminds us of earth. It reminds us that Father Sky and Mother Earth will unite forever.

From the corn we learn to live, we learn the life that is ours, by grinding the corn we learn the footsteps of life. We go through a purification, until we are like dust. The corn came from the dust, from Mother Earth, and it gives life, like from Father Sky.

We are like the kernel that comes from the corn. With it we bring life, like the seed of the corn. Corn is the fruit of the gods; it was brought to us by the creator, that we may remember him. Our lives, we must remember that they are holy. The corn is sacred. We are sacred. We hold the seeds of the gods to the future (p. 4 of prologue).

So distinctive and talented were the Pueblo Indians that it is not surprising that different customs and a distinctive cuisine resulted from their interaction with the Spaniards. In fact, the New Mexico-style Mexican-American cooking of today, which has changed little from the early days, contains many dishes that are seldom, if ever, found in other parts of the Southwest. Tortillas, *posole*, and *atole* made of blue corn; *chicos*; *carne adovada*; green chile sauce; flat enchiladas; and *sopaipillas* are all nearly exclusive to New Mexico. In New Mexico, perhaps more than in any other area, the Spanish ingredients were absorbed by the Indian cuisine.

Historical descriptions of the early cuisine of New Mexico depict the range of early cooking and established traditions. Erna Fergusson, in *Mexican Cookbook*, published in 1934, describes a typical day's meals in early Spanish New Mexico, portraying the customs of a wealthy household that engaged in the type of lifestyle that many less privileged Spaniards came to the New World to find:

The menus are based on meals as served at a gentleman's table before the general adoption of American ways. Then eating was a serious matter, interfered with only by famine, war, or Lent. The day began with a preliminary breakfast in bed; coffee or chocolate and sweet rolls. At nine o'clock came the real breakfast which included eggs or meat and more bread and coffee.

At noon formal dinner was served; a heavy soup, meats and vegetables, and desserts. The service in a wealthy family was of silver; platters, plates, and goblets. As there were no knives, the food was prepared in such a way that it could be managed with the silver forks and spoons. In a typical meal there were several meats and only one vegetable, various health rules not having been discovered. Beans and rice took the place of potatoes, which were neither raised nor imported. Salad was unusual. Wine or beer was served. Water was anathema—it was used for irrigation, washing, and religious purposes, never for drinking.

After this meal, one could indulge in the siesta, and come up refreshed for chocolate and more sweet cakes at four o'clock. Supper, at half past six, was a simple meal: chicken or spareribs, fresh or dried vegetables according to the season, and cornmeal dishes at any time (p. 6).

In *Food of the Conquerors: Native Dishes of New Mexico*, Margaret Abreu gives us a different view by recounting the cooking described to her by her grandmother:

The *metate* and the little *mano*, or grinding stones, were something to conjure with! My grandmother used to tell us that in her childhood home there were so many Indian servants, captive slaves rather, that at least a dozen of the younger ones did nothing all day long but grind the cornmeal for the *nixtamal*. Bending over the *metates* with the clicking *mano* as an accompaniment they sang their grinding songs in a clear yodeling voice. . . .

The preparation of these native dishes, finally mastered by the mistress of the house, was a part of the education of the young ladies of *antaño*. This phase of their training consisted of how to do the proper thing properly, not haphazardly. For instance, the clove of garlic had to be crushed with the butt end of the kitchen knife, not chopped. The chocolate, stirred to a foam not with the spoon but a wooden *molinillo*. The red or green chile had to be pressed with the fingers, not the meat grinder, until the desired result was obtained. . . . If red chile, the finished product was, and should be, a rich, thick smooth sauce. In the case of green chile, this pressing with the hand turned out a delicious concoction called *chile verde*. And how the hand burned (p. 18)!

A look at several of the best-known contemporary restaurants specializing in Mexican-American food will underscore the continuity of that tradition in New Mexico and the specialties of the region. As one example, the story of the establishment of La Posta restaurant in Mesilla, New Mexico, demonstrates the tenacity of the area's Hispanic people and the success of Mexican-American cooking in the area.

One day early in 1939, Katy Griggs, a vivacious girl in her mid-twenties, was ironing diapers in the kitchen of her family's hacienda, just outside of Las Cruces, New Mexico. She looked up at her mother, Josephine Chávez Griggs, who, as usual, was tending to sauces simmering on the stove and said, "Mom, I think I'm going to start a chile joint."

"Where will you put it?" was the skeptical reply.

Katy said she would see if she could rent a room in the museum owned by her uncle George in nearby Mesilla. Although he first warned her she would go broke, she pointed out that the family had not yet emerged from the Depression and that she, at least, couldn't go any "broker." He finally agreed to rent her a room for $8 a month.

Talking about the event over fifty years later, Katy, now Katy Meek, said with a wry smile, "I think he died before I could pay him the first month's rent." Katy was extremely popular in the community, and with her mother's recipes the restaurant, which she named La Posta, was filled the first night and has been so ever since, often serving as many as 1,500 patrons a day.

Now well into her eighties and in poor health, Katy is one of those people who have the kind of personal magnetism that makes success difficult to avoid. However, it was not just Katy's personality that led to the success of La Posta. Katy's father was the son of James Edgar Griggs, who moved from New York to New Mexico in about 1865. Wealthy in his own right, he married a lady of Spanish descent who inherited a huge land grant and went into the mining business. Family legend has it that it was the elder Griggs who originally brought to the West a mining engineer named William Bonney, who was killed in a mine accident, leaving his young son Billy without a family. The future "Billy the Kid" is said to have lived with the Griggs for a short period of time.

The Griggs land grant eventually fell into the hands of more powerful people as did many others, and the Depression depleted the family's wealth. Katy's father inherited the family farm and hacienda, which was about all that was left of the family fortune. Although the Depression was hard on the family, at least they had enough to eat. In fact, Katy's mother often passed the time perfecting her favorite recipes in the big old kitchen. In it hung a sign saying, *"Panza Llena, Corazón Contento"* ("Full Stomach, Contented Heart"). Out of this grew her book *A Family Affair: A Few Favorite Recipes of Mrs. Griggs*. It was with these recipes that Katy began La Posta. (I believe the book may still be for sale at the Griggs restaurants in El Paso.) In addition, Katy Meek has written a book featuring the recipes of La Posta, which is available from that restaurant. It is interesting to see how little the recipes changed from one book to the other. However, Katy takes full credit for the recipe for *Tostadas compuestas*, perhaps La Posta's most popular dish.

As other members of the Griggs family also established restaurants, it became clear that Katy's success was no fluke. Using the same recipes Katy's brother, Edgar, opened the Griggs Restaurant in El Paso. Although no longer owned by Mr. Griggs, the restaurant is still in operation at two locations, and the one in west El Paso houses the Billy the Kid Museum. Yet another family member, Katy's sister Mary Griggs Moore, established La Posta de Rancho Córdova, in Córdova, California.

Perhaps the most successful La Posta offshoot is El Pinto in Albuquerque, New Mexico. Following World War II John Thomas, Sr., came from Manhattan to the University of New Mexico to study engineering on the GI Bill. He grew to love Mexican food and traveled to Mesilla, where he had heard a restaurant called La Posta served some of the best. During his many trips to the restaurant, he became acquainted with an attractive young girl, a family member who was working as a waitress and cashier. They married and moved back to the East Coast. However, after ten years they missed New Mexico and particularly its food so much they returned and opened El Pinto, again using Mrs. Griggs's original recipes. Now run by their twin sons, Jim and John Thomas, El Pinto serves some of the finest New Mexico-style food available.

Another well-known contemporary restaurant known for its New Mexico-style cooking is Rancho de Chimayó, founded in 1965 and located in the village of Chimayó, about 20 to 30 minutes northeast of Santa Fe. A typical northern New Mexico village, Chimayó was Robert Redford's original choice for the filming of *The Milagro Beanfield War*, but one of the residents vetoed the idea and the village of Las Truchas, a few miles away, was chosen instead. Rancho de Chimayó was established by Arturo Jaramillo in what used to be his grandfather's hacienda. Although the restaurant is relatively new and sometimes criticized for its occasional deviations from traditional recipes such as the use of Worcestershire sauce in its red chile sauce, the Spanish colonial ambience coupled with the fine cooking has made this place an institution. Particularly popular are Rancho de Chimayó's *carne adovada* and stuffed *sopaipillas*.

The fact that New Mexico's cuisine still is based upon the early cooking is accounted for by the fact that over a period of 223 years a complete well-rounded society developed. As Joan W. Moore and Harry Pachon state in *Mexican Americans*: "Unlike those in the borderlands of Texas, New Mexico's Spanish-speaking residents had a full range of class structure and a well-established ruling group, able in every respect and interested in retaining political power (p. 15)." Northern New Mexico, where the capital lay, was isolated and remote so that when the railroads came, bringing land speculators and surveyors, they found a well-rounded society with firm traditions. Certainly, much of the land and political power disappeared from Hispanic hands, but not nearly to the extent it did elsewhere. What remained almost completely intact was the cuisine—possibly because it was so good and so suited to the area.

As I explained in my previous book, *El Norte: The Cuisine of Northern Mexico*, New Mexico is unique among southwestern states in that its Mexican cuisine came not from immigrants crossing our border, but from our moving the border south; New Mexico's cuisine, more than that of any other area in the Southwest, developed organically on its own territory and from its own resources, resources that included the Pueblo Indians.

One of the most interesting aspects of New Mexico-style cooking is the numerous types of enchiladas in the state. When ordering enchiladas, you often must decide if you want blue corn, white corn, or yellow corn tortillas; whether you want the enchiladas stacked or rolled; if stacked, whether you want them topped with a fried egg; and finally whether you want a red or green chile sauce—many New Mexicans order both.

Other features and dishes of New Mexico cooking that contribute to its uniqueness, many of which were developed by Pueblo Indian cooks, include the pure red *chile colorado* made from home-grown chiles that are characterized by their complexity of flavor (as well as their heat), and stews such as *carne adovada*, *posole*, and *chicos* that are flavored with it; the green sauces made from the same chiles in their ripe, rather than dried, state that are used on everything from eggs to enchiladas; the blue corn from which tortillas, *posole*, and *atole* are made; the pillow-like, airy crisp *sopaipillas* found almost nowhere else; and, of course, the humble but singular Indian taco.

Texas

In 1519, while Cortés was discovering Mexico, Alonso de Pineda surveyed what is now the Texas Gulf Coast and claimed the territory for Spain. It was on this same coast that Cabeza de Vaca was shipwrecked in 1528, beginning his seven-year journey through the Southwest.

However, the first Texas settlements of any consequence were not established until 1682, 163 years after the territory was first discovered. By 1793, the only permanent colonies remaining were those in San Antonio, Goliad, and Nacogdoches. As in Arizona, the Indians, in this case the Comanches, were too hostile for the traditional mission system to work.

The early Hispanic settlers in the central and eastern parts of the territory, often called *tejanos*, came largely from the bordering northern states of Coahuila, Nuevo León, and Tamaulipas. Those in the western part of the area arrived as part of the Spanish immigration into New Mexico. While these early tough and resilient pioneers were not as far from Mexico City as the Hispanic settlers of California, their wild surroundings effectively removed the *tejanos* from many of the strictures of centralized authority. As a result there was much less Spanish influence in Texas than in New Mexico.

In the early 1800s, Anglos began to move into Texas, and the resulting frictions culminated in 1836 at the battle of San Jacinto, where Texas won freedom from Mexico. Texas remained a republic until 1845 when it was annexed as the twenty-eighth state.

Cattle ranching was the basis of the early Texas economy, and most

Mexican settlements were confined to the far south, with few north of the Nueces River. According to Paul Taylor in *An American-Mexican Frontier, Nueces County, Texas*, by 1859 "all Mexican owned grants but one in Nueces County passed into the hands of Anglo settlers (p. 94)." It was in this way that the pattern of Anglo owners and Mexican cowboys was established.

Texas is a large and often wild place, and even today people frequently have scorn for anything short of total self-reliance. Mexican ranch hands learned to live off the land. Beans, which were easy to carry and prepare, became the staple, something that would keep you alive if all else failed. Tortillas came next as mentioned by Arnoldo De León in *The Tejano Community 1836–1900*, who quotes from J. Frank Dobie's "In the Shadow of History":

> Tortillas ranked second only to *frijoles* as a mainstay and as an article identifying the Tejano way of life. The arduous and intricate process of preparing them required soaking the maize in water and lime to remove the hulls, grinding corn on the *metate*, and finally baking the cake on the *comal* (p. 122). . . .

There was little to distinguish the foodways of the early *tejanos* from those of the Indians found by Cortés.

Chiles, strips from the nopal cactus, goat, inexpensive cuts of meat such as tripe, kidneys, and tongue, as well as game such as turkey, dove, quail, deer, *javelina* (wild boar), and rabbit rounded out the diet of the early Hispanic settlers. As George A. McCall reported in *Letters from the Frontier*: "Around Corpus Christi in the 1840s, *mexicanos* used the stalking horse to get within rifle shot of deer grazing on the plains. Cautiously pushing the dried hide of the head, neck and part of the body of a mustang before them, they advanced stealthily on their breast until close enough to consummate their purpose (p. 436)."

To make beverages, the *tejanos* used the leaves of the maguey cactus as their Indian forbears had for centuries. Quoting Pirtl's *Life on the Range and on the Trail*, Arnoldo De León, in *The Tejano Community 1836–1900* describes the process:

> When Tejanos saw the long leaves of the maguey turning inward at the tips, they knew the time had come for it to bloom. They then dug out the center of the plant in the place where the stalk for the bloom was going to shoot up. Letting the sap or *aguamiel* out into a goat- (or pig- or sheep-) skin bag. After fermenting the sap, Tejanos could enjoy the thick, milky-looking fluid known as *pulque*. Through still other processes, Tejanos derived two ginlike beverages, *mescal* and tequila from maguey (p. 123).

As life became more civilized, gardens yielded onions, tomatoes, fresh corn, and squash; and domestic animals such as goats, pigs, chickens, and cattle were more available. This permitted a major enhancement to the cuisine in the form of cheese. In *The Tejano Community 1836–1900* De León quotes O'Shea's *El Mesquite*, which explains that:

> Aside from the butter it rendered, milk could be clabbered with rennet from the cow or with the juice from the wild *santa pera* plant and made into a variety of cheeses, including *panela*, *azadera* and *queso molido* (used for enchiladas). Finished cheese was placed in a *zarso*, or cloth frame, and hung high on a tree so that nothing could touch it (p. 123).

Mexican cooking, however, was not always accepted among the general population. In *Sixty Years in the Nueces Valley*, S. G. Miller describes her earliest experience with the Mexican ranch staff:

> They tried to be very kind to me, and one of the things which they did in an effort to make me feel at home was to cook their native dishes and bring them to me. Time after

time they presented me with pots of chili, rabbit cooked in
their highly seasoned sauce, prickly pear cooked with eggs,
or dishes of young *paisanos* or birds of paradise. Try as I
would, I could eat none of these rich peppery dishes (p. 15).

This reaction, typical of the times, demonstrates why it took so long for
Mexican cooking to be accepted in the general population.

Today, the differences between Mexican-American cooking in the
western region of Texas and the central and eastern regions still reflect
the historical development of these areas. Early Mexican immigration did
not extend far north of the Río Grande, but Texas is so large that this
was nevertheless more than 800 miles of territory. When cattle ranching
first began, the southern portion of Texas ranged from grassy savannas
in the central and eastern portions of the state to dry grasslands and
desert toward the west; but overgrazing occurred almost immediately,
and today most of south-central and eastern Texas is thick brush country.
The western portion of Texas has always ranged from semiarid grassland
to desert. Settlements in this western area were related mostly to the
northward Spanish explorations to New Mexico, and today west Texas-
style Mexican-American cooking resembles that of New Mexico much
more than the more typical Tex-Mex varieties found in other parts of the
state that were influenced by southern Texas ranch cooking.

Although a considerable number of Mexican-American restaurants
carry on the tradition of Tex-Mex cooking today in Texas, one of the
best west Texas Mexican-American restaurants is unfortunately no
longer open—the Old Borunda Cafe in Marfa. Established in 1910 by
the Borunda family and operated by Carolina Borunda Humphries until
it was closed a few years ago, it was one of the country's unique restaurants and a west Texas institution. If it were still in existence, this establishment would undoubtedly be the oldest continuously operating
Mexican restaurant in the United States.

Carolina Humphries began waiting tables under her father's direction and took over full management in 1938. A fanatic about freshness and quality, she insisted on using only the best ingredients, and they were bought daily, except her dried chiles which came from New Mexico. Everything in the Old Borunda Cafe, most of which was closer to what we think of as New Mexico-style rather than Texas-style cooking, was prepared from scratch on an 1897 wood-burning stove. A friend of mine who operated the butane supply business in Marfa for many years recalls installing a gas oven over Carolina's objections. After trying it she declared it cooked much too fast and refused to use it for anything other than to keep food warm. The Old Borunda Cafe had only a few tables, and although the customers had to wait a long time to be served, the local people did not mind. Carolina allowed her customers to bring in two beers each, and that kept nearly everyone reasonably happy. However, a friend related a story about a disgruntled couple from California who once visited the café while passing through. After a long wait to be served, the man went to the kitchen to complain; Carolina, waving a butcher knife, ordered him to leave!

The most distinctive brand of Tex-Mex cooking, as the Mexican-American cooking in Texas is called, comes from south Texas. While the cooking in west Texas resembles that of New Mexico, the south Texas variety, based upon the ranch country resources of beef and game, as well as *ancho* and *jalapeño* chiles, has its own distinctive stamp.

Mexican-American cooking in Texas was influenced by the cuisine of the border states of Coahuila, Nuevo León, and Tamaulipas, from which so many of its Mexican settlers emigrated. It evolved to its current distinctive forms through the interaction of Mexican cooks with Anglo ranch owners. When thinking about Tex-Mex cooking, the intense beef-flavored sauces redolent of cumin and sizzling *fajitas* come first to mind. But also particularly Tex-Mex are the thick flour tortillas served with *carne guisada*, the small pork- or venison-filled tamales, the puffy tacos, and, of course, the *cabrito*, which is still a very active part of the cuisine.

Arizona

The early Hispanic immigrants to Arizona came almost exclusively from Sonora and had very little effect on the area's culture when compared with early Hispanic influence in other areas of the Southwest. This is explained in one word: *Apaches*. These fierce warriors, whose battle strategies are still studied in military colleges, were the stuff of which the old shoot-'em-up cowboy and Indian movies were made. In reality, until 1886 the Indians were the victors more often than not. The virulence of the Apache campaigns ebbed and flowed over the years, often giving the Mexicans just enough time to rebuild their settlements before the next attack.

A brief review of the territory's history shows why there is a lack of lore about the early Mexican influence on cooking in Arizona.

On his travels through the Southwest, Cabeza de Vaca went through Arizona, and as in New Mexico, Coronado on his search for treasure passed through part of the area in 1540. The next major exploration was by a Spanish party from New Mexico that attempted to convert the Hopi in northern Arizona. The expedition came to an end with the Pueblo Revolt of 1680.

It was not until 1700 that Father Eusebio Kino founded the first mission at Xavier del Bac, just south of present-day Tucson. However, the Apaches soon arrived, and the settlements were touch and go from then on. In fact, in their book *Mexican Americans* Joan W. Moore and Harry Pachon report that by 1856 nearly all the Mexicans in the area, less than 1,000, were concentrated in fortified Tucson (p. 16). In 1848, the United States acquired the northern part of Arizona through the treaty of Guadalupe Hidalgo, and in 1854 the rest of the state with the Gadsden Purchase.

Following 1850, increased Indian attacks, a cholera outbreak, and growing numbers of Anglo immigrants resulted in most Mexicans either going back to Sonora or to California, decreasing Mexican influence in the area's culture, including the cuisine.

Although Arizona was less influenced by the early Spanish and Mexican presence than any of the other southwestern states, it may have the oldest currently operating Mexican restaurant. Founded in 1922 by a family of French extraction which established roots in Arizona prior to the territory's acquisition by the United States, Tucson's El Charro is said to be the longest continually operated restaurant of any kind in Arizona. Jules Flin, a master stonemason, came from France to Tucson in the 1880s to finish the area's first cathedral, San Agustín. He married the daughter of a Frenchman who had come to Mexico during the reign of the Archduke Maximilian. The Flins lived first on a ranch along the Santa Cruz River and later at a home built by Flin on Court Street in what is today downtown Tucson. One of the Flins' eight children, Monica, grew up in frontier Tucson and married a Mexican named Pancho Fernández. Following a short unhappy period in Mexico's interior, she returned to Tucson and established El Charro in 1922. After several moves the restaurant ended up at the Court Street house which Jules had left to Monica.

By all accounts Monica had great personality and style. She was said to love both drinking and serving martinis and got around her lack of a liquor license by serving them from a teapot into tea cups. She also did not believe in income taxes, and made her checks to the IRS payable to *Los ladrones* (the thieves); the checks came back endorsed *Los ladrones*, IRS.

Today, El Charro is managed by Jules Flin's great granddaughter, Carlotta Dunn Flores, and her husband, Raymond Flores. The restaurant serves some of the best Sonora-style Mexican-American food anywhere. Daily, Raymond Flores hoists 30 pounds of beef over El Charro's roof in a huge fly-proof cage, where Arizona's dry air and sunshine do their work. The result is the most perfectly textured, flavorful *carne seca*, or *machaca*, I have ever tasted. Because of the lack of similar dry conditions in other parts of the country, alternate methods for making *machaca* that work very well are included in the recipe section (see p. 156). Many of El Charro's Sonoran specialties, including burritos, enchiladas, and *chimichangas* feature their *carne seca*.

Another place where exemplary Sonoran cooking holds sway in Arizona is Los Olivos in Scottsdale, founded in 1927. One dish that Los Olivos does to perfection is their combination enchilada plate called the Three-color Mexican Flag, an outstanding dish, a version of which I have included in the recipe section (p. 208).

As we have seen, although the Mexican cooking of early Arizona had little lasting effect on the area, the state of Sonora was so close and its food so interesting that, as the story of El Charro demonstrates, it took very little time for the cooking style to reassert itself.

The Mexican-American cooking of Arizona is rooted firmly in the cuisine of the Mexican state of Sonora, with which it shares its entire southern border. The huge paper-thin flour tortillas, *carne seca*, and the burritos and *chimichangas* into which they are made, garnished with guacamole, sour cream, and olives typify this style of cooking. But there are many more aspects of this regional style, such as the large green corn tamales which capture the essence of corn like no others, the creamy soups filled with fresh vegetables, and the Sonora-style enchiladas made with thick patties of dough, or *masa*.

This is not to say that the cooking of Arizona is exactly like the cooking of Sonora. Most of the Mexican dishes have evolved into new and original forms. The giant burritos and *chimichangas* smothered in chile sauce and melted cheddar cheese are rarely found south of the border, nor are the cheese crisps and combination plates completely covered with chile sauce and cheese.

California

Following establishment of the first settlement in San Diego in 1769 by expeditions based in Baja California, Spanish explorers marched northward and in 1770 founded the first colony in Monterey, California. A few years later, Juan Bautista de Anza led an expedition overland from Tubac, Arizona, to Monterey. His party consisted mostly of Sonorans, who were eager to leave Arizona because of the incessant Apache raids. According to James E. Officer in *Hispanic Arizona, 1536–1856:* "Among those accompanying him on the journey of colonization were Tubac residents whose relocation created the first of many kinship ties between *Californios* and *Sonorenses* (p. 21)." The patterns established in the early exploration continued and are, of course, why to this day the cooking of Baja California and Sonora predominate in California.

A prime factor in California's colonization and one which had a significant effect on the culture of Spanish California was the Franciscan missionaries. According to Richard Griswold del Castillo in *The Los Angeles Barrio 1850–1890: A Social History:*

> The California missions were different from the institutions
> that developed in other areas of the Southwest; they were on
> a larger scale and much more prosperous than those of
> Arizona, New Mexico, or Texas. The New Mexico missions
> were small churches located near Pueblo Indian villages.
> Unlike those in Alta California, they owned no lands and
> pursued no program of concentrating diverse tribes into a
> central location (p. 12).

The missions acquired vast landholdings and utilized the local Indians to work the land. After Mexico gained independence from Spain in 1821, the California settlers automatically obtained Mexican citizenship. They also acquired ownership of most of the mission landholdings and Indian labor resources, resulting in the creation of the huge ranchos for which California was known.

The immense ranchos, isolated from outside influences and distant from the central authorities in Mexico, who had little concern for this remote province, produced a unique culture in the grand Spanish tradition. With ample land and Indian labor the owners were able to devote their time to horsemanship, hunting, and entertaining. Shortly before and after acquisition of California by the United States the *californios* (as the early Spanish and Mexican settlers were called) were often vilified by Anglos who resented their wealthy and seemingly indolent culture—and who wanted their land. Later the *californios* were romanticized by a host of fanciful and sentimental movies (such as the Zorro series) and in novels such as Helen Hunt Jackson's *Ramona*. Their image came to be that presented by the actor and personality Leo Carillo.

The flavor of the life and cooking of those days is best depicted in quotes by early settlers such as John Bidwell, who says the following in *In California Before the Gold Rush*, as quoted in *Mexican California: An Original Anthology*, edited by Leslie Parr:

> The kindness and hospitality of the native Californians have not been overstated. Up to the time the Mexican regime ceased in California they had a custom of never charging for anything; that is to say, for entertainment, food, use of horses, etc. You were supposed, even if invited to visit a friend, to bring your blankets with you, and one would be very thoughtless if he traveled and did not take a knife with him to cut his meat. When you had eaten, the invariable custom was to rise, deliver to the woman or hostess the plate on which you had eaten the meat and beans—for that was about all they had—and say, *"Muchas gracias, señora"* ("Many thanks, madame"); and the hostess as invariably replied, *"Buen provecho"* ("May it do you much good") [p. 67].

Father Juan Caballaria, in his *History of San Bernardino Valley from the Padres to the Pioneers 1810–1851*, describes the cooking of the *californios* in the following way:

> It has been said the Mexicans did not know how to cook. Such assertions were made by people who did not know them and had never associated with them. While they do not cook the so-called fancy dishes, their food, especially in days past, was nourishing, wholesome and digestible. Indigestion, dyspepsia and kindred ailments were unknown, while today they are as subject to these diseases as are other people (p. 117).

He goes on to describe cooking arrangements similar to those found today in New Mexico:

> There were no stoves in the early days, but in their stead fireplaces of mud and stones. They were built in a semicircular form, varying from a foot and a half to three feet long, and from one to two feet wide, and about one foot high, with bars across the top to hold the pots. To bake bread *"hornos"* (ovens) were built of bricks and mud, on the same principle as bakers' ovens are built at present. Tortillas were baked on large pieces of iron called *"comales"* (pp. 117–18).

Next, we are given a rare insight into the actual preparation of early dishes:

> Everyone is familiar with the making of tortillas, tamales and enchiladas, but there were other foods prepared which are not so well known, namely, *puchero, estofado, albóndigas* and *colache*.
>
> To make *puchero* select pieces of meat were placed to boil until it bade froth, when that was thrown out. Then to the meat and broth were added green corn, string beans, garlic,

onions, cabbage, squash, carrots and a few of the spicy weeds, and all boiled until the vegetables were well cooked. To prepare *estofado*, some pieces of meat with lard were placed on the fire, and after a short time dry grapes were added and left until well cooked. Then slices of bread, sugar and some spice were added and again placed on the fire for a short while. *Albóndigas* were made from the sirloin of the beef. The meat was well ground on a *metate*, or otherwise; to it were added onions, black pepper, coriander and *yerba buena* (a species of mint). All these were made into a dough or paste, and from this little balls were shaped and cooked in boiling water. *Colache* was a common dish, wholesome and easily cooked. Some lard was thoroughly heated, and in that squash cut up fine, green corn, also cut up, some cheese and meat, all being cooked together (pp. 117–18).

Unlike in other regions of the Southwest, in California there was little interaction between Spanish and native Indian cuisines. The California Indians were the least developed of those in Spanish occupied territories. As José Bandini says in *A Description of California* as cited in *Mexican California: An Original Anthology*, edited by Leslie Parr: "They were wholly unlike the Eastern Indians. They lacked the social organization of the Pueblos. There were no powerful tribes among them, as the Sioux of the north and the Apache of the Southwest (p. 46)." Later, gringo explorers were to nickname them "Diggers" because of their habit of digging for worms and roots which they often ate uncooked. Because there was little social interaction between these Indians and the Spanish, there was little cross-influence on the cuisine. Because of this, the early California settlers maintained a diet more similar to that of their Spanish heritage than in other parts of the Southwest.

Mexican influence in California predominated only until the "Bear Flag" Revolt in 1846, although Mexican ownership of land lasted somewhat longer. What occurred soon after mirrored events in the rest of the Southwest. The gold rush of 1849 soon petered out, and the hordes of miners and other settlers were forced to turn to other means of earning a living, often agriculture.

A terrible drought and the railroad finally dropped the curtain on Mexican primacy. As Joan W. Moore and Harry Pachon state in *Mexican Americans:*

> The final blow (as in all the border states) was the arrival of the railroad, which reached as far west as San Francisco in 1869. In 1876 the railroad was completed to Los Angeles from northern California; the next year, a line to Los Angeles from the East was finished. In 1887 alone the two new railroads brought in more than 120,000 Anglo American settlers. There were by that year only 12,000 Mexicans in all southern California. Thus, almost in one year, the Mexican majority became a local minority (p. 20).

Moore and Pachon go on to conclude:

> Everywhere except in New Mexico, this charter-member minority . . . was reduced to landless labor, and made politically and economically impotent. Socially the long-settled charter-members had become "Mexicans" indistinguishable from the new immigrants from Mexico. Perhaps more important, by now all Mexicans, whatever their isolation from other Mexican communities, had in common a heritage of racial conflict. Only in New Mexico did Mexicans retain some degree of numerical plurality and control in political affairs (p. 20).

It was not until well into the twentieth century that Mexican influence on California cooking began its rebirth. In fact, it was in 1939, about the time Katy Meek opened La Posta restaurant in New Mexico that Ralph Pesquiera, Sr., moved his family from Calexico to San Diego, California. In 1940, he established a *tortillería* which he called El Indio, appropriately located on India Street, just north of the downtown area. Besides making about thirty dozen tortillas a day El Indio sold beans, enchiladas, and sauces as take-out food. If you ask three Mexican-Americans in San Diego the recipe of their mother's enchilada sauce, at least one will probably shrug and tell you sheepishly that it came from El Indio. Over the years, the menu was expanded, a sit-down eating area was added, and a patio was built just across the street. Now operated by Ralph Pesquiera, Jr., who is on the Board of Regents of the University of California, El Indio produces about 6,000 tortillas a day, serves diners in four locations, and has a large catering division.

Another pioneer in the Mexican food business in California is Catalina Gonzáles, the owner of Tony's Jacal, located just north of Del Mar, California. She told me of the close connection her family developed with El Indio over the years, having bought their tortillas since 1947. Tony's Jacal restaurant was established when Catalina, who wanted to get a job, was told by her husband Tony that a job would interfere with the raising of their three children. Instead of seeking outside employment, she opened a restaurant in the house across the street that had been left to them by Tony's parents. At first Tony's Jacal opened only on weekends, and Cataina did everything herself except wash dishes. After about three years people were waiting in line for an hour or two, and Catalina decided she must either keep the restaurant open more days or close it. Fortunately, she decided to keep the restaurant open on a regular schedule.

Catalina came from the southern state of Michoacán. Her family immigrated first to Phoenix, which may explain the Sonoran influence on the cooking at Tony's; however, Tony's also serves *carnitas*, for which Michoacán is famous. While Sonoran cooking predominates in California, as in the case of this restaurant, one often finds influences from other parts of Mexico. Although Catalina, now in her eighties, spends a good part of the year traveling in Europe, Asia, and Mexico, she still manages to keep a sharp eye on the restaurant, which is staffed primarily with her children, grandchildren, and other family members.

Unfortunately, most of the dishes that made California's Mexican-American cooking special have nearly disappeared, along with the *californios* who developed them. The lure of gold and the ease of access to the area created by the railroads resulted in a tide of Anglo settlers and the destruction of the huge ranchos, ending a very special way of life in a unique environment.

Because, at least in terms of cooking, the indigenous Indians were the Southwest's most primitive, the cooking of the *californios* retained more of its Spanish characteristics than Mexican-American food did in other areas. However, the use of chiles and tortillas, as well as the olives, nuts, and fruits that thrived in California's temperate climate, gave the barbecued dishes, the stews, the egg dishes, and the desserts of this region distinctive qualities.

Today, except in the homes of descendants of the original settlers, one rarely finds such dishes. Most of the cooking, and especially that found in restaurants, comes from the same roots as that of Arizona, Sonora— but with some important additions. Many of California's more recent Mexican immigrants have come from Baja California, and they have introduced that area's tradition of seafood cooking to the California cuisine. In addition, immigrants from southern Mexico have been drawn to California perhaps more than to any other part of the Southwest, and consequently elements of the cooking of places like Michoacán, Puebla, and Oaxaca can be found more and more frequently incorporated into the local cuisine.

RECENT IMMIGRATION AND MEXICAN-AMERICAN FOOD

The above historical outline shows why, other than in New Mexico, there was very little Mexican influence on the cooking of the Southwest before 1900. In both Texas and California there was a strong Mexican presence prior to the acquisition of these areas by the United States in the mid-1800s. However, the large numbers and aggressiveness of the Anglo settlers provided a nearly total displacement of the Hispanic culture. In Arizona, because of Indian depredations, there never were more than about 1,000 Mexican settlers, and most of them were crowded into fortified Tucson.

In their book *Mexican Americans*, Joan W. Moore and Harry Pachon refer to Carey Williams's *North from Mexico*, and the Bureau of the Census's *Historical Statistics of the United States, Colonial Times to 1957*, noting that the approximate numbers of Mexicans in the Southwest when the United States assumed control of the area were: 5,000 in Texas, 1,000 in Arizona, 7,500 in California, and 60,000 in New Mexico. It is obvious, therefore, that, except in New Mexico, the current potent influence was a result of more recent immigration (p. 12).

Although recent migration began, in a meaningful way, as early as 1900, it is not immediately apparent why the larger population did not discover Mexican cooking twenty or thirty years earlier than it did. Why did so many years elapse between the time of immigration and settlement and the time when Mexican cuisine became an important aspect of our culture? How did the food prepared in Tony's, El Charro, and thousands of Mexican-American kitchens evolve from its Mexican origins into what it is today?

One of the reasons why Mexican-American cooking was not accepted earlier by the general population was undoubtedly because of the isolation of Hispanics from mainstream American culture. In the early 1900s, Mexicans came to the United States to obtain work and to escape the turmoil of the revolutionary activity in their country. The migration and trade patterns established in the eighteenth and nineteenth centuries continued as immigration routes after 1900. This meant that a majority of Mexicans moving to central and east Texas came from the border states of Tamaulipas, Nuevo León, and Coahuila; those in west Texas and southern New Mexico from Chihuahua; Arizona's immigrants originated in Sonora; and California's came from both Sonora and Baja California.

The early immigrants were employed almost exclusively in three occupations: railroads, mining, and agriculture, and, as Thomas Sowell says in *Ethnic America: A History:*

> These three dominant occupations all tended to isolate Mexican-Americans in enclaves separate from the rest of the American population. Their children grew up in a separate, Spanish-speaking Mexican-American world.
>
> This early isolation was responsible for forming many of our attitudes and subsequent treatment of Mexican-Americans and, of course, their attitudes toward the rest of the U.S. Here were people we saw often during the day at work, but otherwise it was as if they did not exist. They spoke a different language and had different customs and ethics, notably a propensity to put family over work. They also came from a culture where education did not, for all practical purposes, exist so this was not a part of their culture. This flew directly in the face of the United States' early work ethic (p. 249).

Other factors that contributed to the ethnic isolation of Hispanics were the continuing Anglo antipathy toward Catholicism that had been conditioned for several hundred years by England's rivalry with Spain and its denunciations of Catholicism.

Early migrants lived in rural mining, railroad, or agricultural camps, often in poor circumstances with few modern conveniences. The foodways of these new residents were usually those of the areas from which they came. Meat came mostly from goats, cattle, and pigs, but not in neatly wrapped supermarket packages. In order to obtain a steak one butchered the entire animal, and so scarce was food that nothing was wasted. Fat was rendered, pork skins made into *chicharrones*, entrails were used, and heads were smoked in pits in the ground in the centuries-old Indian tradition. Even the blood was used in the making of stews such as *fritada* and *morcilla*.

In referring to C. A. Hawley's *Life along the Border*, Joe S. Graham, in "Mexican-American Traditional Foodways at La Junta de Los Rios" notes that Hawley, who was the business manager for the Chisos Mining Company in Terlingua around the turn of the century, says that California pink beans and white corn were the "main staples in that diet . . . tamales were more-or-less a luxury among the poor, probably because of the expense of the meat. Tortillas and enchiladas were more common among the workers because they were less expensive (p. 7)."

A new set of immigration laws and the Great Depression of the 1930s reversed the immigration process for a time, but then came World War II. The war effort meant that there was a need not only for agricultural labor, but also for factory workers. It was during this period that Mexicans worked and lived in an urban setting with Anglos for the first time. The war also threw thousands of Mexican-American draftees together with their Anglo counterparts.

Consequently, although Mexicans had been living in the Southwest for around 350 years, it was not until the late 1930s that they began to mix in any meaningful way with Anglos. It is understandable that, until this time, the Anglo community knew nearly nothing about Mexican cooking.

As modernization came to Mexican-American communities, their cooking was greatly affected. Technology in the form of food preservation and packaging meant that precious items such as meat could be purchased in small amounts at the supermarket instead of coming from an entire animal, the rest of which would have to be processed and used or preserved. By-products such as blood, variety meats, and pork skins became less important than they had been (and continued to be in Mexico). The availability and low cost of ground beef in the United States led to its frequent use as a replacement for the traditional shredded beef in many Mexican recipes. Inexpensive, packaged cheddar cheeses replaced the white *asadero* cheese that is still used in Mexico and which was formerly made by rural Mexican-Americans. In addition, increased incomes meant larger portions of ingredients were used in recipes.

Even the acquisition of modern gas and electric ovens has had a significant effect on Mexican-American cooking, altering the method of enchilada preparation and, ultimately, the way in which Mexican-American combination plates are served. In Mexico enchiladas are most often prepared by dipping the tortillas into hot oil and then into hot or warm sauce. (The oil makes the tortillas pliable and prevents the sauce from making them soggy.) They are then wrapped around either a cheese or meat filling and served immediately. In Mexican-American cooking the process is the same except that after the enchiladas have been filled and wrapped, they are placed on ovenproof plates, covered with more sauce and cheese, and heated in the oven until the cheese is melted and the sauce is bubbling. It is this final addition of sauce and subsequent heating that accounts for the most substantial difference between Mexican and Mexican-American cooking.

Although a combination plate in Mexico may consist of the same items as one in the United States (an enchilada, a taco, and either a tamale, *chalupa*, *quesadilla*, or other *antojito*, accompanied by rice and refried beans), in Mexico the enchilada is usually prepared as described above, with the sauce limited to the enchilada itself and the other items kept separate, while the Mexican-American combination plate is usually covered with the chile sauce. Food experts often use this somewhat indiscriminate covering of nearly everything on the plate with what I call the "master" sauce as evidence that Mexican-American cooking lacks the finesse of true Mexican cooking. While these critics may be partly correct, there is no doubt that the Mexican-American style of cooking has millions of aficionados, and customer satisfaction is the ultimate criterion.

The forgoing has attempted to trace the development of Mexican-American cooking and to share a few of the stories behind some of the people and places that have made it so incredibly popular in the United States. While the diversity of their backgrounds mocks any attempt at stereotyping, there is one strong commonality—the desire to both preserve and share something in which they take tremendous pride: their families' cooking traditions. It is now time to move on to the recipes that are responsible for the current wave of popularity of Mexican-American cooking.

basics

INGREDIENTS AND EQUIPMENT

In order to keep this section as short as possible, I have limited the descriptions to items that are used throughout the book and have not included items that are explained in the individual recipes. For example, corn and *nixtamal* are explained in the sections on tortillas and *posole* in which they are used.

I have especially kept the section on chiles brief since there are so many excellent books on the subject, such as *The Whole Chile Pepper Book* by Dave DeWitt and Nancy Gerlach.

INGREDIENTS

CHILES

Fortunately for us not nearly as many varieties of chiles are used in Mexican-American cooking as in Mexican cooking. (Actually, it is the same in Mexico if you consider each region individually since just a few kinds of chiles usually predominate in each area.) In fact, the vast majority of Mexican-American dishes can be prepared with dried New Mexico and *ancho* chiles and fresh *serrano* and *jalapeño* chiles. The dried varieties are easily available through the mail-order sources listed in the Appendix and keep indefinitely if stored in airtight jars. The fresh chiles are available in grocery stores throughout the Southwest and in most major cities in other parts of the country.

In the chapter "Pre-Hispanic and Mexican Haute Cuisine Recipes" (p. 26), two exotic chile varieties are specified that, to my knowledge, are not available in this country. These are the *mulato* chile used in *Mole poblano* and the *chilhuacle* chile used in Oaxaca's *mole negro*. In fact, the *chilhuacle* chile, which today costs over $25 a pound, is rarely available outside of Oaxaca. To obtain these chiles, about your only recourse is to visit Mexico and make friends with someone who can send them to you. The experience will be well worthwhile, and maybe you can start an import business!

DRIED CHILES

Ancho: Ancho chiles are the dried version of the *poblano* chiles from which *chiles rellenos* are made. These and the New Mexico chiles are by far the most frequently used chiles for making chile sauces—the most distinctive aspect of Mexican-American cooking.

Chile powders: Chile powders are made from dried chiles, and you can easily make your own with a spice or coffee grinder. If possible, use only the powders made from New Mexico and *ancho* variety chiles rather than the generic brands which often

Ancho chile

contain cumin and oregano as well as garlic and onion powders. Powders can be substituted for whole chiles at the rate of 1 tablespoon per chile.

Chipotle: Chipotle chiles are *jalapeño* chiles that have been smoked. These fascinating chiles were made by the pre-Hispanic Indians and have recently been adopted by many of the talented chefs specializing in new southwestern cooking. *Chipotle* chiles come either dried or canned with an *adobo* sauce. They are very hot but impart a deep smoky flavor to the dishes in which they are used.

De árbol: The chile *de árbol* is very hot and ranges from about 1½ to 3 inches in length and up to about ¼ inch in width.

New Mexico: New Mexico chiles come in several varieties and different heat levels, and have been developed over the years in careful breeding programs. Often called *chiles de ristras* because of the colorful way in which they are often braided and sometimes made into wreaths, they come in mild, medium, and hot. Unfortunately, the labels are often inaccurate so you should always test a new batch and make your own determination.

Regarding New Mexico chiles, there is a product available that is both interesting and a great time-saver—Santa Cruz Chile Paste made by the Santa Cruz Chili & Spice Co. As far as I know, this product is unique, as is the company which produces it. Judy England, owner of the company, located in Tumacacori, Arizona, between Tucson and Nogales, comes from an old Arizona ranching family with a fascinating history.

Usually chile paste and chile sauce are made by reconstituting dried chiles, then grinding them into a paste. At Santa Cruz Chili & Spice Co., however, they take fresh red, ripe New Mexico chiles grown near Douglas, Arizona, which they call "wet reds," and grind them immediately into a paste that is then packed into jars. All you need to do is dilute the paste with water to obtain the basis for New Mexico-style chile sauces. The company also manufactures some excellent sauces and carries a large number of spices. To order these and other products, see the Appendix.

Pasilla chiles

Pasilla: This chile, which is wrinkled like the *ancho* but is much longer and thinner, and more black than reddish brown (like the *ancho*), is not used very often in this country, but is nevertheless available through mail-order sources (see the Appendix). I mention it mainly to note the fact that in California the popular *ancho* chile is often labeled as a *pasilla*. This error also occurs in some cookbooks.

Pequín and Tepín: These are the small, respectively football and round-shaped chiles that are the hottest used in the Southwest. They are quite common and are easily obtained through mail-order sources (see the Appendix). In Mexican-American cooking these chiles are most often crumbled into stews, soups, and other dishes to add some heat, much the way we use ground black pepper. Although they have distinctive flavors, by the time you use enough *pequín* or *tepín* chiles to actually be able to discern their individual character, most people have gotten more BTU's than they want.

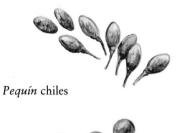

Pequín chiles

Tepín chiles

FRESH CHILES

Anaheim or New Mexico: These are the long, relatively thin chiles from which the dried New Mexico chiles are made. When fresh, they are used primarily to make green chile stews and sauces, but they are also used to make *chiles rellenos*, especially when *poblano* chiles are not available.

Ten fresh whole green chiles equal approximately 1 pound. This weight is reduced to about 9 ounces after they are peeled, stemmed, and seeded. At this point their volume equals about 1⅓ cups.

Jalapeño: Originally from Jalapa, the capital of Veracruz, *jalapeños* are the best-known and most available of all the chiles. They usually range about midway up the heat scale, except that Texas A & M University has introduced a low-heat variety which, unfortunately, is found too often in grocery stores.

Jalapeño chiles

Poblano: The *poblano* is the *ancho* chile before it has been dried. It is the chile that in Mexico is used to make *chiles rellenos* and

Chiles en nogada. However, in Mexican-American cooking the Anaheim or New Mexico-style fresh chile is often used for these dishes. The *poblano* ranges in heat from mild to just a step or two below the *jalapeño*.

Serrano: The *serrano* chile, originally from southern Mexico, is smaller than the *jalapeño* but hotter, so that they are often interchangeable. However, the flavors are different so try to use the one specified whenever possible.

Serrano chiles

ANISEED

These are the aromatic seeds that come from the anise plant, a member of the carrot family. In Mexican cooking they are used to flavor teas and desserts.

AVOCADOS

Avocados have been a part of Mexican cooking since well before Mexico was discovered by explorers from the Old World. My favorite variety in the United States is the haas, with the fuerte a second choice. The large watery and virtually tasteless Florida avocados that are sold during the winter months are not an acceptable substitute.

BEANS

When thinking of beans in relation to Mexican food, it is usually the pinto bean that comes to mind, and occasionally the black bean. In Mexican-American cooking there is no question that the pinto bean is king and that the black bean is rarely seen. There are, however, two other types of beans often used in Mexican-American cooking, the California pink bean and the New Mexico and Colorado bolita bean. The pink bean is a smaller version of the pinto bean, while the bolita is a round, solid-colored, light brown bean that, to me, tastes a bit like a cooked, dried lima bean. The bolita, which is grown mostly in Colorado, is particularly adapted to high-altitude cooking and takes less time than the pinto bean to prepare. Although these different varieties of beans have different characteristics, one may often be substituted for another, and they can, for the most part, be used interchangeably in the recipes in this book.

BELL PEPPERS

These are the sweet green peppers that are found in grocery stores everywhere. Use the more common green variety unless otherwise stated.

CALABAZA/CALABACITA

In Spanish the word *calabaza* usually refers to a squash, pumpkin, or gourd larger than that which is commonly found in United States grocery stores (except around Halloween). The word *calabacita*, which literally means little squash, refers to the more typical varieties of squash that are found domestically, such as zucchini or crooknecked squash.

CHEESE

Many of the early Mexican immigrants who lived in rural settings made cheeses very similar to those they were accustomed to in Mexico, such as *asadero* and *requeson* or *queso fresco*. However, as urbanization became the rule rather than the exception, this changed.

Today, in Mexican-American cooking the most commonly used cheeses are mild cheddar, Colby, longhorn, and Monterey Jack, and these are sometimes mixed together. Other cheeses that can be used include mozzarella, provolone, and farmer cheese. These cheeses, with the possible exception of mozzarella, are quite different from the native Mexican cheeses such as *asadero*, Chihuahua, *anejo*, *queso blanco*, or *queso fresco*. Herein lies one of the major differences between Mexican and Mexican-American cooking. If all other ingredients and methods of preparation remain the same, dishes made with a cheddar cheese, such as enchiladas, are completely different from those made with *asadero*. Recently, American companies such as Cacique have begun introducing cheeses that are very much like those made in Mexico, albeit at prices much higher than those for our common domestic varieties of cheese. It will be interesting to see to what extent they are adopted.

———

NOTE: You have probably noticed the nachos that are sold in fast-food restaurants, movie theaters, and at sports stadiums throughout the country which are made with a Velveeta-like cheese. Although this cheese may resemble melted plastic, such nachos are not entirely unauthentic. This type of cheese, the most inexpensive available, was often a staple in the early immigrant's larder, and I have recently seen nachos made with such cheese in various parts of Mexico as well. However, because this type of cheese is truly inferior I have not specified it in any of the recipes.

CHORIZO

This is the typical Mexican sausage that is usually sold in bulk form, particularly in the southwestern United States. It differs from other types of sausage in that much of its flavor comes from a combination of chile and vinegar.

CILANTRO

This is the fresh coriander leaf which is also called Chinese parsley. Dried cilantro does not work in the recipes, nor is there any other substitute.

Cilantro

COOKING OIL, LARD, AND SHORTENING

Mexican and Mexican-American cooking traditionally rely on lard for nearly all situations where fat is required. However, this is changing as the adverse effects of lard's high cholesterol and saturated fat content become more widely known. Where the strong statement of lard is required, I specify olive oil, which, while different, makes an acceptable substitute. There are, however, a few items for which only lard can be used to achieve the traditional taste of the dish, including tamales and refried beans. Even in these cases shortening and olive oil can be substituted if you decide lard is just not acceptable. In situations where a neutral oil is needed, I prefer canola, peanut, or safflower oils.

CORN HUSKS

Corn husks are used for wrapping tamales. Usually they are purchased dry, then soaked in warm water to reconstitute them. However, occasionally fresh husks are used. This is especially true in the making of green corn tamales in which fresh corn kernels are used. If you are unable to obtain corn husks, a piece of cloth such as from an old pillowcase or bed sheet may be used. However, be careful not to use anything that could bleed potentially poisonous dye into the tamale dough while it is steaming.

CUMIN

Cumin comes as a whole seed and ground into powder. Except in Texas the whole seed is most often used. When ground cumin is required in a recipe, it will be specified. In all other cases use the whole seed.

Jícama

JÍCAMA

A root vegetable that, to me, is best described, both in terms of taste and texture, as a cross between an apple and a water chestnut. It is used as an appetizer and salad ingredient.

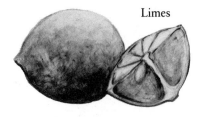

Limes

LIMES

In the United States most of our limes are the large Persian variety. They are quite a bit sweeter than the smaller Mexican limes but make a reasonable substitute.

MASA HARINA

This product, manufactured by Quaker, is a flour that has been made from the dried corn used to make the *masa* that is used to make corn tortillas. Tortillas and tamales made from Masa Harina are not as good as those made from a ground, wet *masa*, but it makes a good substitute.

MESQUITE

This refers to the wood of the mesquite tree, which is the cooking fuel of choice in northern Mexico and in much of the southwestern United States; it is now sold packaged throughout most of the United States. In addition to its distinctive flavor, mesquite is one of the hottest burning woods used in cooking. If necessary, you can substitute hickory or a natural hardwood charcoal. Briquettes should only be used as a last resort because they sometimes contain petroleum-based ingredients that can produce an unpleasant taste.

MEXICAN CHOCOLATE

Mexican chocolate differs from chocolate familiar to us principally in that it is more granular in texture and usually contains ground almonds and cinnamon. Whether it is whipped into the traditional hot chocolate drink or used to make one of the *moles*, the result is a very special taste. Mexican chocolate is usually available in large grocery stores and supermarkets in the United States. It can also be purchased from mail-order companies (see the Appendix). However, if you cannot find it, use some semi-sweet chocolate and add a little granulated sugar and a pinch or two of cinnamon.

NOPALES

In Mexican cooking *nopales* or *nopalitos* refers to the leaves, or paddles, of the nopal cactus. They are used as a vegetable and in salads. The main drawback of *nopales* is that they emit a glute-

Nopal

nous substance much like that of okra. Canned *nopales* do not greatly resemble fresh ones, but they make an adequate substitute, especially for salads since they are usually canned in vinegar.

OREGANO

Oregano comes in the form of crumbled leaves and ground. The ground variety is rarely used and will be specified when it is needed in a particular recipe. A fresh Mexican oregano may be substituted, but the dried version is much more common in Mexican-American cooking.

PILONCILLO

Piloncillo

This is the dark brown, hard cone made of unrefined sugar that you find in Hispanic grocery stores and the ethnic section of southwestern supermarkets. Brown sugar makes an acceptable substitute. In fact, in many cases I have taken the liberty of specifying brown sugar since it is so much easier to use.

PIMIENTO

Pimientos are red bell or other very mild large peppers whose skins have been removed. Pimientos are usually found with the olives and pickles in domestic grocery stores.

PINE NUTS

Pine or piñon nuts are readily available in most supermarkets in the United States. They are particularly characteristic of New Mexico's cooking.

POSOLE

Posole is usually called hominy in this country. It refers to corn which has been dried and then cooked until it is tender. In New Mexico *posole* comes in yellow, blue, and white varieties. If absolutely necessary, canned hominy may be substituted.

TOMATILLOS

Called *tomates verdes* in some parts of Mexico, this small, green tomato-like relative of the gooseberry is very common in Mexican cooking. It is usually boiled until soft before being blended into sauces. *Tomatillos* are easy to grow so consider this option if they are unavailable in your area. There is no substitute.

Tomatillos

EQUIPMENT

Mexican-American cooking like Mexican cooking requires very little specialized equipment. However, there are a few items that make the process both easier and better.

BLENDER

The *licuadora* is now found in the kitchens of even the poorest Mexican families. Its most important function is to replace the *molcajete* in the preparation of large amounts of chile sauce.

COMAL

This is a flat iron griddle used in Mexican cooking. A heavy iron skillet makes a fine substitute.

DEEP-FRY THERMOMETER

This item is especially useful when making *sopaipillas*, fry bread, and *buñuelos*. A good one with a clip to hold it to the side of a pan allows a much better deep-fry result than even the better home-size deep fryers, which either have inaccurate thermostats or do not register temperatures over 350 degrees.

Comal

DOUBLE BOILER

This item is useful in making custards since it allows the custard to thicken more gradually than if the ingredients were placed over an open flame, thus reducing the risk of this dish becoming more like scrambled eggs than a creamy dessert.

ELECTRIC MIXER

Either a stationary or powerful hand mixer is a great help in making desserts, especially those that call for beaten egg whites, and in making the *masa* for tamales.

FOOD MILL

This piece of equipment is extremely useful for straining blended chile puree when making chile sauces.

FOOD PROCESSOR

As with any other cuisine, a food processor allows many short-cuts in Mexican-American cooking. It is particularly useful in making *chorizo*, chopping large quantities of vegetables, grating cheese, making *masa* for tortillas, and in making desserts. A food processor fitted with a plastic dough blade is especially useful for imitating the texture of handshredded meat.

IRONWARE

Iron cookware, skillets, griddles, Dutch ovens, and saucepans are my favorite cooking implements and are very inexpensive. Their only disadvantages are that they are quite heavy and their handles are not insulated from the heat.

LIME SQUEEZER

Manufacturers in Mexico produce a device that is my all-time favorite for extracting the juice of limes. You place a cut lime in the receptacle and squeeze the hinged handles, and with very little effort the majority of the juice is extracted. The only problem is that these items are made with uncoated aluminum, which is believed to be potentially dangerous to the health, especially when combined with acidic foods. This may be why the Mexican juicers are not sold in this country.

MOLCAJETE AND TEJOLOTE

This Indian version of the mortar and pestle is indispensable for grinding garlic, chiles, and spices for sauces. Made from volcanic rock, the *molcajete* is also the best and easiest way to produce guacamole of the right consistency. The only thing comparable is one of the rough-sided Oriental mortar and pestles.

Molcajete and
Tejolote

SCALE

An accurate kitchen scale is useful in many ways. When making large quantities of chile sauce, it is helpful to measure chiles by weight rather than number because their sizes can vary so dramatically. Also, when making items such as tamales, it is much more accurate to weigh ingredients than to measure them.

TORTILLA CHEF

This is a small appliance made by Vitantonio Cookware which resembles an electric waffle iron; it takes much of the labor and need for experience out of making homemade tortillas.

TORTILLA PRESS

This is the old standby for making corn tortillas and is usually available in Hispanic grocery stores or in specialty cookware shops. Although it is effective, it is not nearly as much fun or as easy to use as the Tortilla Chef.

Tortilla press

TORTILLA WARMER

As the name infers this is a device intended to keep tortillas warm. In Mexico this is nearly always achieved by placing the tortillas wrapped in a towel into a basket. In this country devices are made for the purpose, usually out of plastic or Styrofoam. These work well and are great for heating the tortillas in a microwave oven as well as for keeping them warm.

Recipes

Included in this section are the best Mexican-American recipes I have collected during more than eighteen years of research, gleaned from cooks in homes and restaurants in many regions of Mexico and the southwestern United States, as well as from old out-of-print cookbooks, some from around the turn of the century. All recipes were kitchen-tested by me, and personal interpretations are included where appropriate. The most interesting recipes from the old cookbooks were checked with acquaintances in various regions to determine if they were still part of the current cuisine, and then the modern versions were tested in comparison with the original versions to arrive at the best interpretation of each recipe. Most often the final product included in this collection was a result of combining aspects of several different recipes. The general criteria I used for including various dishes were whether the dish was an important part of the cuisine and whether it had universal appeal, although I deviated from these criteria in a few instances, such as in the section on "Variety Dishes," where some dishes of historical importance to the cuisine were included even though they might lack universal appeal.

In order to make this book useful to novice and experienced cooks, as well as creative cooks (those cooks who enjoy using recipes as a springboard for developing their own favorite renditions of a dish), I have used a format that differs from that of other cookbooks. For each category, such as enchiladas, I first provide a detailed description of the dish's preparation and a discussion of its variations; I then give the recipes of my favorite versions of the dish. Accordingly, the cook new to Mexican food will have all the detail necessary to be able to prepare the dishes; the experienced cook can skip the explanatory section and go straight to the recipes; and the creative cook is provided with all the elements necessary to produce a result that is more personal.

In addition, for health-conscious individuals or those on low-fat, low-cholesterol diets, I have included "nutrition hints" in many sections of the book that indicate how various recipes might be adapted to meet particular health needs.

Bebidas
DRINKS

hen one thinks of Mexican drinks, the margarita, tequila sour, and tequila sunrise spring to mind. The impression that these drinks are somehow Mexican comes from the fact that they are made with tequila and are very popular in Mexican-American restaurants. Interestingly, most of these drinks were either invented by bartenders during the border town heyday of Prohibition, or in Cuba. The truth is that tequila taken straight or with *sangrita*, beer, *mescal*, *pulque*, *sangría*, or brandy are the majority of alcoholic beverages traditionally imbibed south of the border.

Mexico's real contributions to thirst quenching are nonalcoholic drinks such as herb teas and fruit and rice- or corn-based beverages such as *horchata* and *atole*. To these traditional Indian beverages the *californios*, mostly of Spanish ancestry, added wine. The Mexican-American drink repertoire, as with the cuisine, evolved from the Mexican favorites but was limited by availability of ingredients and financial considerations.

While this section contains some favorite cocktails that are traditional gringo favorites when partaking of Mexican food, it also includes some of the lesser-known drinks that immigrants brought north with them.

MARGARITA

How can the margarita be placed anywhere but first in any heirarchy of Mexican drinks? This is, of course, regardless of the fact that, other than in establishments catering to tourists, it is difficult to find a bartender in Mexico who knows how to make a margarita. This famous drink and beer are the overwhelming choices of gringos when partaking of Mexican food.

The margarita's origin is just as steeped in mystery and controversy as some other aspects of Mexican cooking. The main difference is that people tend to be more passionate about margaritas than about, say, nachos. The invention of the margarita is variously ascribed to bartenders in Ciudad Juárez, Baja California, and Los Angeles, as well as to a San Antonio socialite who claims to have invented it at her villa in Mexico.

The fascinating stories revolving around the margarita and associated lore will be in a forthcoming book on tequila by food and horticultural expert Lucinda Hutson. Lucinda was kind enough to provide the following recipe, which is her favorite, but with one caveat: she warned that the real margarita is strong, more like a martini than some of the watered-down versions served in restaurants. She also advised that silver tequila, the variety with less age than the gold varieties, is preferred because its flavor is not dominated by the other ingredients.

LUCINDA'S MARGARITA

Pour the ingredients over ice in a cocktail shaker, shake for 30 seconds, then serve on the rocks garnished with a lime wedge. *Serves 1.*

2 *ounces silver tequila*

1 *ounce Cointreau*

1 *ounce Mexican lime juice*
   Salt to coat the glass's rim (optional)

1 *lime, cut into wedges*

BORDER TOWN MARGARITA

1½ *ounces tequila*

1½ *ounces Cointreau*

1½ *ounces lime juice*

　　Salt to coat the glass's rim (optional)

1 *lime, cut into wedges*

From Nogales, this margarita, not too strong and not too weak, is my favorite. The equal ingredient amounts make it easy to remember.

Pour the ingredients over ice in a cocktail shaker, shake for 30 seconds, then serve on the rocks garnished with a lime wedge. *Serves 1.*

FROZEN MARGARITA

1¼ *ounces tequila*

1¼ *ounces water*

1¼ *ounces triple sec*

3 *ounces lime juice*

　　Generous bar spoon of sugar

　　Salt to coat the glass's rim (optional)

1 *lime, cut into wedges*

This is a good refreshing drink with a fine flavor. Its main advantage is that it allows serious, chile-induced thirst quenching without the kick of the preceding recipes.

Place the ingredients in a blender with ice and blend. Serve garnished with a lime wedge. *Serves 1.*

TEQUILA SUNRISE

1½ *ounces tequila*

　　Orange juice

　　Grenadine

　　Maraschino cherry and orange slice for garnish

Another popular drink with Mexican food, particularly at brunch, is the Tequila Sunrise.

Pour the tequila over ice in a tall glass. Fill the glass with the orange juice, add a dollop of grenadine, and serve garnished with a cherry and orange slice. *Serves 1.*

CUBA LIBRE

This famous drink is the old standby rum and Coke with a healthy squeeze of lime juice.

1½ *ounces dark rum*
      Coca-Cola
¼ *lime*

Pour the rum over ice in a tall glass, fill it with Coca-Cola, and squeeze in the juice from the lime wedge. *Serves 1.*

SANGRITA

Although by far the most popular accompaniment to tequila in Mexico, *Sangrita* has not caught on in the United States for some reason. However, it is such a perfect marriage with tequila that its popularity cannot be far away. *Sangrita* can either be sipped as a chaser with straight tequila or mixed with it over ice as you would a Bloody Mary, sometimes with the addition of soda. The latter drink is called a *vampiro* and is popular in northern Mexico, especially in Nuevo León.

    Sangrita can be purchased, but the following recipe is quite easy and much better.

1 *cup orange juice*
½ *cup tomato juice*
1 *tablespoon grenadine*
1 *teaspoon salt*
   Pinch to ¼ teaspoon
      cayenne pepper,
      depending on individual
      taste

Mix all ingredients together and serve as described above. *Serves about 2 as a* vampiro *or about 6 as a chaser with tequila.*

CHOCOLATE

1 *pint milk*
1 *pint condensed milk*
6 *ounces milk chocolate*
½ *teaspoon powdered cinnamon*
1 *teaspoon vanilla*
   Sugar to taste

In Mexican and Mexican-American households chocolate is one of the favorite and most traditional drinks. In Mexico the chocolate is usually mixed with water or milk, but this Mexican-American recipe combines whole milk with condensed milk for a rich variation.

Mix 1 cup of the milk, the condensed milk, and the cinnamon and bring the mixture to a boil over medium heat.

Meanwhile, heat the remaining 1 cup milk over low heat and melt the chocolate in it. Pour the melted chocolate mixture into the rest of the milk, add the vanilla and sugar to taste, and whip the drink with a wire whisk or *molinillo* (the wooden device used in Mexico) until it is frothy. *Serves 4.*

TEAS

Most Mexican-American teas are taken as much for medicinal reasons as for their interesting tastes. These natural brews are both tasty and comforting.

TÉ DE YERBA BUENA
Mint Tea

5 *cups water*
   Heaping tablespoon dried mint leaves
   Heaping tablespoon sugar, or to taste

Bring the water to a boil, add the mint leaves, and simmer for 5 minutes.

Stir in the sugar, remove the pot from the heat, and allow to steep, covered, for 10 minutes. Serve hot or cold. *Serves 4.*

TÉ DE ANIS

Anise Tea

If you like anise, you will enjoy this refreshing drink. It is also useful in making pastries and breads flavored with anise.

5 *cups water*
2½ *teaspoons aniseed*
Heaping tablespoon sugar, or to taste

Bring the water to a boil and add the aniseed.

Remove the pot from the heat and allow to steep, covered, for 20 minutes; then strain out the seeds.

Stir in the sugar and either serve the tea at room temperature, chilled, or reheated. *Serves 4.*

TÉ DE CANELA

Cinnamon Tea

Bring the water to a boil, add the cinnamon, and simmer for 15 minutes.

5 *cups water*
4 *cinnamon sticks*
4 *teaspoons sugar, or to taste*

Stir in the sugar, remove the cinnamon sticks, and serve. *Serves 4.*

WINE

Wine was popular with the early Spanish settlers in both California and New Mexico. However, it was in California that wine became a part of the larger tradition.

Early California Hospitality by Ana M. Bégué de Packman is one of the most important sources of information on the cooking of early California. She was a secretary of the Historical Society of Southern California; a historian of first families of California; a former custodian of Casa Figuroa; and the author of *Leather Dollars*. In *Early California Hospitality* she describes two of early California's most popular wines as follows:

VINO
Wine

One cannot think of early California without her claret or zestful *Angélica* wine. The broad acres of mission grapes produced one of the most important industries of Alta California.

Fill a fifty-gallon open-top barrel with crushed mission grapes. No water. In early California the padres taught the Indians to crush the grapes by stomping upon them in the vats with their bare feet. Today, the *americano*'s invention of a small hand-press will do the work.

Every day stir the mixture with a long paddle so as to turn what is on top today to the bottom. On about the tenth day all the roughage will mass and sink to the bottom of the barrel. Never leave the pulp which rises to the top exposed for more than six hours, because the air sours it and when turned under it will spoil the whole barrel.

To clear, draw the strained liquid off into a smaller covered-top barrel, and allow to stand without a cork. Just cover the bunghole with a light piece of cloth to keep out the gnats. Never move the barrel.

Here it must ferment for ten more days. Then very carefully syphon the clear liquid into a clean charred barrel. Be sure it is sweet and not sour. This is now wine, and it must be well sealed for at least three months to age.

ANGÉLICA
California Sweet Wine

To make the famous *angélica de California*, use only the clear liquid pressed from the mission grape. Allow to ferment in an open barrel for ten days, then syphon off the settled liquid into a kettle to cook.

Boil the clear wine and add to every gallon one pound of sugar and one quart of grape alcohol. Allow to stand sealed in a well-charred barrel for six months before bottling.

Angélica was served at the end of the meal with the desserts or at the *merienda* (p. 79).

Atole

Cornmeal Drink

This is one of the oldest recipes on our continent. Originally made with water, this recipe, made with milk, is even better. In fact, according to Ana M. Bégué de Packman, the *californios* called it *Nech'-atole*, a colloquialism for *leche y atole*, or milk with *Atole*. *Atole* was a common drink at the *merienda*, or afternoon tea, following the daily siesta.

½ *cup Masa Harina*
5 *cups milk*
4 *tablespoons brown sugar*
¼ *teaspoon cinnamon*
1 *teaspoon vanilla*

Put the Masa Harina in a bowl and whisk in the milk, little by little.

Pour the milk mixture into a pot and add the brown sugar and cinnamon. Bring to a boil and simmer for 5 minutes, stirring constantly to keep it from becoming lumpy and sticking. Stir in the vanilla and serve in mugs. *Serves 4.*

CHAMPURRADO

Chocolate Drink

There are many recipes for this famous drink of Aztec origin. As with the other *Atole*-type recipes in this book, I have substituted milk for the traditional water. That is how it is usually made today, and it is much tastier made with milk.

Follow the drink recipe for *Atole* (p. 95) and add 1 ounce of chocolate with the sugar. *Serves 4.*

Tortillas y Pan
TORTILLAS AND BREAD

mexican-American cooking, as does that of Mexico's interior, relies extensively on the tortilla. But there are other breads, no less distinctive; most of these are derived from Indian recipes. The *sopaipilla*, one of the showpieces of New Mexican cooking, is the best example.

While Mexican-American breads appear simple, they have many subtleties that, fortunately, are easy to master with a little practice. Each region has its specialty, from the thick flour tortillas of Tex-Mex cooking to the huge paper-thin variety used in the Sonora-based concoctions of Arizona. One of the basic differences between an average and a great meal lies in the quality of the tortilla or bread that is used. After all, you wouldn't serve Wonder bread with a fine Italian meal.

TORTILLAS

The tortilla, more than anything else, symbolizes the cooking of Mexico. Invented by the pre-Hispanic Indians, this simple circle of baked corn was their bread as well as their knife, fork, and spoon. Although originally made from corn, the tortilla was later also made from wheat, which flourished under Spanish cultivation, especially in northern Mexico.

Very few meals are served in Mexican or Mexican-American homes without a basketful of steaming flour or corn tortillas. These are used the way Europeans use bread, and to fold up and consume the last bits of meat and vegetables on the plate. In its more familiar incarnations the tortilla is fried to various degrees of crispness to make tacos, *taquitos*, *flautas*, enchiladas, *tostadas*, and the chips that greet customers in Mexican-American restaurants.

CORN TORTILLAS

The ingredients in corn tortillas have not changed over the centuries, nor has there been a great deal of modification in their preparation. In cities and villages throughout Mexico, cooks still soak dried corn in a solution of water and dolomitic lime, boil it, and then remove the tough outer skins from the swollen kernels. This results in the hominy that is used to make *posole*. The hominy is then ground by hand on a *metate* into a dough called *masa* from which individual tortillas are patted out by hand. The tortillas are then baked on hot *comales*, or griddles.

In these same cities and villages, *tortillerías* go through exactly the same process, soaking, boiling, grinding, forming, and baking. The only difference is that machinery performs the vast majority of the work. In between these extremes are various pieces of equipment used by small restaurants and families, some manually operated, some powered by electricity, that partially mechanize the process.

Throughout the southwestern United States and in most cities in other areas, corn tortillas are sold in grocery stores. It is unfortunate that the vast majority of these products taste more like cardboard than the fragrant soft tortillas found in Mexico and in a few *tortillerías* in the United States. A major problem is that tortillas should be consumed shortly after being made. A week on the shelf makes even a well-made tortilla too dry. Another problem is that some manufacturers cut corners by using corn flour rather than grinding the hulled corn into *masa*.

If you have access to a *tortillería,* buy your tortillas there. If there is no nearby *tortillería,* use the store-bought variety for taco shells, *tostadas,* enchiladas, and the like. But for soft tacos that are made without frying the tortilla and when the tortillas are to be used as a table bread, you should make your own.

Until recently making corn tortillas was a rather difficult and thankless chore. The only alternative to patting the tortillas out by hand, a skill that looks as if it would be easy to acquire but is not, was to use a tortilla press. The press is used to squish rounded pieces of *masa* placed between plastic wrap or waxed paper into tortillas. The formed tortillas are then carefully transferred to a *comal* or griddle over medium heat. After a little practice the process can be accomplished with some degree of efficiency, but it is never a lot of fun.

A few years ago I purchased a *tortilladora* in Mexico, a small handcranked machine that works something like a pasta machine. Once you get the hang of it, which takes considerable practice, it turns out lots of tortillas quickly and efficiently. Unfortunately, I have not seen these machines for sale in the United States.

However, Vitantonio Cookware now manufactures a device called the Tortilla Chef that resembles a Teflon-coated, electric waffle iron with smooth surfaces. While it does not produce perfect corn tortillas (at least mine doesn't), it makes tortillas better than the ones found at most markets. It also takes most of the work out of the process and adds a little fun.

To Make Corn Tortillas:

THE DOUGH:

The first step in producing corn tortillas is to make or buy the *masa,* or dough, from which they are made. If you have access to a *tortillería,* you can buy the *masa* already made. If not, you can make your own very easily by buying a package of MaSeca, a

newly imported product from Mexico, or the more familiar Masa Harina. Just mix the corn flour with water according to the directions on the package.

If you want to make the *masa* from scratch, you will need dolomitic lime and a grinder made especially for the purpose. The latter are sold in most hardware stores in Mexico, but I have not seen them in this country.

FORMING CORN TORTILLAS:

If you are using the Tortilla Chef described on p. 85, all you need to do is follow the directions that come with it. If you do not have this device, you should purchase a tortilla press at a specialty kitchenware shop.

To make tortillas with a tortilla press, first preheat a *comal* or griddle over medium heat. Pinch off a piece of *masa* about the size of a golf ball or slightly smaller and roll it into a ball. Open the tortilla press and put a piece of waxed paper or Handi-Wrap on the bottom plate. Place the *masa* ball just to the rear of the press's center, top with another piece of waxed paper or Handi-Wrap, and press down firmly to squeeze out a tortilla. Lift the completed tortilla from the press, carefully remove the top piece of paper or plastic, and, also carefully, invert the tortilla onto the *comal* or griddle. Cook the tortilla for 20 to 30 seconds; then turn it over and cook the other side for about 30 seconds. If the heat is right, the process should not take much longer than this, so make any necessary adjustments.

In case you do not have a tortilla press, there is another way of forming the tortillas that is often used in Mexico. First, cut out a tortilla-size circle of waxed paper, about 5 to 6 inches in diameter. Make the *masa* ball and press it into the center of the waxed paper, which should be placed on a flat work surface. Continue to press on the dough, turning the waxed paper as you press until the tortilla is formed. *Yields 6 tortillas per cup of Masa Harina (dry mix) or per approximately each 10 ounces of prepared* masa.

FLOUR TORTILLAS

In recent years flour tortillas have become nearly as well known as the more traditional corn tortillas. This is not surprising since flour tortillas are as popular or more so than those made from corn in northern Mexico where so many Mexican-Americans originated. It is also far easier to make top-quality flour tortillas at home or in a small restaurant than it is to make corn tortillas.

Fine flour tortillas can be made with no more equipment than a rolling pin made from a broomstick. However, the Tortilla Chef and a food processor make producing them a real joy. Many if not most recipes for flour tortillas do not call for baking powder. Certainly fine results can be obtained without it, but, after many conversations with expert tortilla-makers and much experimentation, I have concluded that the use of baking powder produces a lighter, more tender result. The only exception to this is when making the huge, paper-thin Sonora-style tortillas that are used for burritos and *chimichangas*. With these the baking powder can cause excessive rising that leads to burst bubbles in the dough.

Different recipes call for tortillas of different sizes and thicknesses. For example, a typical Tex-Mex flour tortilla may be 5½ to 7 inches in diameter and fairly thick, while a Sonora-style tortilla used to make burritos in Arizona will be 12 inches to 18 inches in diameter and paper-thin. The following recipe provides the amounts of dough and instructions for these most common variations. However, please note that it takes considerable practice to make a proper Sonora-style tortilla. In tortilla factories an electric dough-roller is used to form the extremely thin tortillas, and then they are stretched by hand, much the way you see dough being shaped in pizzarias.

NUTRITION HINT: According to tradition, flour tortillas should be made with lard or, in some Sonoran cooking, with beef suet. However, good sense and current nutritional guidelines emphasize the health hazards of animal fats. Fortunately, excellent flour tortillas can be made using vegetable shortening that is low in saturated fat. For those on low-fat diets, the quantity of fat can also be cut up to 75 percent; however, if you cut it more, the result is too noticeable, with the tortillas lacking flexibility and becoming quite heavy. On the other hand, many family cooks often use more fat than this recipe calls for. So remember that the recipe can be made with as little as 1 tablespoon of vegetable shortening or as much as 6 tablespoons of lard.

You will notice that the following recipe calls for unbleached all-purpose flour. I find that this works much better than high-gluten bread flour which, being much more elastic, makes it more difficult to form the tortillas, especially very thin ones. For this same reason flour tortilla dough should be worked as little as possible since it is the kneading that produces the gluten.

If you do not remember anything else, remember that the secrets to making the best flour tortillas are to let the dough rest for at least 20 minutes before rolling them and to use the proper temperature when cooking them. The first is easy, and the second comes with just a little practice.

To Make Flour Tortillas:

THE DOUGH:

2 cups unbleached all-purpose flour

½ teaspoon salt

½ teaspoon baking powder (except when making Sonora-style tortillas)

¼ cup vegetable shortening

Approximately ½ cup hot water

To make the dough, mix the dry ingredients in a bowl. Some cooks now "cut" in the shortening as you would to make pie dough, but I find it much easier to melt the shortening in the water, then stir it into the flour. Form the dough into a ball, knead it for about 1 minute, then let it rest for 5 minutes, covered with a damp cloth.

Making the dough is much quicker and easier with a food processor fitted with a steel blade. Just put the dry ingredients in the bowl; then with the machine running add the water and melted shortening until the dough just comes together. Allow the machine to knead the dough for a maximum of 15 seconds, then let the dough rest as explained above.

After the dough has rested briefly, cut it into 12 equal pieces. This will produce flour tortillas with a diameter of approximately 6 to 7 inches, the usual size for table use and for *Tacos al carbón* (p. 191).

Form each piece of dough into a ball, cover it with a damp cloth, and allow it to rest for at least 20 minutes. The reason for this is that if you try to form the tortillas immediately, the dough will be difficult to stretch. After resting, the dough is less elastic and much easier to form.

FORMING AND COOKING FLOUR TORTILLAS:

This is where the Tortilla Chef machine really shines. It enables you to make very thin, light table-size flour tortillas. When it is used in combination with a *comal*, it also allows the cook to produce a large number of tortillas very quickly. Simply press out a tortilla on the machine, allow it to cook for a few seconds, then transfer it to the *comal* on your stove and proceed. This way you can cook at least 3 tortillas at the same time, rather than only 1.

If you do not have a Tortilla Chef, you must roll the dough balls into tortillas. First, whether you are using a Tortilla Chef or not, dust the dough balls with flour to keep them from sticking. Next, flatten the balls with the palm of your hand and roll them out using a small rolling pin. It helps if you turn the tortilla a ⅓ to ½ turn after each roll and turn them over after every 3 or 4 rolls. Dust the tortillas with a little more flour during the process, if necessary.

Regardless of how you form the tortillas they should be cooked in the same manner, on an ungreased griddle or skillet for just the right amount of time. The former is easy; the latter comes quickly with practice. You will have to experiment to find the best temperature setting on your particular stove, remembering that it will differ depending on the thickness of the tortillas. As a general rule I set my stove just below the medium setting. In any case, when you place the uncooked dough on the griddle it should lightly brown portions of the first side within 30 seconds. At this point, turn the tortilla and replace it on the griddle. Within 15 seconds it should begin to puff and brown. When it is fully puffed, the tortilla will either be done or it will need to cook just a few more seconds on the first side. When properly cooked, the tortilla should have some browned areas on both sides, but should still be mostly white. The major difficulty is in getting the tortilla cooked through without burning or overbrowning it, which will cause it to lose its flexibility. Again, just a little practice will give you the right timing.

Immediately after each tortilla is done place it in a tortilla warmer or wrap it in a towel. This both keeps the tortillas warm and

makes them pliable.

The above recipe produces nice thin, light flour tortillas when the dough is rolled out to 6 to 7 inches. To make the thicker Tex-Mex variety, divide the dough into 8 pieces and roll each to a diameter of about 6 inches. To make Sonora-style tortillas, divide the dough into 6 pieces and roll out to 10 or 11 inches in diameter; then stretch the dough by hand to a final diameter of 12 plus inches. (I have not provided instructions for larger versions up to 18 inches in diameter since home skillets and griddles are usually no larger than 12 inches in diameter.)

INDIAN FRY BREAD

2   *cups unbleached white flour*
½   *teaspoon salt*
1½ *teaspoons baking powder*
¼   *cup evaporated milk*
    Water to make a medium moist dough, about ¾ cup

This New Mexico specialty is alternatively called Navajo fry bread after the tribe with which it is usually associated. Even though fry bread is basically Indian in origin, I am including it since it should be of interest to many readers, particularly in relation to its cousins the *sopaipilla* and *buñuelo*. Fry bread is eaten with honey as a treat, or it is made into Indian Tacos (in my opinion its best use), which are found on reservations and in nearby towns, especially in far northern New Mexico.

Sift the dry ingredients together; then add the milk and water and form into a dough, kneading as little as possible.

Form the dough into 4 balls; then allow them to rest, covered with a damp towel, for 20 minutes.

Roll the dough into circles about 8 inches in diameter and about ¼ inch or a little less thick.

Heat the oil in a deep fryer to 350 degrees; then lower a piece of dough into it. The dough will begin to puff in an irregular manner almost immediately. Fry the bread until just browned on the bottom, then turn and fry it on the other side.

When the bread is finished, remove it and drain it on absorbent towels. Either serve the breads with honey or use them in making Indian Tacos (p. 200). *Serves 4.*

SOPAIPILLAS

These famous puffed breads from New Mexico are most probably refinements of the simpler Indian fry bread. *Sopaipillas* are
served in virtually every Mexican-American restaurant in New
Mexico as bread with the meal, with honey as dessert, or stuffed
with chile as an entrée. Because of their popularity with both
New Mexicans and tourists I have always marveled that *sopaipillas* are virtually unobtainable in other parts of the country. And
when you do find them they are usually heavy and greasy, nothing like the airy little pillows of New Mexico.

One reason they are not universal may be that while it is easy
to make an average *sopaipilla*, making a great *sopaipilla* is a bit
tricky. Do not be daunted by this, but please realize that you will
have to experiment a bit. The good news is that once you get the
right combination for your particular circumstances you will be
able to turn out *sopaipillas* like a pro! First, the temperature must
be just right. Virtually all cookbooks call for *sopaipillas* to be
fried at 400 degrees. I have found this to be a good average, but,
as with all deep-fried foods, altitude is a factor. For example,
water which boils at 212 degrees at sea level boils at just 198
degrees in Santa Fe, New Mexico, which is at about 7,000 feet.
Since deep-frying occurs when moisture within the food evaporates (i.e. boils), it follows that the higher the altitude, the lower
the oil temperature must be to obtain the same results. Another
difficulty with *sopaipillas* is that the thickness must be just right.
Unfortunately, they are too thin to measure accurately, but ⅛ inch
is a good starting point.

Experiment with the temperature and the thickness and after a
couple of attempts you will be an expert. The best way to check the
temperature is with a good deep-fry thermometer, the kind that clips
on to your pan. Use this to check the settings on your deep fryer or,
even better, use a medium-size high-sided pot set on a burner. To
check the accuracy of your thermometer, first find out at what temperature water boils at your altitude. See the chart at right.

Bring some water to a full boil and place your thermometer in
it. If, for example, you are at sea level and the reading is 210

2 *cups all-purpose flour*
2 *teaspoons baking powder*
½ *teaspoon salt*
2 *tablespoons lard or*
  shortening
½ *cup water*
½ *cup evaporated milk*

FAHRENHEIT READINGS

Sea level	212 degrees
2,000 feet	208 degrees
5,000 feet	203 degrees
7,500 feet	198 degrees
10,000 feet	194 degrees

degrees, you will know that your thermometer is low by 2 degrees. Now you can experiment cooking *sopaipillas* at various temperatures. You should find the best temperature for your particular situation at between 380 and 405 degrees.

To determine the best thickness, roll pieces of dough to different thicknesses and fry them, beginning with one about ⅛ inch thick. This task is simple if, like most New Mexico restaurants, you own a $3,500 electric dough-roller. Fortunately, it is also easy if you have a $30 pasta machine. I find the best thickness on my handcranked Atlas machine is at the thickest or next to the thickest setting. You will also find that making the dough in a food processor simplifies matters.

While most cookbooks call for *sopaipillas* to be made entirely with water, the following recipe specifies a combination of water and evaporated milk. You can use either method, but the dough made with the milk yields a softer result.

Either sift the dry ingredients together or accomplish the same purpose by whirling them a few times in a food processor.

Cut in the lard or shortening, mix the water and milk together, and add just enough of it to make your dough. The dough should be just at the point where it ceases to be wet and sticky but should not be actually dry.

Knead the dough for 1 or 2 minutes, wrap it in a damp towel, and allow it to rest for 20 minutes. This is important, especially if you are going to roll the dough by hand, since the resting allows the dough to "relax," making it pliable enough to roll very thin.

Roll the dough out until it is about ⅛ inch thick; then cut it into 5-inch squares. You can make the *sopaipillas* in this shape or cut them diagonally to make them in the shape of right triangles.

At this point make certain your oil is heated to 400 degrees (or the temperature you found best for your situation after experimentation); then drop in a cut piece of dough. It will sink to the bottom of the fryer then immediately rise to the top. It should now begin to puff. You can help this process by spooning some hot oil over the top of the *sopaipilla*. As soon as the bottom is browned, about 15 to 20 seconds, turn the *sopaipilla* and continue to cook until the other side is browned, about 10 to 15 seconds.

Remove the finished *sopaipilla* to drain on absorbent towels and repeat. *Serves 8 to 12.*

CORN BREAD

Mexican-American cooking is replete with corn bread recipes, from those made with all fresh ingredients to those made with all dried ingredients and all sorts of combinations in between.

FRESH CORN BREAD

This is a simple, rustic dish that is nevertheless comforting. Its fresh, clean taste makes an excellent foil to spicy entrées. Served hot it makes an appropriate accompaniment to a breakfast of ham or *chorizo* and a fine snack when served cold.

    The dish can be made with frozen corn, but be sure and measure it after thawing since the loss of water shrinks the amount considerably. It will still have a higher moisture content than fresh corn so after the first 45 minutes of cooking, turn the heat down to 350 degrees and cook an additional 15 to 20 minutes.

3 *cups fresh corn kernels, or substitute frozen corn*

2 *tablespoons lard or shortening*

2 *eggs, beaten*

1 *tablespoon sugar*

½ *teaspoon salt, or to taste*

Mix all the ingredients well and pour them into a small well-greased baking dish.

Bake the mixture for 45 minutes in an oven preheated to 400 degrees. *Serves 4.*

PAN DE MAÍZ CON CHILE VERDE

Corn Bread with Green Chile

1 *cup white or yellow cornmeal*

1½ *teaspoons baking powder*

¼ *teaspoon salt, or to taste*

1 *cup canned creamed corn*

2 *eggs, lightly beaten*

⅓ *cup cooking oil*

1 *cup Monterey Jack cheese, grated*

¼ *cup green chile, peeled and minced*

This recipe combines dry cornmeal with creamed corn to produce a very interesting texture and flavor.

Preheat your oven to 350 degrees.

Mix all the ingredients together, place in a lightly greased baking dish, and bake for approximately 35 to 45 minutes. Before removing from the oven, check to make sure that a knife inserted in the bread comes out clean, indicating that the corn bread is done. *Serves 4.*

PAN DEL RANCHO

Ranch-style Bread

3⅓ *cups flour*

4 *teaspoons baking powder*

½ *tablespoon salt*

½ *tablespoon sugar*

⅔ *cup lard*

1¼ *cups milk*

This is the south Texas *vaquero*'s version of camp biscuits. It goes well with *Frijoles de olla* (p. 130) and any of the chile-based stews, which is fortunate since such dishes were often the only choices cowboys had. The most authentic way to bake this bread is in a Dutch oven set over mesquite coals, with more coals piled on the lid. With the understanding that there are limits to the need for authenticity, here is the oven version.

Preheat your oven to 450 degrees.

Mix together the dry ingredients; then cut in the lard or shortening. A food processor fitted with a metal blade makes this task easy.

Add enough milk to make a firm dough; then knead it for about 2 minutes.

NUTRITION HINT: The only way this dish will taste authentic is when made with lard. However, it can be made just as successfully, though not as authentically, with shortening. This will eliminate the large amount of cholesterol, but the bread will still contain too much fat for those with restricted diets.

Roll the dough into a circle about ½ inch thick, place it on a greased baking sheet, prick the top with a fork or score it with a knife, and bake it for 15 to 20 minutes or until the bread is puffed and browned.

Remove the bread from the oven, cut it into squares, and serve. *Serves 4.*

Salsas para la Mesa
TABLE SAUCES

hese are the picante sauces that are the mainstay of the chips and salsa appetizer in Mexican-American restaurants, and that are never far away from diners in Mexican households.

I am nearly always disappointed at the quality of the table sauces in restaurants. The basic problem is that restaurants use a fantastic quantity of these sauces and their cost is a major factor in the cost of the entire meal. Therefore, to make life easy for themselves and to save money, they rely on canned ingredients. The results cannot help but reflect this. However, most Americans have been so conditioned to this particular taste, bad as it might be, and by the salsas on grocery store shelves that they do not seem to mind. For purposes of comparison, I have included a recipe for picante sauce that is very close to that of the most popular bottled salsas so the difference in ingredients and amount of salt and other additives used in these and home-style sauces are apparent. The other recipes included in this section reflect the best of the home-style sauces that are made by discerning cooks.

SALSA DE CHILE VERDE
Green Chile Sauce

Although rarely found in public establishments except when it is heated and used as an enchilada sauce in New Mexican restaurants, this is one of the most traditional table sauces found in Mexican-American home-style cooking. Interestingly, while this sauce was also ubiquitous in early California (where the word *sarsa* rather than *salsa* was often used), I found much less evidence of it having been used in early Arizona and almost none in Texas. Green Chile Sauce goes particularly well with broiled meats, especially when they are chopped up for *Tacos al carbón* (p. 191). It was a traditional accompaniment of early California barbecues.

Prepare the chiles (see pp. 36–37). Although I find it easier to remove chile skins after deep-frying them quickly, the more traditional broiling method, especially if done over mesquite coals, adds a smoky flavor that is well worth the extra effort.

Combine the ingredients and allow to macerate for ½ hour. *Yields enough sauce to serve 4 with chips or with a meal.*

8 *large New Mexico or Anaheim chiles, or substitute* poblano *chiles, seeded, peeled, and coarsely chopped*

2 *medium tomatoes, finely chopped*

1 *small onion, finely chopped*

½ *teaspoon salt, or to taste*

½ *cup loosely packed cilantro, chopped*

1 *tablespoon vinegar*

SALSA SONORA

Sonora-style Sauce

1 ancho *chile, stemmed and seeded*

4 de árbol *chiles, stemmed and seeded*

½ *pound tomatoes*

½ *tablespoon vinegar*

   Heaping ¼ *teaspoon salt, or to taste*

This sauce is one of the better sauces prepared in homes and restaurants in Arizona.

Place both types of chiles in a bowl, cover them for 15 minutes with boiling water, then remove them to the container of a blender. Broil the tomatoes by placing them on a cookie sheet or pizza pan as close to the oven's preheated broiler as possible until they are soft but not too charred, about 15 minutes.

Add the broiled tomatoes, vinegar, and salt to the blender and blend for 1 minute. The sauce can either be strained or left as is. *Yields enough sauce to serve 4 with chips or with a meal.*

PICO DE GALLO

Tomato-Chile Relish

2 *medium tomatoes, seeded and chopped (peeling is optional)*

¼ *cup onion, finely chopped*

2–4 serrano *chiles, minced*

¼ *cup loosely packed cilantro, chopped*

1 *tablespoon lime juice (optional)*

Pico de gallo, often called *salsa mexicana* in Mexico, is the relish that is the traditional accompaniment to *fajitas*. The name means "rooster's beak" and probably comes from the fact that the *serrano* chiles from which it is made resemble that appendage. They also have quite a bite, or, more properly, peck. In addition to *fajitas*, *Pico de gallo* can be served with just about any *antojito* or meat dish and makes a colorful garnish.

Some upscale restaurants now peel the tomatoes before removing the seeds and chopping them. I think this is worth the trouble since it produces a more sophisticated result. To peel the tomatoes, place them in boiling water for 1 minute, then put them in cold water until they are cool enough to peel.

Combine the tomatoes with the remaining ingredients and serve immediately since *Pico de gallo* does not keep well. *Yields enough sauce to serve 4 with chips or with a meal.*

SALSA PICANTE DE OLIVOS

Olive Hot Sauce

This old California sauce, which is splendid on broiled pork, has a particularly interesting texture. The chiles are first toasted and then crushed; and the seeds are ground before being mixed with the remaining ingredients. The sauce is easily made in a food processor.

Rinse the chiles and toast them in an oven preheated to 275 degrees until they are fairly crisp but not burned, about 10 to 15 minutes.

Remove the stems, veins, and seeds, reserving the latter.

In a small ungreased skillet toast the seeds over medium heat until they are just beginning to brown. To crush the seeds, you can grind them in a *molcajete* or mortar and pestle, but the task is far easier if you have a spice or coffee grinder. To crush the chiles, you can chop them with a chef's knife and then grind them in a *molcajete*, but I recommend a food processor fitted with a steel blade.

Combine the chiles and seeds with the remaining ingredients and allow to sit, covered, in the refrigerator for at least 2 hours before serving.

As mentioned above, this sauce is delicious with roast or grilled pork, and it also makes a wonderful sandwich when combined with Monterey Jack cheese on French bread. *Yields enough sauce to serve 4 with chips or with a meal.*

3 *mild dried New Mexico chiles*
½ *cup onion, minced*
2 *green onions, minced*
2 *cloves garlic, minced*
½ *teaspoon oregano*
¾ *cup black California olives, minced*
½ *cup pimientos, minced*
1 *tablespoon olive oil*
½ *cup white vinegar*
½ *teaspoon sugar*
½ *teaspoon ground black pepper*
¼ *teaspoon cayenne pepper*
¾ *teaspoon salt*

PICANTE SAUCE

Commercial-style Hot Sauce

½ *cup tomato puree*

1 *cup water*

½ *cup plus 2 tablespoons*
    ordinary white vinegar

3 *tablespoons* jalapeño
    chiles, seeded and
    minced

½ *cup onion, minced*

2¼ *teaspoons salt*

⅛ *teaspoon MSG*

This sauce is different from any other in this book or, for that matter, most of those in other books. The reason is that rather than being a traditional sauce handed down through families it is basically an invention of the American food industry. However, the amount of space devoted to this product on supermarket shelves testifies to its popularity. Because of this I decided to include this recipe so that if you wish you can make this popular sauce, very much the way the big food companies do and at a considerable savings. Please note the high level of salt and the use of MSG.

Place all ingredients in a saucepan, bring them to a boil, and simmer slowly until the onion and chiles are soft and the sauce is thickened, about 15 to 20 minutes. *Yields enough sauce to serve 4 with chips or with a meal.*

SALSA RANCHERA

Ranch-style Sauce

This is one of the best and most popular home-style Tex-Mex sauces I have tried. It is also used as the sauce for Texas-style Ranch Eggs (p. 310).

Heat the lard or olive oil over medium heat, add the chiles and onion, and cook until they begin to soften, but do not allow them to brown.

Add the remaining ingredients except for the water or broth and cook, stirring frequently, for ½ hour over very low heat.

Add just enough broth or water to make the sauce a little soupy and continue cooking an additional 10 minutes. The sauce should be thick enough to coat a spoon without immediately running off, so add more liquid or cook a while longer, as necessary. *Yields enough sauce to serve 4 with chips or with a meal.*

2 **tablespoons lard or olive oil**

2 **tablespoons** jalapeño *chiles, seeded and minced*

½ *cup onion, chopped*

2 *cups tomatoes, chopped*

2 *teaspoons vinegar*

¼ *teaspoon ground black pepper*

½ *teaspoon salt, or to taste*
   Light beef broth or water

SALSA CRUDA
Uncooked Sauce

2 *medium to large
tomatoes, chopped*

½ *cup onion, chopped*

2–3 *tablespoons* jalapeño *or
serrano chiles, minced*

¼ *cup cilantro, chopped*

½ *teaspoon salt, or to taste*

Perhaps the most universal hot sauce of all in Mexican-American cooking, *Salsa cruda* is "crude" only in the sense that it is uncooked. This sauce and variations of it are made in various textures, from completely pureed in a blender to coarsely ground in a *molcajete* to roughly chopped. My favorite way to prepare it is to grind it in a *molcajete*. If you do not wish to do this, a reasonable facsimile of the texture this method produces can be achieved in a food processor fitted with a steel blade.

Grind, chop, or blend the ingredients together to make a sauce of the consistency you prefer. *Yields enough sauce to serve 4 with chips or with a meal.*

SALSA DE TOMATILLO

Tomatillo Sauce

1 *pound* tomatillos

2 *green tomatoes (optional)*

2–4 serrano *chiles*

¼ *cup onion*

½ *teaspoon salt, or to taste*

½ *teaspoon sugar (optional)*

⅓ *cup cilantro (optional)*

This sauce is very popular in Mexico, but, until lately, was not used as much in Mexican-American cooking, especially the restaurant variety. However, with the advent of new Southwest cooking it has been discovered and is found more and more frequently.

Tomatillos range in taste from slightly acidic to bitter. Taste the sauce after blending and, if necessary, add the optional sugar. Alternatively, add 1 or 2 green tomatoes to the recipe and cook with the *tomatillos*. This rounds out and sweetens the sauce without changing its appearance. The optional cilantro makes a nice addition if the sauce is to be used as a table sauce but is usually not included if it is going to be used as an enchilada sauce.

Place the *tomatillos*, green tomatoes, if used, and chiles in a pot and cover with water. Bring the water to a boil over *medium* heat. If you use high heat, the *tomatillos*, which become delicate when soft, can easily disintegrate if the water is allowed to boil too swiftly.

When the *tomatillos* and chiles have become quite soft, about 5 to 10 minutes, discard the water and place them in a blender. Add the onion and salt and blend, using pulses, until the sauce is roughly chopped. Taste the sauce and add the sugar, if necessary, and the cilantro, if desired.

If the sauce is to be used as table sauce, simply pulse a time or two more to incorporate the optional ingredients. This should leave the sauce with a chunky, handground texture. If the sauce is to be used in enchiladas, blend it for about 15 seconds or until it is smooth. *Yields enough sauce to serve 4 with chips or with a meal.*

NUTRITION HINT: This sauce, which is extremely easy to make, can be used as a table sauce or as a very low-fat sauce for enchiladas. For those not so concerned with fat content, the sauce, when it is to be used for enchiladas, is best made with 2 tablespoons oil (see recipe for Mexican-style *Tomatillo* Enchilada Sauce, p. 181).

Aperitivos y Botanas

APPETIZERS

In Mexican-American as in Mexican cooking there is a fine and sometimes indistinct line between what is an appetizer and what is not. Many hold the view that the *antojitos mexicanos,* or corn- and tortilla-based foods like tacos, enchiladas, and tamales, are really appetizers. Since these foods are so distinctive and usually, at least in the United States, taken as a main meal, I feel that they deserve a separate section. However, even so there are still questions such as is a cheese crisp which resembles a giant nacho an appetizer?

In this section I have included only those items that, to me, are obviously appetizers in the sense that they would be eaten as a snack before dinner or at a cocktail party.

CHIPS AND SALSA

The hot tortilla chips and bowl of picante sauce that arrive at your table soon after being seated in most Mexican-American restaurants constitute what is undoubtedly the best-known, and possibly the most enjoyed, of the cuisine's appetizers. In truth, overindulgence in Chips and Salsa often defeats the purpose of an appetizer by sating rather than stimulating the appetite. But this is a natural consequence of the enjoyment produced by the "gift" of the restaurant.

Serving Chips and Salsa at home is very easy. After all, grocery store shelves are filled with packages of tortilla chips and jars of picante sauce. However, the experience can be improved significantly if you make both your own Chips and Salsa.

To make the chips, heat a deep fryer to between 350 and 375 degrees, then deep-fry 12 or more tortillas which have been cut into 4 pie-shaped wedges. You will have to do this in several batches, depending on the size of your fryer. The chips are done when they stop sputtering and begin to turn a light golden brown.

Serve the chips with your favorite sauces from the chapter on "Table Sauces" (p. 110). *Serves 4.*

BLACK BEAN DIP

4   *slices bacon, chopped*

4   *cloves garlic, minced*

¼   *cup onion, chopped*

1   *pound black beans,
    picked over and washed*

4–5   *cups water*

1   *pound Monterey Jack
    cheese, grated*

1   *pound mild cheddar
    cheese, grated*

2   *tablespoons pickled
    jalapeño chiles, minced*

2   *tablespoons juice from
    jalapeño can*

½   *cup onion, minced*

¼   *cup sour cream*

1   *large avocado, chopped*

¼   *cup cilantro, minced*

The following recipe makes a superb dip, nacho topping, or burrito filling.

In a large pot fry the garlic and ¼ cup onion with the bacon over medium heat until the onion is soft.

Add the beans to the pot with 4 to 5 cups water. Bring the liquid to a boil and simmer, partially covered, until the beans are tender, adding additional water as necessary.

When the beans are tender, pour off all but a little of the liquid from the pot and place them in an ovenproof serving dish. Mix in the cheeses, chiles, chile juice, and ½ cup minced onion. Bake the dip at 350 degrees until the cheese has melted and is bubbling, about 10 minutes.

Serve topped with the sour cream, avocado, and cilantro. *Serves 10 as an appetizer.*

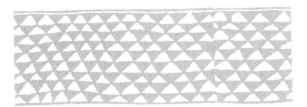

CHILE CON QUESO

Chile with Cheese

In Mexico *Chile con queso* is usually made with the white, slightly astringent *asadero* cheese, which is melted into a pan in which some onion and green chile have been sautéed. Sometimes a little milk or cream is added. While Mexican-American versions are usually made with cheddar cheese, they are too often made with less desirable ingredients such as canned cheese soup and melted Velveeta cheese. The following recipe combines aspects of the original Mexican-style *Chile con queso* with the use of cheddar cheese and evaporated milk, making the dish uniquely Mexican-American.

Melt the butter in a saucepan over medium heat. Add the onion and green chile and sauté until the onion is soft but not browned.

Turn the heat to low, add the milk, oregano, salt, and pepper and bring to a boil. Add the *jalapeños* and their juice, if you are using

2   *tablespoons butter*

1   *cup onion, chopped*

½   *cup green chile, peeled, seeded, and chopped*

1   *cup evaporated milk*

¼   *teaspoon oregano*

½   *teaspoon salt*

½   *teaspoon ground black pepper*

2   *tablespoons pickled jalapeño chiles, minced (optional)*

1   *tablespoon juice from the jalapeños (optional)*

1½   *cups mild cheddar cheese, grated*

1½   *cups Monterey Jack cheese, grated*

this option. (It will make a spicier, less subtle dish.) Remove the pan from the heat, add the cheeses, and stir until they are melted and combined with the other ingredients. The mixture may seem a bit thin at first, but it will thicken with subsequent warming.

Place the *Chile con queso* over a low flame or on an electric warmer to keep the sauce hot. Serve with tortilla chips or flour tortillas. *Serves 4 as an appetizer.*

NACHOS

Like so many things in Mexican cooking (margaritas and *fajitas* come to mind) there is a mystery as to who invented nachos. Discussions on the matter can become heated. Frankly, I don't care who invented nachos; I'm just glad they did. Undoubtedly, the original nacho was a simple tortilla chip topped with melted cheese and a piece of pickled *jalapeño*, and this simple version is still something one comes back to after the palate tires of more complicated renditions.

Restaurant patrons are often surprised at the cost of this appetizer. When you try these recipes, you will understand that, through the laws of geometry, these delectable morsels require ingredients in substantial quantities.

How to Make Nachos:

To make quick nachos, you can use packaged tortilla chips. However, these commercial chips are never as good as those you make yourself. To make your own, cut each of 3 tortillas into 4 pie-shaped wedges and deep-fry them at between 350 and 375 degrees until they are golden brown and crisp. For more details,

---

NOTE: Each recipe below is designed to make 1 dozen nachos. This should provide a sufficient appetizer for 4 people. However, these are so good that you might want to consider doubling the recipes!

see "Chips and Salsa" (p. 119).

The cheese, chiles, and any other ingredients are placed on top of the tortilla chips, which are then placed under a preheated broiler. A baking sheet or pizza pan works well for this task. Be very careful to leave the nachos under the broiler only until the cheese is melted. If left too long, the cheese will become dry and grainy. *Makes 1 dozen.*

REGULAR NACHOS

Preheat your broiler.

Place the chips on a baking sheet or pizza pan. Top each chip with a slice of cheese, then a slice of *jalapeño* chile.

Place the chips 2 to 4 inches under the broiler and cook just until the cheese is melted. You must be careful since the cheese can easily burn and become dry and grainy. *Makes 1 dozen.*

1 *dozen tortilla chips*
½ *pound mild cheddar or Monterey Jack cheese, cut into slices ⅛ inch thick by 1 inch wide by 2 inches long*
12 *slices pickled* jalapeño *chiles*

NACHOS COMPUESTOS

This is the deluxe version of traditional Mexican-American nachos and, if the recipe is doubled, it can make an entire meal.

Preheat your broiler.

Place the chips on a baking sheet or pizza pan.

Mix together the Refried Beans and *Picadillo* II and put 1½ to 2 tablespoons of the mixture on each tortilla chip.

Sprinkle half the cheese over the tortilla chips, then place a slice of *jalapeño* chile on each chip. Pour 1 or 2 teaspoons of picante sauce over each chip, then top with the remaining cheese.

Place the nachos 2 to 4 inches under the broiler and cook just until the cheese is melted. Be careful not to overcook since the cheese will become dry and grainy. *Makes 1 dozen.*

1 *dozen tortilla chips*
¾ *cup Refried Beans (p. 132)*
¾ *cup* Picadillo *II (p. 150)*
½ *pound mild cheddar cheese, grated*
12 *slices pickled* jalapeño *chiles*
Picante sauce

CRAB NACHOS

1 *dozen tortilla chips*

1 *cup black beans, cooked
   and pureed*

½ *pound cooked crabmeat
   (imitation crab but not
   canned crab can be
   substituted)*

½ *pound Monterey Jack
   cheese, grated*

1 *recipe* Tomatillo *Sauce
   (p. 116)*

½ *cup sour cream*

¼ *cup cilantro, minced*

1 *or 2 limes, cut into wedges*

This is more a restaurant invention than anything else, but it makes a nice addition to any Mexican meal.

Mound 1 to 2 tablespoons of the pureed beans on each tortilla chip, then top with some crabmeat, some cheese, and finally a tablespoon of sauce and ½ tablespoon of sour cream.

Place the nachos 2 to 4 inches under the broiler and cook just until the cheese is melted. Do not overcook or the cheese will become dry and grainy.

Garnish the nachos with the cilantro and serve with the lime wedges. *Makes 1 dozen.*

Arroz y Frijoles

RICE AND BEANS

Rice and beans are the usual accompaniment to *antojitos* and to almost everything else in Mexican and Mexican-American cooking. Unfortunately, in Mexican-American restaurants little consideration is often given to these essential elements of the cuisine. More often, in Mexican-American homes as in Mexico, beans and rice (particularly the latter) are given the care they deserve, especially when served as a separate course as a part of the *comida*, or main meal. However, rice and beans are a significant part of any meal, especially a combination plate, so why not make them as good as everything else you serve?

NUTRITION HINT: Nutritionists tell us that, when eaten together, beans and rice create a "complete" protein that is an acceptable substitute for meat. For an elaboration of this, see, for example, Frances Moore Lappé's book *Diet for a Small Planet*.

ARROZ MEXICANO
Mexican Rice

Mexican Rice can be served alone or in combination with refried beans as an accompaniment to *antojitos* and entrées. Prepared properly, this is one of the finest ways of cooking rice, and one which yields a greater quantity than nearly any other method. For example, the following recipe produces about 7 cups of cooked rice, a cup more than a similar amount of boiled or steamed rice. This is because the rice is first fried, and then cooked covered with liquid, which means each grain will not just expand but literally explode, creating an extremely light and tasty product.

Please note that some cooks do not cover the rice during the first 15 minutes or so of the cooking process, only adding the top to the pot for a final steaming. They also use more liquid to make up for the increased amount lost to evaporation. This is certainly a viable alternative, but, to me, produces a less distinctive and interesting result.

Also, you will notice that the recipe calls for the tomatoes to be broiled before being blended. To me, this precooking of the tomatoes creates a result with better texture, color, and flavor than the more usual procedure of blending the uncooked tomatoes.

While some recipes suggest soaking the rice in hot water before cooking, I have found that this makes no difference when using good quality American rice since ours has been well cleaned, and there is no discernible difference in the grain's expansion.

Finally, if you are fond of garlic, you will find the dish much improved if you blend some additional cloves with the water or broth before adding it to the pot.

Broil the tomatoes by placing them on a metal sheet (a pizza pan works well) 1 to 3 inches below the oven's broiler. Cook until the skins are well charred, about 10 to 15 minutes.

Heat the oil in a heavy pot or Dutch oven, over low to medium heat, until a drop of water sputters immediately upon contact (being careful not to burn yourself with spattering oil during the testing process). Add the rice and cook, stirring often, until it is a

2 *small or 1 large tomato, a total of about 10 ounces, broiled (This will equal about 1 cup after blending.)*

1½ *cups olive, peanut, safflower, or other good quality cooking oil*

1½ *cups good quality long grain rice*

⅓ *cup onion, chopped*

2 *large cloves garlic (or 3 medium), peeled*

¾ *teaspoon salt, or to taste*

2⅓ *cups water or very mild chicken broth*

2–3 *cloves garlic (optional)*

⅓ *cup carrots, peeled and grated, or julienned (optional)*

⅓ *cup frozen peas, thawed (optional)*

very light brown but not at all burned. This usually takes 5 to 8 minutes.

While the rice is browning place the tomatoes, onion, garlic, and salt in a blender and blend until pureed, about 15 seconds. Also, at this time, if you are using the additional, optional garlic, blend it with the water or broth until it is totally incorporated, about 2 to 3 minutes.

When the rice is browned, drain the oil (using a strainer) and save it for future use. Return the rice to the pot, turn the heat to medium, and add the tomato mixture. Cook, stirring fairly continuously, until the liquid has been absorbed and the rice grains no longer stick together, about 5 to 7 minutes.

Add the water or broth and carrots (if used) and mix well. Bring the rice to a boil, cover it, and turn the heat to very low; then allow it to cook for 20 minutes. Remove the cover, add the peas (if using them), and gently stir them into the cooked rice. Replace the cover and cook an additional 5 minutes. Remove the pan from the heat and leave it, still covered, for 15 minutes.

Serve immediately or allow the rice to cool and refrigerate it. Mexican Rice reheats fairly well in a microwave oven, if tightly covered during the process. *Serves 4.*

NUTRITION HINT: You might think that the recipe calls for a lot of oil, but nearly all of it is strained out of the rice after the rice is browned. I have tried cooking this dish with a smaller amount of oil, say 2 to 3 tablespoons, as recommended in some cookbooks, but it requires more stirring and makes it more difficult to brown the rice evenly. If you measure the oil before and after use, you will find that the amount actually incorporated in the dish is only about 1 to 2 tablespoons. However, if you do not want to go to the extra effort involved in using this amount of oil, simply fry the rice in 3 tablespoons olive oil. To avoid wasting the strained oil, store it in a bottle or jar for the same or another future use.

Arroz estilo Español

Spanish Rice

2½ tablespoons olive oil

1 piece bacon, minced

½ cup onion, sliced thin

3 cloves garlic, minced

½ cup green pepper, sliced thin

¼ cup pimiento, chopped

¼ cup black California olives, chopped (optional)

1½ cups long grain rice

1 14½-ounce can tomatoes, well drained, seeded, and chopped

1 teaspoon paprika

½ teaspoon salt

17 ounces water

The thought of Spanish Rice reminds many of us of the soggy canned variety that was our first introduction to the genre. What distinguishes Spanish Rice from its Mexican cousin is that the former contains more vegetables and is somewhat damper in texture. Unfortunately, cooks in New Mexico, which is about the only area in the Southwest where Spanish Rice (as opposed to Mexican Rice) is served with regularity, often do not do much better than Chef Boyardee. Some even cook the rice and vegetables separately, then mix them at the last minute before serving. This method reduces the soggy quality of the dish, but the rice has none of the flavor that it has when properly cooked with all the ingredients—the reason for preparing the recipe in the first place. The best alternative is to cook Spanish Rice in the Spanish fashion, which calls for cooking without a cover on the pan for most of the process.

The following version of Spanish Rice is somewhat more elaborate than the usual New Mexico rendition but is well worth the extra effort.

In a pot or Dutch oven heat the olive oil over medium heat; then add the bacon, onion, garlic, and green pepper. Cook until the pepper and onion are just beginning to soften, about 2 minutes. Add the pimiento, olives (if used), rice, and tomatoes and continue cooking, stirring often, for an additional 2 minutes.

Mix the paprika and salt into the water and stir into the rice. Bring the mixture to a boil, then immediately turn the heat down until the water barely simmers. Continue to cook the dish without touching the ingredients until nearly all the liquid has evaporated, about 15 to 20 minutes. You may need to insert the point of a knife in the rice to determine how much moisture remains, but disturb it as little as possible.

When the liquid is gone, cover the pot and continue to cook over the very lowest heat for 5 minutes. Remove the pot from the heat and allow to steam an additional 5 to 10 minutes. *Serves 4.*

BEANS

1½ cups pinto beans (a little
    over ½ pound), or
    substitute pink beans

1 ounce salt pork, in 1 piece
    (a chunk that looks like
    about 2½–3 tablespoons)

⅓ cup onion, chopped

2 cloves garlic, peeled and
    mashed

6 cups water

½ teaspoon salt, or to taste

The Mexican affinity for beans is no myth. This food was a staple of early Amerindian cooking and remains nearly as important in the cuisine of their descendants, in both Mexico and the United States. While the different beans described in the chapter "Basics: Ingredients and Equipment" (see p. 73) have different characteristics, they can, for the most part, be used interchangeably in the following recipes.

FRIJOLES DE OLLA

Beans from the Pot

Although seldom eaten with *antojitos*, *Frijoles de olla* are the first step in making refried beans, which are part of nearly every *antojito* meal. If possible, *Frijoles de olla* should be prepared a day ahead of serving to allow the flavors to concentrate overnight in the refrigerator.

One question that always arises is should you soak the beans overnight? I find little difference in the end result except that unsoaked beans require longer cooking. However, some authorities contend that soaked beans can have a slightly bitter flavor. Also, few Mexican cooks I know soak their beans.

Frijoles de olla seems to have more flavor if cooked in a hand-made clay pot, but this may be imagination at work. If a clay pot is not available, use an iron, stainless steel, or ceramic pot, but never aluminum. A Crock-Pot also works well, but the beans will require a longer cooking time.

Place all ingredients except the salt in the pot, bring to a boil, and simmer, partially covered, until the beans are tender but not so soft they lose all texture. This can take anywhere from 30 minutes to 2 hours or more depending on the age of the beans and

NUTRITION HINT: Beans contain very little fat, so they are a good diet food. As is the case with baked potatoes it is the fat that is added that makes a dish like refried beans a plague to the slim crowd.

whether they were soaked. The best advice I have had on cooking beans is that after the initial expansion of the beans you should keep no more water in the pot than necessary. There should always be just enough liquid to cover them.

After the beans have cooked, add the salt only if *Frijoles de olla* is to be the end result. If you are preparing refried beans, the salt will be added later.

Finally, remove the beans. For *Frijoles de olla,* serve immediately or allow them to cool, still partially covered, and refrigerate them until you are ready to use them. Properly chilled, the beans will keep up to three days. *Serves 4.*

FRIJOLES REFRITOS

Refried Beans

1 *recipe* Frijoles de olla,
   including broth (p. 130)

½ *teaspoon salt, or to taste*

1 *teaspoon ground cumin
   (optional)*

⅓ *cup lard*

2 *cloves garlic, peeled and
   mashed*

6 *¼-inch-thick slices onion*

2 *tablespoons queso anejo, or
   substitute grated feta
   cheese (optional)*

8 *tortilla chips (optional)*

These beans are not really refried at all since the only previous preparation is that of *Frijoles de olla*, which are not fried. The Spanish prefix *re*, in this case, denotes the dish as something extra special. Refried Beans are either a part of, or eaten with, nearly all *antojitos*. They do not keep well in the sense that they do not take to reheating or, for that matter, refrying, so serve them as soon as possible.

Remove the salt pork from the *Frijoles de olla*; then drain them, reserving the broth.

Traditionally, the beans are prepared by pouring them, with some of the broth, into the heated lard, where they are mashed with a special tool resembling a potato masher. However, this is often a messy job and more work than necessary. Instead, put the drained beans into a food processor fitted with a steel blade and process, using 1-second pulses, until the beans are pureed but still slightly chunky in texture. Add just enough of the broth to get the texture you wish.

New Mexico cooks usually do not serve their Refried Beans completely pureed. To prepare this style, puree only about a third of the beans; then mix the puree with the whole beans and proceed. Place the processed beans in a mixing bowl.

Stir the salt and cumin, if used, into ½ cup of the reserved broth and pour it into the beans, mixing them together carefully until they are just combined. The beans can be prepared to this point then finished just before serving.

Heat the lard in a heavy skillet over medium to medium-high heat until it is melted. Add the garlic and onion slices and cook them until just before they begin to color. Do not allow them to burn since this will give the beans a bitter taste.

After removing the garlic and onion, add the bean mixture. Stir the beans into the lard and keep stirring frequently (as you would for scrambled eggs) until they are done. As the liquid evaporates they will begin to "set" just like eggs. Some people prefer their Refried Beans slightly runny, while others like them firmer and browned on the outside. With just a little practice adjusting the heat and cooking time, you will be able to control the texture with accuracy.

When the beans are done, either serve them immediately or place them in a bowl to keep them from drying out in the hot skillet. Also remember that if they are to be served on a hot plate, as with enchiladas, they will continue to cook a bit so allow for this, leaving them slightly more runny than you want the end product to be.

Refried Beans are often served garnished with some *queso anejo* and a couple of tortilla chips. Grated feta cheese is an excellent substitute for *queso anejo*. Just sprinkle about ½ tablespoon over each serving and stick a couple of chips in it. *Serves 4.*

FRIJOLES RANCHEROS

Ranch-style Beans

1 *recipe* Frijoles de olla
   (p. 130)

3 *pieces bacon, chopped*

½ *cup onion, chopped*

2 *cloves garlic, minced*

2 serrano *or* jalapeño *chiles,
   diced*

2 *medium-size tomatoes,
   chopped*

½ *teaspoon oregano*

Often called *Frijoles á la charra*, or Beans Horsewoman Style, this dish is very popular in Mexico, especially in the north. Not surprisingly, it is universally popular in the southwestern United States as well.

Prepare the *Frijoles de olla* until they are about 30 minutes from being done.

Heat a skillet over medium heat. Add and fry the bacon until it is just beginning to brown. Add the onion, garlic, and chiles and continue cooking, stirring often, until the onion is well browned.

Add the tomatoes and oregano and cook 5 more minutes. Add the cooked vegetables to the beans and continue cooking until they are tender.

Serve the beans in bowls with the liquid and vegetables. *Serves 4.*

NUTRITION HINT: Cholesterol can be greatly reduced by substituting 2 table-spoons of olive oil for the bacon. Total fat can also be much diminished by using just ½ tablespoon olive oil.

FRIJOLES REFRITOS CON CHORIZO

Refried Beans with Sausage

Make these just like regular Refried Beans (p. 132) until the stage where the lard is heated in the skillet. After the lard has been heated, add ⅓ pound *chorizo* and cook, stirring constantly to break up the meat, until it is browned. Proceed to cook the beans as in the recipe for Refried Beans. *Serves 4.*

NUTRITION HINT:
DIET REFRIED BEANS
Diet recipes are often a difficult task for cookbook writers. On the one hand, there is the desire to provide directions for an authentic dish; on the other hand, there is the wish to make the result as palatable as possible for those on low-fat diets. Fortunately, all of the following variations give an acceptable result.

Variation 1

If you wish to eliminate cholesterol, substitute olive oil for the lard. To more drastically reduce the fat content as well (while still having a reasonable substitute), do the following:

Variation 2

Instead of processing the beans alone, heat them with ½ cup broth. When they are hot, add 1 tablespoon olive oil in which you have heated 1 clove garlic, peeled and mashed until just soft; then process the beans. (The garlic clove may be left in or discarded.)

Variation 3

For those with an extreme need to maintain a low-fat diet, use no oil at all. *All recipes serve 4.*

Sopas y Ensaladas

SOUPS AND SALADS

oup is a very important item in Mexican-American cooking since it is such an economical and nourishing way to use nearly any ingredient. Although there are countless varieties, fortunately most of the soups are variations on just a few basic themes. In fact, most are based on meat, poultry, and vegetables, the only thing differentiating them from stews being the amount of liquid used. *Posole* and *menudo* are good examples of dishes that could be considered in either category. In this chapter I have provided my favorite versions of the basic soups.

SOUPS

SOPA ESTILO SONORA
Sonoran Cheese Soup

This soup is a specialty of Sonora, many variations of which are found in and around Tucson.

In a large pot melt the butter over medium heat. Add and sauté the onion, green onion, and garlic until the onion is soft but not browned.

Add the flour and stir into the onion mixture. Continue to cook until the flour is cooked, but not browned, about 1 minute.

Remove the pot from the heat and stir in the heated milk, a little at a time to prevent lumping. When about half of the milk has been added, return the pot to the heat and stir in the rest. Bring to a simmer and cook, uncovered, for 5 minutes.

Add the remaining ingredients except the cheese and continue simmering, uncovered, until the potatoes are done, about 10 to 15 minutes. Then add the cheese and continue cooking, stirring constantly, until it is just melted. Serve the soup with flour tortillas and butter. *Serves 4.*

- 3 *tablespoons butter*
- ¼ *cup onion, chopped*
- ¼ *cup green onion, minced*
- 1 *clove garlic, minced*
- 2 *tablespoons flour*
- 1½ *quarts milk, heated*
- ½ *cup green chile, peeled, seeded, and chopped*
- 1 *pound potatoes, diced*
- 1 *cup frozen corn kernels*
- ¼ *teaspoon ground oregano*
- ¼ *teaspoon thyme*
- ¼ *teaspoon ground cumin*
- ½ *teaspoon black pepper*
- ½ *teaspoon salt, or to taste*
- ½ *pound Monterey Jack cheese, grated*

SOPA DE FIDEO

Noodle Soup

1 *tablespoon olive oil*
½ *pound lean ground beef*
½ *cup onion, chopped*
1 *clove garlic, minced*
5 *cups water*
1 *14-ounce can tomatoes and green chiles*
¼ *cup tomato paste*
½ *teaspoon salt, or to taste*
½ *pound* fideo, *or substitute angel-hair pasta*
1 *cup mild cheddar cheese, grated*

Fideo is the favorite Mexican-American pasta. It comes in tightly wrapped coils, about the size of angel-hair pasta.

Heat the olive oil in a large pot over medium heat. Add the ground beef, onion, and garlic and cook until the beef is browned and the onion is soft.

Add the water, canned tomatoes and chiles, tomato paste, and salt. When the ingredients have been well combined, bring them to a boil and simmer 5 minutes, covered.

Remove the cover and add the *fideo*. Cook, uncovered, until the pasta is tender but not mushy, 8 to 10 minutes.

Serve the soup immediately, topped with the cheese. *Serves 4.*

CALDO DE POLLO

Chicken Soup

At Mexican-American restaurants in south Texas noontime means *caldo*, usually *Caldo de pollo* or *Caldo de res*. These hearty dishes are more brothy stews than soups and are often served in huge bowls, accompanied by rice, lime wedges, chopped cilantro, and thick, hot flour tortillas.

Place the cut-up chicken in a large stewpot; add the water and bring to a boil. Simmer the chicken, covered, for 30 minutes.

Grind together and add the garlic, cumin, and peppercorns. Add the remaining ingredients except the rice, limes, cilantro, and tortillas and continue to simmer, covered, for another 30 minutes. You may need to add additional water during the cooking process, so check the soup every once in a while.

Serve the soup with the rice, lime wedges, cilantro, and flour tortillas. Diners may add the rice to the soup or eat it separately. *Serves 4.*

1	*3½–4½ pound chicken, cut into serving pieces*
2	*quarts water*
4	*cloves garlic*
½	*teaspoon cumin*
½	*teaspoon peppercorns*
½	*teaspoon oregano*
½	*teaspoon marjoram*
½	*teaspoon thyme*
¼	*teaspoon sage*
1½	*cups carrots, chopped*
½	*cup onions, chopped*
2	*large tomatoes, chopped*
½	*cup celery, chopped*
1	*teaspoon salt, or to taste*
1	*recipe Mexican Rice (p. 126)*
2	*limes, cut into wedges*
½	*cup cilantro, chopped*
1	*dozen thick flour tortillas*

CALDO DE RES

Beef Soup

1 *pound beef brisket or 2 pounds short ribs, or a combination of both*

2½ *quarts water*

½ *cup tomato puree*

4 *cloves garlic*

½ *teaspoon cumin*

1 *teaspoon oregano*

½ *cup onion, chopped*

1 *cup cabbage, chopped*

2 *large tomatoes, chopped*

½ *cup sweet bell pepper, chopped*

2 *ears corn, cut into 2-inch lengths*

1 *teaspoon salt, or to taste*

1 *recipe Mexican Rice (p. 126)*

2 *limes, cut into wedges*

½ *cup cilantro, chopped*

1 *dozen thick flour tortillas*

This Tex-Mex companion to *Caldo de pollo* is made with many different cuts of meat. My favorites are beef brisket and beef short ribs. In either case remove as much of the fat from the meat as possible.

In a large stewpot cover the meat with water and bring to a boil. Skim off the scum which rises to the surface and add the tomato puree. Grind together in a *molcajete* or mortar and pestle the garlic, cumin, and oregano and add the mixture to the soup. Simmer the soup, covered, for 1 hour and 15 minutes, adding additional water if necessary.

Add the remaining ingredients except for the rice, limes, cilantro, and tortillas and continue to simmer, covered, for ½ hour.

Serve with the rice, lime wedges, chopped cilantro, and tortillas. *Serves 4.*

SOPA DE TORTILLAS

Tortilla Soup

Tortilla Soup comes in many forms, from clear broth to a highly flavored one like the following. The only necessity seems to be that it contain fried pieces of tortilla. This recipe is my all-time favorite. It is excellent and not to be missed.

Place the tomatoes and 2 *ancho* chiles in a blender and blend for 1 minute. Add as much of the chicken broth as your blender will hold and blend until well mixed.

Pour the contents of the blender into a soup kettle, add the remaining ingredients except the fried tortilla strips, cheese, and sour cream, including the remaining chicken broth and 4 *ancho* chiles. Bring the liquid to a boil and simmer for 10 to 15 minutes.

Place ¼ of the tortilla strips and ¼ cup of the cheese in each of 4 soup bowls.

Place 1 of the boiled *ancho* chiles in each bowl, then ladle in the soup. Top the soup with a large spoonful of the sour cream and serve. *Serves 4.*

10 *medium-size tomatoes, peeled, seeded, and coarsely chopped*

6 ancho *chiles, stemmed, seeded, and deveined*

20 *ounces chicken broth*

1 *teaspoon salt*
Juice from 2 limes

2 *tablespoons sherry*

¼ *teaspoon Tabasco sauce*

4 *tortillas, cut into ½ inch by 2-inch strips and fried crisp*

1 *cup Monterey Jack cheese, grated*

½ *cup sour cream*

SOPA DE ALBÓNDIGAS

Meatball Soup

½ pound ground pork
½ pound ground beef
½ teaspoon salt, or to taste
1 piece bread
1 egg, beaten
1 teaspoon chile powder
3 hard-boiled eggs, chopped
1 tablespoon lard
5 tomatoes, peeled and
   crushed
¼ cup onion, chopped
1 teaspoon chile powder
4 cups beef broth

The following recipe for this popular dish is from *One Hundred & One Mexican Dishes*, compiled by May E. Southworth. Published in 1906, this is the oldest book on Mexican cooking published in the United States according to the Library of Congress. I have left the instructions intact but have added the list and quantities of ingredients. I also increased the amount of broth given so the recipe would serve 4.

> Take equal parts of fresh pork and beef, chop fine, add salt, a piece of soaked bread, one egg well beaten, and one teaspoonful of chile powder. Mix thoroughly and make into small balls, putting into each a piece of hard-boiled egg. In a tablespoonful of hot lard put five peeled and crushed tomatoes, a little chopped onion, salt and chile powder; add one cupful of broth and let boil a few moments; then put in the meatballs and boil until the meat is thoroughly cooked. *Serves 4.*

SALADS

Salads as we know them are not big items in Mexican cooking, and it is the same in the Southwest's Mexican-American kitchens. Most Mexican cookbooks give recipes for salads that are about the same as what most Americans eat every day. However, among the few notable exceptions are the recipes included in this section.

ENSALADA ESTILO TACO

Taco Salad

The Taco Salad is probably the result of a cook combining numerous leftovers from a Mexican kitchen, for this is basically what it is. In restaurants this salad is usually served in a huge corn or burrito-size flour tortilla which has been fried into the shape of a bowl. Unfortunately, most home cooks cannot obtain corn tortillas of sufficient size, so we usually have to use flour tortillas. But this is fine, especially if you garnish the salad with a few corn tortilla chips.

A further problem is that many home deep fryers do not have sufficient capacity, either of width or depth, to allow for the proper shaping of a tortilla shell. However, this problem can be overcome by frying several smaller tortillas into flatter than usual shapes and overlapping them on the plate. Another solution is to either mix corn tortilla chips into the salad or to serve them on the side. For making and frying tortilla shells, see the recipe for *Tostadas compuestas* (p. 229).

All the ingredients should either be chilled or at room temperature.

DRESSING:

Use your favorite dressing or ⅓ cup olive oil whisked with ⅓ cup vinegar and ⅓ cup of your favorite salsa.

Fried tortilla shells (p. 229) or tortilla chips

1¼ *cups Mexican Rice (p. 126)*

1¼ *cups Frijoles de olla (p. 130), drained*

1¼ *cups canned corn kernels*

1¼ *cups Picadillo II (p. 149) or Spicy Shredded Chicken Filling (p. 158)*

1¼ *cups tomatoes, chopped*

3 *cups lettuce, shredded*

1¼ *cups black California olives, sliced or chopped*

1¼ *cups Monterey Jack or mild cheddar cheese (or a combination of both), grated*

1¼ *cups jícama, thinly sliced*

3 *green onions, chopped*

2 *avocados, peeled, seeded, and sliced*

Tortilla chips

Combine all ingredients except the avocados and tortilla chips, toss with the dressing, and place equal portions on each plate (on top of the tortilla shells if you are using them). Garnish each salad with the avocados and tortilla chips. *Serves 4.*

GUACAMOLE

2   *medium to large avocados,*
      peeled and seeded

½   *tablespoon fresh lime or*
      lemon juice (optional)

¼   *cup onion or green onion,*
      minced (optional)

1   *tomato, peeled, seeded, and*
      chopped (optional)

1   serrano *chile, seeded and*
      minced (optional)

1   *pickled* jalapeño *chile,*
      minced (optional)

½   *tablespoon juice from*
      jalapeño *can (optional)*

2   *pieces bacon, cooked crisp*
      and minced (optional)

¼   *cup cilantro, minced*
      (optional)

      Corn tortilla chips

Guacamole could be classified as either an appetizer-type dip, a sauce, or a salad, depending on how it is to be used. It is one of those items like nachos that can be as simple or as complex as your mood. Many of the jazzier variations offered in restaurants are served not necessarily because they are better but because they are cheaper. Adding items like lettuce, tomato, and onion is an inexpensive alternative to a salad of pure avocado. However, these items are also a great deal less fattening than avocado, a much more valid reason for using them.

You should use the richest avocados (with the highest fat content) you can find. In this country that usually means either haas or fuerte avocados, but never the watery Florida varieties.

Please note that Americans often put way too much lime or lemon juice in Guacamole. There should be just enough to keep the Guacamole from turning dark before it is served. The truth is that if you are using really rich, well-ripened avocados, the Guacamole will taste best with no juice added. In any case, never use anything but fresh lime or lemon juice.

Another common mistake made even by restaurants is to blend or process the Guacamole to a totally smooth consistency. Good Guacamole should be chunky, and the best way to achieve this consistency is to mash it by hand in a *molcajete*.

The following recipe lists all ingredients except the avocados and tortilla chips as optional so that you can make Guacamole as simple or as complicated as you wish. Except for the addition of bacon, which is seldom used, this Guacamole is essentially the same as the Guacamole made in pre-Hispanic Mexico (see p. 28). Mix and mash the ingredients together and serve garnished with tortilla chips. *Serves 4 as an appetizer or as a garnish for tacos.*

ENSALADA DE COL O LECHUGA

Shredded Cabbage or Lettuce Garnish

This is the garnish that rounds out many of the *antojito* plates served in Mexican-American restaurants. Unfortunately, most restaurants do not take the trouble to use a dressing on this item. The slight extra trouble and expense would do much to enhance the entire plate.

The following recipe is very similar to that served at La Posta restaurant in Mesilla, New Mexico.

Toss all the items together and serve as a garnish on *antojito* plates. *Serves 4.*

3 *cups cabbage or lettuce, shredded*

1½ *tablespoons cider vinegar*

3 *tablespoons cooking oil*

¼ *teaspoon pepper*

⅛ *teaspoon salt, or to taste*

ENSALADA DE NOPALITOS

Cactus Paddle Salad

THE DRESSING:

- 1½ *tablespoons cider vinegar*
- ½ *tablespoon liquid from a can of pickled* jalapeño *chiles*
- 4 *tablespoons olive oil*
- ½ *teaspoon oregano*
- ¼ *teaspoon salt*
- ¼ *teaspoon pepper*

THE SALAD:

- 3½ *cups* nopalitos, *fresh or canned*
- 3½ *cups canned corn kernels*
- ¼ *cup green onions, minced*
- 2 *avocados, peeled, seeded, and chopped*

If you like okra, you will probably like *nopalitos,* cactus paddles from the nopal cactus; if not, the opposite will more than likely be the case. The reason is that the cut cactus leaves give off the same mucus-like texture that is a characteristic of okra, and no matter how fresh or how well cooked the cactus leaves are, it never seems to completely go away. In the following recipe you can use canned *nopalitos* as well as fresh. Their flavor will be different, since vinegar is usually added to the canned variety, but the result will be fine. In any case you can substitute cut green beans for the *nopalitos* in this recipe with great results.

Mix the dressing ingredients together.

To prepare fresh *nopalitos,* first make sure all the thorns have been removed. Then cut them into pieces about ¼ inch wide by 2 inches long. Finally, boil them in salted water for about 15 minutes.

Mix the *nopalitos* with the remaining salad ingredients; then stir in the dressing and serve. *Serves 4.*

*W*hether you are making tacos, enchiladas, tamales, burritos, *chimichangas*, or any of the other common *antojitos*, you will find the same basic fillings used over and over again. Shredded beef and pork, ground beef and pork, and shredded chicken and turkey are the staples of a majority of recipes. To avoid repetition, I have included the most universal fillings in this chapter, accompanied by their principal variations.

I have also made suggestions for using the fillings in addition to the ways they are used in other recipes in the book.

PICADILLO
Ground Meat

In Mexican cooking *picadillo*, which means "minced meat" or "hash," refers to any ground meat stuffing. In Mexico ground meat is not nearly as common as in this country. This is certainly one reason why, south of the border, *picadillos* are seldom used to stuff tacos or other *antojitos* except *chiles rellenos*. Mexican immigrants, however, found ground beef to be their cheapest source of meat and later discovered it was much easier to prepare than the more traditional shredded meat. So Mexican-American *antojitos* are more likely to be filled with a *picadillo* than anything else.

There are really two types of *picadillos* used for *antojitos*, one that is relatively dry, made almost completely of meat, and one that contains other ingredients, including potato, bread, and tomato. The later type was undoubtedly developed because it "extends" the meat but was later found to be ideal as a stuffing for items that are to be fried, such as tacos, *taquitos*, and *flautas*. Not only does this type of filling remain moist after frying, but it also holds its shape and tends to stick to the tortilla, making it much easier to shape and cook. The first recipe, *Picadillo* I, is for this type of stuffing, while *Picadillo* II is a drier version that is ideal for use in soft tacos and flour tortilla tacos.

2 tablespoons olive oil
1 pound lean ground beef
2 medium tomatoes, chopped
1½ medium onions, chopped
3 cloves garlic
3 slices bread, chopped
¼ teaspoon ground cumin
½ teaspoon oregano
½ teaspoon salt, or to taste
½ teaspoon ground pepper

PICADILLO I
Filling for Fried Antojitos

Place the oil and then the ground beef in a skillet that has been heated over medium heat. Lightly brown the meat, stirring and chopping it with a cooking spoon to break it up.

NUTRITION HINT: In addition to the recipe for Low-fat *Picadillo* provided on p. 151, all recipes for fillings will be improved from the standpoint of healthy eating, with little or no loss in flavor, if you use extra-lean meat.

Meanwhile, blend the remaining ingredients to a paste.

As soon as the meat has been lightly browned add the blended ingredients and stir until well combined. Turn the heat to medium low and continue to fry for about 15 minutes, stirring often until most of the liquid has evaporated.

This filling keeps well in the refrigerator and is ideal for filling *tacos dorados*, *taquitos*, and *flautas*. *Makes approximately 2 cups.*

PICADILLO II
Filling for Unfried Antojitos

Heat a skillet over medium heat and add the olive oil, onions, and potatoes, if used. Cook the onions until they are soft but not browned and add the ground beef in small pieces. Brown the meat, breaking it up with a cooking spoon.

Grind together the garlic, oregano, and cumin in a *molcajete* or mortar and pestle and stir it into the meat. Next, add the chile powder, if used, and salt. Turn the temperature to very low, cover the skillet, and simmer the filling for 20 minutes, stirring occasionally.

Use as a stuffing for soft tacos, flour tortilla tacos, enchiladas, *empanadas*, and *chiles rellenos*. *Makes approximately 3½ cups.*

1½ *tablespoons olive oil*
½ *cup onions, minced*
½ *cup potatoes, cut into ¼-inch pieces and rinsed (optional)*
1½ *pounds very lean ground beef*
4 *cloves garlic*
1 *teaspoon oregano*
½ *teaspoon cumin*
1½ *teaspoons chile powder (optional)*
½ *teaspoon salt, or to taste*

PICADILLO III

Chorizo/Beef Filling

2½ *tablespoons olive oil*
⅔ *cup green chiles, minced*
⅔ *cup onions, minced*
⅔ *cup potatoes, minced*
3 *cloves garlic, minced*
1 *cup tomatoes, diced*
  Heaping ¼ teaspoon salt, or to taste
  Heaping ½ teaspoon ground cumin
½ *teaspoon oregano*
8 *ounces* chorizo
1¼ *pounds very lean ground beef*

This is a terrific filling for taco shells and flour tortillas. It is also the basis for the best breakfast tacos I have ever had.

Heat the olive oil in a skillet over moderate heat and add the green chiles, onions, potatoes, and garlic. Sauté the vegetables until they are well browned, adjusting the heat as necessary, about 8 to 10 minutes, stirring often. You may have to add a little more olive oil to keep the vegetables from sticking.

Add the tomatoes and continue cooking for 3 minutes, stirring often. Then add the salt, cumin, and oregano and cook for 1 minute.

Add the *chorizo*, breaking it up with a cooking spoon and stirring it into the vegetables. When the *chorizo* is browned and has released most of its fat, add the ground beef, breaking it up and mixing it with the other ingredients.

When the ground beef is browned, cover the skillet, turn the heat to very low, and simmer, stirring occasionally, for 10 minutes. *Makes approximately 4 cups.*

LOW-FAT PICADILLO

Put all the ingredients into a large pot and cover them with water so that the water is 2 inches above the solid ingredients. Bring the water to a boil; then simmer, covered, for 20 minutes. At first it may seem as if you are creating a soupy mess, but have faith!

Refrigerate the *picadillo* overnight. The next day skim off any congealed fat from the surface. When you are ready to use the *picadillo*, bring the contents of the pot to a boil, strain out all the liquid, and return the solid ingredients to the hot pot to evaporate any excess moisture before using. *Makes about 3 cups*.

1 *pound very lean ground beef*
½ *pound potatoes, peeled and chopped*
½ *cup onion, chopped*
½ *cup green chile, chopped*
1 *medium tomato, chopped*
3 *cloves garlic, minced*
1 *teaspoon ground cumin*
1 *teaspoon oregano*
½ *cup tomato sauce*
Salt, to taste

NUTRITION HINT: This filling is very easy to make and is an acceptable substitute for the other *picadillos* for people on low-fat diets.

CHORIZO

Mexican-style Sausage

1½ *pounds ground pork*
2 *tablespoons chile powder*
1 *tablespoon paprika*
1 *teaspoon garlic powder*
1 *teaspoon onion powder*
½ *teaspoon ground black
     pepper*
½ *teaspoon ground cumin*
½ *teaspoon ground oregano
     (optional)*
1 *teaspoon salt*
3 *tablespoons ordinary
     white vinegar*

Chorizo is called for in many fillings and nearly always in break-fast tacos. While *chorizo*, usually in link sausage form but some-times in bulk, is found in most grocery stores in the Southwest, this is not always the case in other parts of the country. However, even when it is available, the commercial product is usually infe-rior to homemade varieties. Too often it contains cereal fillers, potentially dangerous preservatives, and too much vinegar and salt. *Chorizo* should be mildly assertive with a nice balance of fla-vors, not pungent, oversalted, or greasy. Although in Spain, where it originated, *chorizo* is often sold in true sausage form, that is wrapped in a natural casing, Mexican-American *chorizo* is nearly always intended to be used in bulk form and consequently is stuffed into plastic casings.

The following recipe for bulk *chorizo* is so good and so easy to prepare that you should use it or your own variation whenever possible. Be sure and use pure chile powder, either from *ancho* or New Mexico chiles. If that is not possible, omit the cumin and half the garlic and onion powder from the recipe. In general, I am usually very much against the use of garlic and onion powders because of their artificial taste, but they work very well in this recipe.

Chorizo can be mixed by hand or with an electric mixer. However, a food processor fitted with a steel blade does a much better job since it cuts the meat into smaller bits, thereby imitat-ing the fine grind of commercial meat grinders used to make this type of sausage.

Place all ingredients in a food processor fitted with a steel blade and pulse until well mixed.

To cook the *chorizo*, fry it over medium heat until completely cooked through and crisped to your preference. Use wherever *chorizo* is specified. *Makes approximately 3 cups.*

TRADITIONAL CHORIZO

Traditionally, *chorizo* is made with whole chiles rather than powder, and it is still made this way in some Mexican-American families. I have conducted several informal, "blind" taste tests between the traditional version and the easier one above, and the latter usually is preferred. However, if you cannot obtain pure chile powder and do have access to the whole chiles or just want to make *chorizo* in the traditional manner, here's how to adapt the preceding recipe for *chorizo*.

Omit the chile, garlic, and onion powders from the preceding recipe and substitute the ingredients at the right.

2 ancho *chiles*
4 *cloves garlic, chopped*
¼ *cup onion, chopped*

Remove the stems, seeds, and veins from the chiles; then simmer them in water to cover for 15 minutes.

Place the chiles, garlic, and onion in a blender, add the 3 tablespoons vinegar, and blend to a paste. Add the paste to the pork with the remaining ingredients and process as directed in the preceding recipe. *Makes approximately 3 cups.*

CARNE DE RES DESHEBRADA
Shredded Beef

¼   *cup cooking oil*

2½–3   *pounds beef brisket, the smaller, thinner end, trimmed of all fat*

1   ancho *or New Mexico dried chile, stemmed and seeded*

3–4   *slices onion*

3   *cloves garlic*

1   *bay leaf*

½   *teaspoon oregano*

This is the traditional Mexican stuffing for tacos and most other *antojitos* that is still used by many Mexican-American cooks. In fact, I have heard many gringos say that such and such a restaurant is more "authentic" because it uses shredded rather than ground meat.

You can use any lean stew or braising meat to make this filling. I prefer beef brisket because its coarse texture makes it ideal for the purpose and because it is a flavorful cut. While beef brisket has a fair amount of fat, about 25 percent by weight, it is easy to remove prior to cooking. In the following recipe the quantity given is before the fat has been removed.

Preheat your oven to 300 degrees.

Heat a Dutch oven over medium-high heat, add the oil, and brown the beef on all sides. Pour off as much oil as possible and just barely cover the meat with water. Bring the liquid to a boil, skim off any scum that rises to the surface, and add the remaining ingredients. Cover the pot and place it in the oven until the meat is tender, 2 to 2½ hours.

Remove the meat, reserving the broth for another use. When the meat is cool enough to handle, shred it. Although traditionally meat is shredded by hand or pounded in a *molcajete*, by far the easiest way to do this is to cut the meat into 1-inch pieces and process it in a food processor equipped with a plastic blade. Ten to 15 pulses usually produces a nicely shredded filling that can be used by itself with the addition of a little salt and pepper or as the basis for a more elaborate stuffing such as *Carne seca* (p. 156). *After shredding, the recipe should yield 4½ to 6 cups of filling.*

This recipe is used to make the mock version of *Machaca*, or *Carne seca* (p. 156), which is one of the best fillings I have ever found for burritos, *chimichangas*, tacos, *taquitos,* and so forth. It is also used to make *Salpicón* (p. 291), the wonderful Mexican-style meat salad.

CARNE DE PUERCO DESHEBRADA
Shredded Pork

Shredded pork is not used nearly as much in Mexican-American cooking as it is in Mexican cooking. I find it makes a nice change from shredded beef in tacos, *taquitos*, and *flautas*. It is also good mixed half-and-half with shredded beef. When partially shredded, the cooked meat is the basis for my favorite version of *carnitas*.

Place the meat in a large pot or Dutch oven and pour in enough water to cover it by 2 inches.

Bring the liquid to a boil and, using a small strainer, remove the scum that rises to the top. Add the remaining ingredients; then simmer the meat, uncovered, adding water as necessary, for 45 minutes to 1 hour, or until it is tender but not dry.

When the liquid has cooled, strain it and reserve it for another use (it is excellent when used to make Mexican Rice, p. 126). Then shred the meat, by hand, in a *molcajete*, or in a food processor with a plastic blade. *Makes approximately 4 cups.*

2½ *pounds lean pork loin, cut into 1-inch pieces*
1 *onion, cut into quarters*
1 *carrot, cut into 4 pieces*
2 *cloves garlic, whole*
2 *bay leaves*

MACHACA O CARNE SECA

Mexican-style Jerky

Machaca is the marvelous *Carne seca,* or dried beef, for which the Mexican state of Sonora is justly famous. *Machaca,* like so many other Sonoran specialties, quickly found its way to Mexican-American restaurants in Arizona.

Unfortunately, if your humidity rises above the 5 percent to 15 percent found in the Southwest deserts, you cannot safely make *Machaca* without a dehydrator since the meat may spoil well before it dries. I do use a dehydrator and make *Machaca* with 2 pounds of lean meat cut less then ¼ inch thick that I have marinated for 1½ hours in ⅓ cup lime juice and ⅓ cup water blended with 6 cloves garlic. I dry the meat at 145 degrees for about 3½ hours in my unit, which has a fan, or until it is nearly but not completely dry. The drier and more brittle the meat, the harder it is to shred, even with the steel blade of a food processor. The result has an authentic texture, but it lacks a certain something that sun drying produces. If you dehydrate your own meat, follow the instructions for the following recipe beginning after the meat is "dried" in the oven.

A good *Machaca* substitute can also be produced in the oven. Before trying the following recipe, which is adapted from one suggested in Tucson's El Charro restaurant cookbook, I was skeptical. However, while the following recipe is not quite as good as the best sun-dried *Machaca,* it comes very close and makes one of the best fillings I have ever tried. In fact, this is how a majority of restaurants make their *Carne seca* since few are willing to go to the trouble that El Charro does to produce the real thing.

You will notice that the recipe calls for garlic puree. Carlotta Dunn Flores, owner of El Charro, uses this product extensively. Her instructions call for blending an entire head of peeled garlic in 8 ounces of water. I blend 16 cloves of peeled garlic in just under 1 cup water so that 1 tablespoon equals 1 clove garlic. After trying it I have found it to be extremely useful and always have a jar of it in the refrigerator.

Preheat your oven to 325 degrees.

To "dry" the meat, toss it with the lime juice and 2 tablespoons garlic puree, place it on a cookie sheet or pizza pan, and bake it for 15 minutes, stirring occasionally. The meat should be quite dry and beginning to stiffen. If not, continue cooking a few more minutes. The meat can be prepared to this point and then refrigerated, if desired.

To prepare the filling, heat a large skillet over moderate heat. Add the oil, then the onion, and sauté it until it is just soft but not browned, 2 to 3 minutes.

Add the green chile, tomato, dried meat, salt, pepper, and 2 tablespoons garlic puree and cook, stirring often, for 3 to 5 minutes. *Yields approximately 4 cups.*

4 cups Shredded Beef (p. 154)

Juice of 1 lime

2 tablespoons garlic puree (see instructions above)

¼ cup olive or cooking oil

⅓ cup onion, minced

½ cup green chile, peeled, seeded, and chopped

1 tomato, chopped

½ teaspoon salt, or to taste

½ teaspoon pepper, or to taste

2 tablespoons garlic puree

POLLO O PAVO DESHEBRADO

Shredded Chicken or Turkey

Chicken or turkey breasts, skin removed

Most shredded chicken and turkey is made from the breast, but feel free to substitute dark meat if you prefer it. Also, both shredded chicken and turkey can be made from boneless breast. My experience is that using bone-in meat seems to produce a more tender result.

Simmer the chicken or turkey in water to cover until just done. Remove the meat, reserving the broth for another use. When the meat is cool enough to handle, remove it from the bones, cut it into 1-inch pieces, and shred it in a food processor fitted with a plastic blade. The yield will depend on the size of the cut used. *Two medium- to large-size chicken breasts (4 split breasts) will yield approximately 2½ cups shredded filling.*

RELLENO DE POLLO SAZONADO

Spicy Shredded Chicken Filling

2 tablespoons olive oil

4 cloves garlic, minced

4 jalapeño *chiles, stemmed, seeded, and minced*

1 onion, chopped

6 small to medium tomatoes, chopped

Shredded Chicken from 2 breasts (p. 158), approximately 2½ cups

2 teaspoons oregano

½ teaspoon salt, or to taste

1 cup chicken broth

This filling is particularly delicious in *flautas*, Tacos dorados (p. 189), and enchiladas.

In a skillet or Dutch oven heat the olive oil over medium heat and sauté the garlic, chiles, and onion until soft but not browned.

Add the tomatoes, shredded chicken, oregano, salt, and enough chicken broth to barely cover the ingredients. Simmer, stirring frequently, until nearly all the liquid has evaporated. *Yields approximately 2½ cups shredded filling.*

Salsas de Chile Colorado
RED CHILE "MASTER" SAUCES

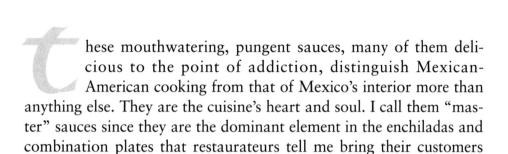

these mouthwatering, pungent sauces, many of them delicious to the point of addiction, distinguish Mexican-American cooking from that of Mexico's interior more than anything else. They are the cuisine's heart and soul. I call them "master" sauces since they are the dominant element in the enchiladas and combination plates that restaurateurs tell me bring their customers back time after time.

It is not just the way these sauces are *made* (there are similar sauces in Mexico) but rather the way they are *used* that makes them unique to Mexican-American cooking. In Mexico one rarely finds combination plates or even enchiladas that are totally smothered in a thickened chile sauce and topped with melted cheese, except occasionally in the north. Much more common are enchiladas whose tortilla has been merely dipped in a sauce, often a rather thin one. The other items on the plate usually come with no sauce at all. (An exception are the enchiladas, sometimes found around Puebla and Mexico City such as *Enchiladas con crema*, p. 33, whose cream bases strongly suggest French influence.) In theory this distinction may not seem of great importance, but the differences in the taste, texture, and eye appeal of the dishes are significant.

While delicious green chile or *tomatillo* sauced enchiladas are served throughout the Southwest, it is the red chile sauces that predominate in the combination plates and that give each cook or restaurant a distinctive imprint.

New Mexico-style master sauces are traditionally based upon chiles and water with the addition of garlic, oregano, salt, and sometimes a little vinegar. These sauces are, like the area's architecture, simple but elegant. The sauces of other regions, most notably Texas, usually contain some tomato or tomato sauce, and are often strongly flavored with meat, producing a result that might be described more accurately as a gravy than a sauce.

While these sauces are very easy to prepare, even small variations in the ingredients produce important differences and these variations are virtually endless. It is these differences in the master sauces, often subtle ones, that distinguish one cook's or restaurant's dishes from another's.

Some distinctions depend on what variety of chile is used. Most of the recipes for these sauces call for either New Mexico variety dried chiles or *ancho* chiles, each of which produces very different effects. Some cooks combine these chiles in various proportions, creating further variations. Still other distinctions depend on whether whole dried chiles or chile powder, or a combination of both, is used.

Additional distinctions are due to the choices and subtle combinations of other ingredients. A sauce based upon beef will be totally different from one based upon pork or one based on a combination of both meats. In the latter, the proportion in which the beef and pork are blended creates yet further variations. Sauces that use no meat are just as unique. Also, the amount of flour used to thicken the sauce makes a difference as does whether it was first browned in fat to make a roux or simply mixed with water and added later. The type of fat used—a neutral cooking oil, olive oil, lard, or butter, or a combination of fats—also creates differences, and so on. While on a superficial level these sauces appear simple, one quickly learns that they are actually pervaded with subtleties.

Finally, the amounts and types of seasonings used are also of major importance. New Mexico-style sauces may contain no cumin whereas the same quantity of Tex-Mex sauce can include 2 tablespoons or more of the powdered variety. The ways that cooks customize their sauces are nearly limitless. Your only real challenge is to decide which you like best.

I have divided this section between the major variations of chile

Appetizer plate of mixed *antojitos*.

Buñuelos, *Biscochitos*, and *Sopaipillas* with honey.

New Mexico Stacked Enchiladas.

Three-color Mexican Flag Enchiladas.

"Master" sauce preparation.

Fajitas.

Pre-Hispanic shrimp salad and potato soup.

Puebla's famous *Mole poblano.*

Eyes of the Ox.

Tex-Mex combination plate.

Enchilada-style burrito.

Isabel Salcido's California-style Stacked Enchiladas.

sauces, including the traditional New Mexico varieties, the Tex-Mex versions, and an all-purpose one that is much like those from other areas. The latter usually consists of combinations and variations of the first two categories. The basic differences relate to what type of chile or combination of chiles is used and to whether broth or water is used. I suggest you try those recipes that appeal to you, then experiment with any variations that seem of interest. In the process you will create a sauce that bears your own signature.

WHOLE CHILES VERSUS CHILE POWDER

The finest Mexican-American cooks know that the best sauces are made from whole dried chiles rather than chile powder. The difference is important since a sauce made with chile powder will never have quite as smooth a texture and as rich a flavor as one made from dried chiles. The ground chile never emulsifies like whole chiles, which means the texture will be grainier; and even the best chile powders seem, to me, slightly bitter. To approach the texture of whole chiles, a ground chile sauce relies on the use of more flour to hold the grainy bits in suspension. While in whole chile sauces the rule is the more chiles the better, with those made of chile powder, the less you use (up to a point), the smoother your sauce will be.

This is not to say that a fine sauce cannot be made with chile powder. My informal surveys indicate that while most Mexican-American cooks admit that whole chiles produce a superior result, they use chile powder much more frequently because of its greater convenience. In fact, unless you make sauces of whole chiles and chile powder side by side you will probably not be disappointed. If you do use chile powder, you must select one of high quality made from the chile specified in the recipe, usually either *ancho* or New Mexico dried chiles, and without additional additives. Never use generic chile powders, which usually contain powdered cumin, oregano, and garlic, not to mention preservatives and other items not specifically noted on the labels. As a rule you can substitute 1 tablespoon chile powder for 1 whole chile in the recipes.

But why not cook with the best ingredients? Mexican cooking has become so popular that most supermarkets in the Southwest carry whole dried chiles, and most urban areas elsewhere have at least one local source. There are also many mail-order sources, some of which I have included in the Appendix; others can be found in *Chile Pepper* Magazine.

NEW MEXICO-STYLE "MASTER" CHILE SAUCES

NEW MEXICO CHILES

New Mexico chiles vary in heat and flavor depending on the soil, seed variety, and climate. These chiles, more than any others, have a complexity of flavor that reflects the soils and clear, dry climate in which they are grown. Their aroma is to many chile aficionados what the aroma of fine wine is to oenophiles.

As you will see, the fact that New Mexico chiles vary so widely in heat makes it difficult to write one recipe that will work for every situation, except when chile powder is specified. After exhaustive experimentation I have concluded that there is no way to take all the adventure out of cooking these sauces—but this is part of the fun.

Most recipes specify the number of chiles required, but since the chiles come in various sizes, you can often not rely on numbers to achieve the desired result. Although I have found that gauging the amount by weight is more reliable, particularly for the inexperienced cook, this method is also less than perfect because of the variability of the chiles' heat. For example, even within the category of mild chiles there can be considerable differences in piquancy. For these reasons the best approach to assuring the desired result in a particular recipe is to do a small test batch with the chiles you are using. This will allow you to adjust the recipe to your own taste. As a starting point I have provided quantities by weight as well as by the number of chiles.

Preparing the Chiles:

In the old days New Mexican cooks removed the chile "meat" from the tough skins by hand, either with their fingers, with a scraper (like a boning knife), or with the *mano* of a *metate*. To facilitate this, the chiles were first simmered for 30 minutes or more to reconstitute them and loosen the skins. I have done this many times, and occasionally the meat is simple to remove; but more often the process is tedious. Nevertheless, if you are really interested in this type of cooking, I recommend that you try the hand method at least once. It is the only way to ensure that you are getting only the pure "meat" without any skin. To me, this method produces the smoothest, most full-bodied sauce.

However, the modern and by far the easiest method is to use the combination of a blender and food mill or strainer. This produces fine results with very little effort. It also allows you to blend in the other ingredients, such as garlic, if you are after an ultra smooth sauce. On the other hand, if you want a truly rustic dish that allows you to imagine the sauce was prepared over a wood stove in a turn of the century adobe, omit the straining. The bits of skin will add the extra texture that was surely part of rural cooking where cooks did not always have the extra time needed to completely remove all the skin.

Thickening the Sauce:

New Mexico chiles are usually sold in packages labeled either hot or mild (as are the chile powders that are made from them). I suggest you use the mild variety, not because they are mild (after all, New Mexico cooking is the hottest of all the Mexican-American styles) but because you can use more of them. And the more chiles you use, the more the sauce will thicken naturally and the less flour will be necessary. I find that the natural thickening from the chiles produces a full-bodied, nicely colored sauce with a more natural, smooth, and rustic texture. The objective is to thicken the sauce with the chiles and use just enough flour to bind it together. For example, the recipe that follows, if made with mild chiles, uses only about 2 teaspoons of flour, whereas one made with hot chiles requires about 2 tablespoons.

In any case, an additional thickening agent is desirable to "bind" the sauce. Some cooks make a roux, which is a combination of oil, butter, or lard and flour that is cooked until the floury flavor is eliminated. They then stir the liquid to be thickened into it at the beginning of the cooking process. While this works well with sauces such as the Tex-Mex variety, the problem with a New Mexico-type sauce that has a lot of natural thickening from the chiles is that it is difficult to accurately gauge the amount of flour that will be necessary before the natural thickening has taken place. To solve this problem, some cooks add a little flour and water toward the end of the cooking process. However, there is some danger of the flour not completely blending and leaving minidumplings in the sauce as well as the raw taste of uncooked flour. To eliminate this problem, other cooks make a separate roux to be added later in the cooking process. The flour is coated with oil, allowing it to completely blend with the sauce. This method also ensures that there will be no floury flavor in the sauce. This is the method I suggest.

In making a roux, 1 tablespoon of oil will accommodate at least 2 tablespoons of flour, but 1 tablespoon of butter will absorb only 1 tablespoon of flour. To make a roux, heat the oil over moderate heat and stir in the flour. Continue to cook, stirring constantly, until the flour just begins to brown and gives off a nutty aroma. Do not allow the roux to scorch since this will ruin the sauce. If you want to extend the sauce (as do many New Mexico cooks, particularly in restaurants), simply use more flour in the roux and add water to the sauce. The use of additional flour and water is also necessary if even the mild chile varieties are too hot for your taste.

A few cooks also use the Chinese method of thickening with cornstarch and water because the mixture can be introduced directly to the sauce without danger of separating. To me, because of the difference in flavor between raw cornstarch and cooked flour, using a roux is superior and is very little extra trouble.

GARLIC AND OREGANO

All the New Mexico red chile sauces call for garlic and oregano. These items can be blended with the chiles before straining to make a very smooth sauce, or they can be ground separately in a *molcajete* and added to the sauce later. This latter method results in a more rustic effect.

VINEGAR AND BAY LEAVES

You will note that the following recipes call for bay leaves and a small amount of vinegar. While these items are not found in all the old recipes, I learned from a fine Mexican cook that they round out the flavor of the sauce in a way that, though virtually imperceptible, is nevertheless desirable. The bay leaves produce a hint of complexity, while the vinegar adds a barely detectable fruity aspect, a nice foil to the mild bitterness of the chiles.

NUTRITION HINT: In the following recipes I have used olive oil rather than the more traditional lard for health reasons. While many modern New Mexico cooks use a less assertive oil, I find that olive oil better reproduces the earthy quality of the lard it replaces. Of course, if you want a truly authentic sauce, use lard.

SALSA DE CHILES COLORADOS AL ESTILO NUEVO MÉXICO CON CHILES ENTEROS

Basic New Mexico Chile Sauce with Whole Chiles

PREPARING THE CHILES:

2 ounces, approximately 8 hot; 2½ ounces, approximately 10 medium; or 3½ ounces, approximately 14 mild, dried New Mexico chiles

4 cloves garlic

1 teaspoon whole oregano

2 tablespoons olive oil

2 bay leaves

½ tablespoon vinegar

½ teaspoon salt

Roux made from 1 tablespoon oil and 2 tablespoons flour

Rinse the chiles in cold water; then toast them by placing them on a cookie sheet in an oven preheated to 275 degrees for about 5 minutes, checking them often. They should be fragrant but not scorched.

Allow the chiles to cool; then remove the stems and most of the seeds. Tear the chiles into pieces and place them in a pot with at least 5 cups of water; then barely simmer them for at least 15 minutes, or 30 minutes if you intend to remove the chile "meat" from the skins by hand-scraping.

Remove the chiles, reserving the chile water, and place the chiles in a blender. Add the garlic, oregano, and 2 cups of the water in which the chiles were soaked and blend for 1 minute. (As explained on p. 165 you can also grind the garlic and oregano and add them to the sauce later.) Strain the chile sauce into a large measuring bowl; then add enough of the remaining soaking water to total 3½ cups.

THE SAUCE:

Heat a saucepan over medium heat, add the olive oil, and then stir in the blended chile sauce. Add the bay leaves, vinegar, and salt and simmer the sauce, stirring frequently, for about 20 minutes; then remove the bay leaves. Add a little of the roux and stir it into the sauce. How much you add will depend, in large part, on whether you used a lesser number of hot chiles or a greater number of mild chiles. The more chiles you use, the less roux you will need. In any case, add just enough roux so that after about 2 minutes of cooking the sauce thickens just slightly. Cook the sauce another 5 to 10 minutes or until it has thickened enough to just coat a spoon. Remember, if the sauce is used on enchiladas, the 10 minutes baking time will further thicken the sauce. *Yields approximately 2 cups.*

SALSA DE CHILES COLORADOS AL ESTILO NUEVO MÉXICO CON POLVO DE CHILE
Basic New Mexico Chile Sauce with Chile Powder

This sauce, as with all those made of ground chiles, is quicker and easier to make than one made with whole chiles.

As mentioned in the introductory remarks on "New Mexico-style 'Master' Chile sauces" (p. 162), when using chile powder it is better to use a medium or medium-hot variety than a mild one in order to minimize the quantity needed. As also noted, it is necessary to use more roux made of oil and flour than with a whole chile sauce. This creates a smoother result, decreasing the tendency of chile powder to create a grainy texture. Because chile powder does not have the same thickening capabilities as whole chiles the amount of flour necessary to thicken them is more predictable. For this reason the following recipe calls for the roux to be incorporated at the beginning of the process.

2½ tablespoons olive oil or 3 tablespoons lard

5 cloves garlic, minced

3 tablespoons flour

½ cup medium or medium-hot New Mexico chile powder

3¼ cups hot water

1 teaspoon whole oregano

½ teaspoon salt

1 teaspoon vinegar

2 bay leaves

MAKING THE SAUCE:

Heat the olive oil or lard over medium heat. Add the garlic and cook, stirring constantly, for about 15 seconds. Stir the flour into the oil and garlic and cook, stirring constantly, until the roux begins to brown and produces a nutty aroma.

Meanwhile, place the chile powder and water in a blender and blend for a few seconds to mix thoroughly.

Remove the cooked roux from the burner and stir a little of the chile and water mixture into it. (A wire whisk is good for this task.) Replace the pan on the burner and add the remaining chile and water in small batches, stirring constantly so that it is completely incorporated after each addition.

Add the oregano, salt, vinegar, and bay leaves. Bring the sauce to a boil and simmer it uncovered, stirring often, for 20 to 30 minutes or until it is properly thickened. *Yields approximately 2 cups.*

Salsa de chiles colorados al estilo Nuevo México con carne de puerco

Basic New Mexico Chile Sauce with Pork

This sauce, which is a simple variation of the Basic New Mexico Chile Sauce with Whole Chiles is my favorite New Mexico-style enchilada sauce. It takes very little extra effort to make, and the result is definitely worth it. Before proceeding, read the recipe for Basic New Mexico Chile Sauce with Whole Chiles (p. 166).

Follow the recipe for Basic New Mexico Chile Sauce with Whole Chiles up to the point where the extra liquid is added to the chiles to total 3½ cups. For this recipe, however, you add enough extra liquid to total 4¼ cups.

Next, heat the olive oil in a saucepan over medium-high heat and just before it begins to smoke add 6 ounces of lean pork loin, cut into pieces no bigger than ¼ inch. Cook the pork until it is crispy brown; then add the strained chile puree and remaining ingredients, except the roux. Cover the saucepan and simmer for 20 minutes. Remove the top and simmer an additional 20 minutes; then thicken the sauce with the roux. *Yields approximately 2 cups.*

TEX-MEX-STYLE "MASTER" SAUCES

The procedures for making Tex-Mex sauces have much in common with those for making New Mexico-style sauces such as the methods of processing the chiles. For that reason I will limit my explanations primarily to the differences in procedures, the type of chiles used, and the broth with which they are cooked.

THE CHILES

Tex-Mex sauces are made with *ancho* chiles, which are somewhat sweeter than the New Mexico varieties. With *ancho* chiles, giving the quantity by weight is less accurate than specifying the number of chiles. This is because they are more "meaty" than the New

Mexico varieties, and therefore the differences in weight between a fully dry and a partially dry chile are much greater. A freshly cured *ancho* chile can weigh more than twice as much as one that has been on the shelf for some time. Because of these factors I only give the *number* of chiles required for the following recipes.

THE BROTH

One thing I learned long ago is that with Mexican-American cooking, much of which was born out of economic necessity, less is often more. While the best Tex-Mex sauces are made with a mild, homemade beef broth, it must be very mild, that is, it should be made with very little beef. Years ago when I first started making these sauces I always used too much meat. The results tasted too much like Texas-style chile, which has only a nodding acquaintance with Tex-Mex cooking. (For a genuine Tex-Mex Chile see p. 254 in the chapter on "Entrées".)

The amount of meat specified gives a good average for this type of sauce. However, some cooks do use more meat. If you prefer a more meaty sauce, experiment using up to 12 ounces. If you do not wish to make your own broth, substitute 1½ cups of Swanson beef broth mixed with 1½ cups water.

To make the sauce with chile powder rather than whole chiles, follow the recipe except do not add the powder to the broth for the first 15 minutes as you do the whole chiles. Rather, put it directly into the blender.

CUMIN

Although eschewed by many experts, I have specified ground cumin since this is what is used by so many Tex-Mex cooks. If you want to use whole cumin, use only 1 tablespoon and either blend or grind it with the garlic and oregano.

SALSA ESTILO TEX-MEX

Basic Tex-Mex Sauce

4 *medium to large* ancho
    chiles
2 *tablespoons olive oil*
6 *ounces lean stew meat,
    cut into ¼-inch pieces
    or smaller*
5 *cups water*
½ *onion, cut in half*
2 *teaspoons oregano*
5 *cloves garlic*
¼ *cup ground cumin*
1½ *tablespoons olive oil*
1½ *tablespoons butter*
3 *tablespoons flour*
½ *cup tomato puree*

PREPARING THE BROTH:

Toast the chiles in an oven preheated to 275 degrees for 5 to 10 minutes; then stem, devein, and seed them.

Heat a pot over medium-high heat and add the first 2 tablespoons of olive oil. Just before the oil begins to smoke add the meat. Cook the meat until it has just browned, stirring constantly.

Add the water, onion, and chiles. Cook the sauce at a bare simmer, covered, for 15 minutes; then remove the chiles, placing them in a blender.

Cover the pot and continue simmering for 1 hour (1 hour and 15 minutes total). When the meat has cooked, remove it and its broth to a bowl. Some cooks leave the meat in the sauce while others use the broth for something else, such as a taco filling. Try both ways, but remove and reserve the meat at this point. While the difference may seem subtle, it is important. In either case, there should be at least 3 cups of broth remaining. If there is more, pour some off; if there is less, add some water.

PREPARING THE SAUCE:

Add the oregano, garlic, and cumin to the blender with the chiles, or mash them in a *molcajete* or mortar and pestle.

Next, add 1 cup of the broth to the blender and blend for 1 minute to fully incorporate the chiles. Add the remaining 2 cups broth and blend to mix.

As with New Mexico-style sauces at this point you can either strain the sauce or not strain it, if you want a more rustic effect.

Heat the pot you used or another similar one over medium heat and add the remaining olive oil and the butter. As soon as the butter is melted add the flour and stir the roux until it just begins to brown and produce a nutty aroma.

When the roux is done, remove the pot from the heat and add about ½ cup of the chile mixture, stirring well until it is incorporated with the roux. Replace the pot on the heat and continue adding the chile mixture in small quantities, stirring well after each addition. Add the reserved meat at this time.

If you ground the cumin, garlic, and oregano separately, add them to the sauce at this time. Add the tomato puree. Bring the mixture to a boil and simmer, uncovered, stirring frequently, until the sauce has thickened properly, about 20 minutes. *Yields approximately 2 cups.*

NUTRITION HINT: I specified a combination of olive oil and butter, although many cooks use either all lard or butter or a more neutral oil. For health reasons the only recipes I use lard in are tamales and refried beans (because shortening is just not an adequate substitute), and I do not eat them often. I limit use of butter for the same reason. I think the specified combination bears a good resemblance to the richer varieties, but the choice is yours.

SALSA PARA ENCHILADAS ESTILO TEJAS ANTIGUA
Old-style Texas Enchilada Sauce

3 ancho *chiles, seeded and stemmed*

8 *ounces* tomatillos

1 *canned* chipotle *chile, seeded*

4 *cloves garlic*

1 *teaspoon oregano*

¼ *cup onion, chopped*

2 *tablespoons lard or olive oil*

½ *teaspoon salt, or to taste*

Although this sauce is very common in Mexico, it is rarely found in Mexican-American cooking today. I am including it because it is used in the recipe for Old-style Texas Enchiladas (p. 215), which unfortunately are not served in many modern restaurants.

Rinse the chiles; then toast them by placing them in an oven preheated to 275 degrees for about 5 minutes. Be careful not to allow them to scorch.

Soak the chiles in 2 cups or more of hot water for at least 15 minutes; then place them in a blender, reserving the water in which they were soaked.

Simmer the *tomatillos* in water to cover until they are tender, about 5 to 10 minutes; then add them to the blender with the *chipotle*, garlic, oregano, and onion. Add 1½ cups of the reserved soaking water and blend for 1 minute. Do not strain the sauce.

Heat the lard or olive oil in a saucepan over medium heat; then add the blended sauce and salt. Simmer the sauce until it has thickened, about 15 minutes. *Yields approximately 2 cups.*

ALL-PURPOSE ENCHILADA SAUCE

Mild beef broth

2 *New Mexico and 2 ancho chiles, or 2 tablespoons each of chile powder made from* ancho *or New Mexico chiles; or 4 chiles or 4 tablespoons powder made from either type of chile*

1½ *tablespoons olive oil*

2½ *tablespoons flour*

4 *cloves garlic*

1 *teaspoon whole oregano*

½ *teaspoon whole cumin*

¼ *cup tomato sauce*

Salt to taste

This sauce is a hybrid of the two distinctive sauce styles, Tex-Mex and New Mexico, and is similar to many of the sauces used in California and Arizona. To put your own signature on the sauce, try different types of whole chiles or chile powders. I suggest you start by making it with one-half New Mexico and one-half *ancho* chiles, or powder made from these varieties. Another option is to include whole chiles of one variety and powder of another.

To make the broth, simmer 4 ounces of lean beef in 5 cups of water, covered, for 1 hour and 15 minutes. If you do not care to make your own broth, use 6 ounces of Swanson plus enough water to make up the 3½ cups in the blender.

If you are using whole chiles, rinse them and toast them in an oven preheated to 275 degrees for 5 to 10 minutes, making certain that they do not scorch. When the chiles have cooled, remove the stems and seeds and soak them in hot water for 20 minutes. Place them in a blender, add 1 cup of broth, and blend for 1 minute. (If you are using the canned broth, use it for the initial blending; then add water in which the chiles were soaked.) Add more broth until the mixture measures 3½ cups. Using a sieve or food mill, strain the chile broth into a suitable container to remove the bits of chile skin. If you are using chile powder, blend it with 3 cups broth.

To make the roux, heat the olive oil in a large saucepan over medium heat, add the flour, and cook, stirring constantly, until it begins to brown and produces a nutty aroma. A wire whisk works well for this task.

Remove the saucepan and begin adding the chile liquid, little by little, whisking or stirring to mix thoroughly after each addition.

Meanwhile, grind the garlic, oregano, and cumin to a paste using a *molcajete* or mortar and pestle and add it to the saucepan. Then add the tomato sauce.

Bring the liquid to a boil; then simmer, stirring frequently, until it is thickened to the consistency of a medium-thin milk shake, 20 to 30 minutes. *Yields approximately 2 cups.*

SALSA PARA ENCHILADAS ESTILO CALIFORNIA ANTIGUA
Old-style California Enchilada Sauce

3 ancho *chiles*

2¼ *pounds tomatoes, chopped*

⅔ *cup raisins*

⅓ *cup blanched, slivered almonds*

¼ *cup olive oil*

1½ *cups onions, chopped*

4 *cloves garlic, minced*

½ *cup black California olives, sliced*

1 *teaspoon oregano*

1 *teaspoon salt, or to taste*

Place the chiles in an oven preheated to 275 degrees and toast them for 5 minutes, taking care that they do not scorch. Remove the chiles and, when they are cool enough to handle, remove the stems, veins, and seeds. Soak the chiles in hot water for 20 minutes; then drain them and place them in a blender.

Add the tomatoes to the blender; blend with the chiles for at least 1 minute, and then strain the mixture into a bowl. This is best accomplished in 2 batches.

Return 1 cup of the strained tomato and chile mixture to the blender and add the raisins and almonds. Pulse the blender until the nuts and raisins are well chopped but not pureed; then mix them with the remaining sauce.

Heat the olive oil in a medium-size saucepan over moderate heat; add the onions and garlic and cook, stirring often, until the onions are browned to the point of being caramelized, about 20 to 30 minutes. You will have to lower the heat as the onions cook to keep them from burning. When the onions are nearly done, add the olives and cook until the onions are ready.

Stir the contents of the blender into the onions, add the oregano and salt, bring to a boil, and barely simmer, uncovered, for 20 minutes or until the sauce has thickened and is no longer watery. *Yields approximately 2 cups.*

MEXICAN CHILE

This recipe is simple and very good. It is particularly interesting as the true *pasilla* chile is seldom used in these sauces, and because it comes from *One Hundred & One Mexican Dishes*, published in 1906, the oldest Mexican cookbook in the United States according to the Library of Congress. I have reproduced the recipe verbatim, including the misspelling of *chiles pasillas:*

> Toast ten *chiles anchos* (the dried pepper in the broad shape) and ten *chiles posillos* [*sic*] (the dried pepper in the thin shape), take out the veins and seeds and soak them in a quart of boiling water. Pass through a sieve twice, getting out all the pulp, and fry this chile liquor in two tablespoonfuls of boiling lard, which has been thickened with a tablespoonful of browned flour. While boiling add salt, a pinch of Mexican sausage, a pinch of sugar, a teaspoonful of cider-vinegar and a tablespoonful of oil. Cook all together in the lard for fifteen minutes.

SALSA ESTILO TEX-MEX CON CARNE DE RES
Tex-Mex Chile-Beef Enchilada Sauce

The preceding Tex-Mex sauce is usually found in better restaurants and in homes with the most discriminating cooks, while the following sauce is one you are more apt to find at hole-in-the-wall cafés and homes all over south Texas.

This sauce will be far better if made with a chile powder from *ancho* chiles, but the generic grocery store brand will, in reality, probably be more authentic in the sense that it is used by more *tejanos*. If the sauce is too strong for you, simply reduce the amount of chile powder and/or cumin.

Heat the oil in a large saucepan over medium heat. Add the ground beef and brown, stirring constantly to break it up.

Add the flour and cook for 1 to 2 minutes.

Place the chile powder in a blender and blend with 3 cups water.

Slowly stir the chile-water mixture into the meat, making sure that, in the early stages, it is well mixed in before adding additional water.

Add the remaining ingredients; then simmer the sauce, uncovered, until it is the thickness of a medium-thick milk shake, 45 to 60 minutes. It should still be a bit soupy since it will thicken further when you use it to make enchiladas. *Yields approximately 2 cups.*

Salsas Verdes

GREEN CHILE SAUCES

*t*here are three basic types of green chile sauce that are used to make enchiladas and to cover other items on combination plates. The first two come from the home of the finest green chiles, New Mexico. One of these, the most basic and possibly the best, is simply a cooked version of a green chile table sauce. The second, and the one most popular in New Mexico, is a cooked sauce thickened with flour. The third version, often found in Arizona, California, and Texas, is a pureed version of the second type with the significant addition of *tomatillos*.

Salsa para enchiladas de chile verde estilo Nuevo México

New Mexico Green Chile Enchilada Sauce

2   *teaspoons olive oil*

2   *cloves garlic, minced*

1½ *cups green chile, peeled, seeded, and chopped*

1   *cup onion, chopped*

½   *cup tomato, chopped*

½   *teaspoon salt*

1½ *cups water*

This sauce is a perfect example of the "less is more" rule in Mexican cooking. The preparation could not be simpler or the result more delicious.

The following version is very similar to that first prepared by Josephine Chávez Griggs and now served at La Posta restaurant in Mesilla, New Mexico, by her daughter Katy Meek. The only difference between the two is that Mrs. Griggs did not use onion. You will note that the recipe calls for a small amount of olive oil, which neither Mrs. Griggs nor Katy Meek included. I think the oil spreads the subtle garlic flavor throughout the sauce, binds it together, and rounds it out, but feel free to omit it.

Heat a saucepan over medium heat; add the oil and sauté the garlic for 1 or 2 minutes or until it is just soft but not browned.

Add the remaining ingredients, bring them to a boil, and simmer them for 10 to 15 minutes or until the liquid is almost gone and the remaining sauce is fairly thick. *Yields approximately 2 cups.*

NUTRITION HINT: This sauce is ideal for people on low-fat diets, especially if the olive oil is omitted and the sauce is used to make turkey or chicken enchiladas.

SALSA ESPESADA DE CHILE VERDE

Thickened Green Chile Enchilada Sauce

This sauce can be made without the pork, but, to me, the result lacks depth and complexity. The objective is to produce a sauce that is not floury or pasty, something that is all too common in restaurants.

The recipe calls for chicken broth, although water can also be used. While broth produces a superior result, it is better to use water than canned broth, which is too salty (even current reduced salt versions).

Heat the olive oil in a large saucepan over medium-high heat. Add the pork and cook, stirring constantly, until it is browned. This is an important step since, to properly put its stamp on the recipe, the pork should be cooked to a crispy brown rather than just darkened.

Turn the heat to moderate, add the onion, and cook it until it is soft but not browned. Add the garlic and continue cooking for about 30 seconds, but do not allow it to brown or the sauce will be bitter.

Turn the heat to medium low, add the flour, and cook until it gives off a nutty aroma, 2 to 3 minutes.

Remove the pan from the heat; add and stir in a little broth or water. The sauce should thicken instantly. Keep adding more liquid, a little at a time. This process is important since adding all the water at once can result in a sauce with little cooked balls of flour, like dumplings.

Replace the pot on the burner and add the green chiles, oregano, and salt. Bring the sauce to a simmer and cook for 30 to 40 minutes. The result should be thick enough so that after baking the enchiladas it is not watery, but not so thick that it is gummy. *Yields approximately 2 cups.*

3 *tablespoons olive oil*

3 *ounces lean pork, cut into ¼-inch pieces*

½ *cup onion, chopped*

2 *garlic cloves, minced*

2 *tablespoons flour*

3½ *cups chicken broth or water*

1¾ *cups green chiles, skinned, stemmed, seeded, and chopped*

½ *teaspoon whole oregano*

½ *teaspoon salt*

SALSA PARA ENCHILADAS DE CHILE VERDE ESTILO TEX-MEX

Texas-style Mild Green Chile Enchilada Sauce with Tomatillos

1 *pound* tomatillos, *peeled and rinsed*
½ *large bell pepper, seeded and chopped*
½ *medium onion, chopped*
1 serrano *chile*
1 *tablespoon cooking oil*
2½ *teaspoons garlic powder*
1 *teaspoon salt, or to taste*
 Chicken broth
 Roux made with 1 tablespoon oil and 1½ tablespoons flour

This mild flavorful recipe is from San Antonio's El Chaparral restaurant. Owner Carlos García's cooking has definite creole overtones and reflects his aversion to overly picante or fatty foods.

Place the *tomatillos*, bell pepper, onion, and chile in a medium-size saucepan, cover with water, and bring to a boil. Simmer the vegetables until they are tender, about 10 minutes.

Pour off the water, place the cooked vegetables in a blender, and blend for 30 seconds; then strain the mixture using a sieve or food mill with a very fine blade.

Heat a medium-size saucepan over moderate heat and add the oil. Stir in the pureed vegetables, the garlic powder, and salt.

At this stage you may adjust the sauce's consistency and flavor to your taste. To do this, first simmer the sauce for 15 minutes adding a little chicken broth. This is done either to thin it or to reduce the *tomatillo* flavor if it is at all bitter, or for both reasons. When the 15-minute cooking time is nearly complete, stir in about ½ tablespoon of the roux and continue cooking for 1 minute. The sauce should be just thick enough so that it is not runny when placed on the enchiladas.

Because there is so little oil and thickener in this sauce the normal 10-minute oven heating time produces a dry result. To avoid this: 1) either heat the enchiladas, covered with sauce, in a microwave or 2) heat them in the oven without the sauce for 5 minutes, then top with sauce, which should be kept heated just below a simmer, and continue heating for 1 more minute. *Yields approximately 2 cups.*

SALSA VERDE ESTILO MEXICANO

Mexican-style Tomatillo Enchilada Sauce

This is *tomatillo* sauce as it is usually served in Mexico.

Heat a large saucepan over medium heat, add the olive oil, and then stir in the *Tomatillo* Sauce. Simmer the sauce for 5 minutes or until it is slightly thickened. *Yields approximately 2 cups.*

2 *tablespoons olive oil*
1 *recipe* Tomatillo *Sauce (p. 116)*

Antojitos Mexicanos
LIGHT MEALS / SNACKS

*a*ntojitos or, more properly, *antojitos mexicanos* is that special category of foods that, to most people, typifies Mexican cooking. This is probably because the vast majority of items on the menus of Mexican-American restaurants come from this category. While the word *antojito* literally means a whim or snack, *antojitos mexicanos* refers to the corn- and tortilla-based dishes such as tacos, enchiladas, tamales, and *quesadillas* that were developed by the early Indians and later modified as they absorbed European introduced ingredients such as beef, pork, and cheese. The introduction of lard also provided cooking fat in quantities that made it practical to make the fried *antojitos* such as crispy tacos and *flautas*.

This section includes recipes for the most popular *antojitos* that are prevalent throughout the major regions of Mexican-American cooking.

TACOS

Certainly a contender for the title of the world's most versatile food, the taco is what first comes to mind when most people are asked about Mexican food. Tacos are classified in three basic ways: by the type of tortilla used (corn or flour), the consistency of the tortilla (crispy, medium crisp, or soft), and according to the filling used (chicken, meat, fish, and so forth).

The first part of this section orients the reader by describing the basic types of tacos found in Mexican-American cooking. The second section provides the best recipes I have encountered for each type of taco mentioned in the first section. I want to stress that these recipes are only a few of those that I think are special. I want to urge the reader to use the descriptions in the first section and the specific recipes that follow as a basis for creating his or her own favorite tacos.

CORN TORTILLA TACOS

Tacos made with corn tortillas, the most popular item in the Mexican food repertoire, come in three basic forms: crispy, medium crisp, and soft. Only one of these types, the crispy taco, is generally known among Anglos. This is the taco made with a corn tortilla that is first fried into a crisp turnover shape, then usually filled with a ground beef *picadillo* or shredded chicken, and, finally, topped with lettuce, tomato, cheese, and hot sauce.

Probably because it is so easy to prepare the crispy taco made with prefried taco shells has become the staple at Mexican-American restaurants and fast-food outlets. However, it has a basic problem. The fact that this taco's shell is crispy means that when you bite into it, it tends to shatter. This means that unless your crispy taco comes in a paper envelope you will find that a majority of the filling and garnish often end up in your lap.

Precisely because of their inconvenience it is difficult to find crispy tacos in Mexico or in Mexican-American households. When they are encountered, you will discover that the filling has been enclosed in the tortillas before frying and that no subsequent attempt has been made to pry them open and place the garnish inside; instead, it is placed on top of the tacos. Most Mexican cooks make *flautas* or *taquitos* when they want the crispy taco experience. These are both easy to prepare and to eat. So there are actually two types of crispy tacos—the one made of preformed taco shells and the more authentic variety that is made from scratch.

Outside of restaurants the most common versions of tacos made from corn tortillas are the medium-crisp and soft varieties. Medium crisp simply means that the tortilla is fried just long enough to give it the proper taco shape and a medium-crisp texture. These tacos, which are both easy to fill and eat because they do not break, are most often filled with stewed meat or chicken.

Soft tacos are usually made by toasting the tortillas on a *comal* or griddle until they are steaming hot and pliable before wrapping them around the stuffing. The most common filling for soft tacos is meat cooked *al carbón* (charbroiled). An advantage of this type of soft corn taco is its low fat content. Occasionally, another type of soft taco is found which resembles an enchilada more than a taco. These are either softened on a griddle or in hot oil, wrapped tightly around a filling, then served topped with a cooked sauce or garnish, and eaten with a fork rather than the fingers.

Yet another type of corn taco is the Tex-Mex puffy taco. I have never found this hybrid of the medium-crisp taco in Mexico. Puffy tacos are made by deep-frying the formed tortilla dough rather than baking it on a *comal*. Upon contact with the oil they burst into soft, easily filled little pillows, much like small, thin *sopaipillas*. They are then drained of excess oil and filled.

Finally, I have recently come across a completely original variation of the taco—the taco cone. Shaped like a giant ice cream cone, the taco cone has a great responsibility resting on its crispy foundation. Apparently it will be the basis for success or failure of a new fast-food operation. My experience was that the cone was proportioned so that it was impossible to bite into one side without the other side touching your forehead. This, in turn, meant that it was difficult to keep your nose out of the filling, garnish, and sauce. Because of the requirement for specialized equipment and an unusually large tortilla (difficult to find or make) I have not provided a recipe or instructions for making a taco cone.

FLOUR TORTILLA TACOS

Tacos made with flour tortillas are nearly always soft. In fact, about the only time flour tortillas are fried is to make *chimichangas*, *chimiquitos,* and edible "bowls" for taco salads. The only exception that I have seen is practiced by San Antonio's La Fogata restaurant, which brushes a small amount of butter on their flour tortillas while heating them. The result produces a unique flavor and texture.

Flour tortillas are most often the basis for tacos filled with meat or chicken cooked *al carbón.* While the size and texture of corn tortillas made in the United States does not vary greatly, that of flour tortillas does, and therefore the effect on tacos made with them. Flour tortillas are big or small, thick or thin, and each type produces a very different effect. Directions for these variations are given in the chapter on "Tortillas and Bread" (p. 97).

FAVORITE TACOS

Before trying these recipes please read the general information about tacos (p. 183).

TACOS ESTILO TEX-MEX

Tex-Mex Tacos

Cooking oil
12 *corn tortillas*
 1 *recipe Refried Beans (p. 132)*
 1 *recipe Guacamole (p. 144)*
 1 *recipe Picadillo II (p. 149)*
 1 *pound mild cheddar cheese, grated*

These tacos are simply the best of their variety I have ever had. I learned this recipe many years ago from an old friend, Pauline Zamudio, who also provided the recipe for *Fideo* (p. 292). Once the various elements of the filling have been assembled, they are easy to put together at the last moment.

These tacos are medium crisp, which means the tortillas are fried just until they begin to crisp and hold their shape. To prepare the tortillas, heat about 1 inch of the cooking oil in a small- to medium-size skillet over moderately high heat. When a drop of water sputters, instantly perform the following steps:

1) Using kitchen tongs, immerse a tortilla in the hot oil. It should immediately start to bubble and puff up. If it does not do this, the oil is not hot enough. 2) Immediately fold the tortilla in half and let it cook for a few seconds. 3) Turn the now folded tortilla over and fry for a few seconds on the other side. As soon as the tortilla begins to hold its new shape remove it from the oil and drain it on paper towels. The shell should be at the stage where it is just beginning to become crisp but is still pliable. A little practice on the first couple of tortillas should provide all the experience you need.

Once all the taco shells have been fried and drained, fill them in the following fashion: 1) Open the shell and spread some Refried Beans on one side and some Guacamole on the other. 2) Put a mound of the *Picadillo* II between the Guacamole and Refried Beans, sprinkle on some cheese, and serve with your favorite hot sauce. *Serves 4.*

El Chaparral's Soft Creole Tacos

The only difference I can find between soft tacos and enchiladas is that the tacos are not usually heated after the sauce has been added. This version from Carlos García's El Chaparral restaurant in San Antonio, Texas, is a perfect choice for people who want authentic taste without a lot of chile heat.

Place equal portions of the *picadillo* on each tortilla and roll them as for enchiladas, putting 2 on each of 4 serving plates.

Top the tacos with the sauce and serve them with Mexican Rice (p. 126).

Place a heavy skillet over medium heat and coat it with the oil. Add the ground beef and brown it, stirring constantly and breaking it into small pieces with a cooking spoon.

Turn the heat to low, add the onion, tomato, salt, and pepper and simmer for 10 minutes, stirring frequently.

Heat a large saucepan over medium heat; add the oil and then the onion and bell pepper. Cook the vegetables until just soft, stirring frequently.

Add the remaining ingredients, bring to a boil, and simmer for 15 minutes or until the sauce is thickened. It is difficult to describe the proper thickness of the sauce. Carlos says it should be thick enough to coat a dipped tortilla; if it runs off, it is too thin. When properly thickened, the consistency resembles that of canned tomato sauce. *Serves 4.*

8 *corn tortillas, softened as for enchiladas (see p. 205)*
Picadillo
Creole sauce

PICADILLO:

1 *teaspoon cooking oil*
¾ *pound very lean ground beef*
2 *tablespoons onion, minced*
2 *tablespoons tomato, minced*
½ *teaspoon salt*
¼ *teaspoon pepper*

CREOLE SAUCE:

2 *tablespoons cooking oil*
2 *cups onion, chopped*
1⅓ *cups bell pepper, chopped*
4 *cups tomato, chopped*
2 *tablespoons celery, minced*
6 *tablespoons tomato puree*
1 *tablespoon garlic powder*
1 *teaspoon salt*
½ *teaspoon pepper*

NUTRITION HINT: As Mexican food goes this dish does not have a lot of fat. To reduce it even more, substitute the Low-fat *Picadillo* (p. 151), soften the tortillas with the spray oil microwave method (see p. 205), and reduce the amount of oil in the sauce to ½ tablespoon.

DRIVE-IN TACOS

12 *prepared taco shells*

1 *recipe* Picadillo III *(p. 150)*

1½ *cups cheddar cheese, grated*

1 *large avocado, pitted, peeled, and cut into ⅛-inch slices*

2 *tomatoes, seeded and chopped*

2 *cups shredded lettuce*

½ *cup black California olives, minced (optional)*

⅓ *cup feta cheese, finely grated (like Parmesan)*

Hot sauce

Much as I dislike tacos made from preformed taco shells because they fall apart when you are eating them, there is no question that they save time and effort, particularly when cooking for a crowd. This recipe makes what is usually a very ordinary taco into one you can be proud of. The feta cheese makes a fine substitute for such Mexican cheeses as *queso cotija* or *queso anejo*.

Warm the taco shells by placing them in an oven preheated to 250 degrees for 1 minute.

Heat the *Picadillo* III and put 2 to 3 tablespoons of it into each taco shell. Sprinkle some grated cheddar cheese over the filling and top with avocado slices, tomatoes, shredded lettuce, and olives (if used); then sprinkle on some feta cheese. Serve the tacos with your favorite salsa or a choice of several. *Serves 4.*

12 *flour tortillas*

1 *recipe* Picadillo III *(p. 150)*

1½ *cups cheddar cheese, grated*

1 *large avocado, peeled, pitted, and sliced about ⅛ inch thick*

2 *tomatoes, seeded and chopped*

2 *cups lettuce, shredded*

Hot sauce

TACOS DE TORTILLAS DE HARINA ESTILO TEX-MEX
Tex-Mex Flour Tortilla Tacos

Heat the tortillas on a griddle and place them in a tortilla warmer or wrap them in a towel.

Heat the *Picadillo* III and place 2 to 3 tablespoons of it in each tortilla. Top with the cheese, avocado slices, tomatoes, and shredded lettuce. Serve with your favorite salsa or a selection of several. *Serves 4.*

TACOS DORADOS
Crispy Tacos

Dorado means golden, which, in this case, reflects the golden brown color of these fried tacos. *Tacos dorados* are the closest of all the Mexican-American tacos to those traditionally served throughout Mexico, especially when made with a shredded meat filling. This version, filled with turkey, is typical of the cooking in southern California, much of which comes from Baja California.

One of my favorite variations of this dish is to make it with *Picadillo* I (p. 148). Garnished with grated cheddar cheese, shredded lettuce, and chopped tomato, this makes a very typical Mexican-American taco.

Fill a small skillet with about 1 inch of cooking oil. Heat the oil over medium-high heat until a piece of bread browns almost immediately. The oil should not be so hot that it smokes.

Using kitchen tongs, soften the tortillas by placing them one at a time in the hot oil for just a second or two or until they become limp and pliable. Remove the tortillas to drain on paper towels.

When the tortillas are cool enough to handle, fill each one by placing 2 to 3 tablespoons of the shredded turkey down the center and folding it in half. At this point some cooks use a toothpick to secure the taco in its folded position. However, because the taco will be fried in a completely closed position this virtually precludes placing the garnish inside the shell without cracking it. I prefer to lower the filled and folded tortillas into the oil with the tongs, then, as the tacos begin to become crisp, use the tongs to hold them open about ¾ inch or enough to accept the garnish. As you finish frying each taco drain it and place it on absorbent towels to remove the excess oil.

Once the tacos have been fried, put a little lettuce and tomato in each one, sprinkle on some of the feta cheese, and serve with hot sauce. Note: if you used the toothpick method, simply sprinkle the lettuce, tomato, and feta cheese over the tacos as they do in Mexico. *Serves 4.*

Cooking oil for frying the tortillas

12 *corn tortillas*

1 *recipe Shredded Turkey (p. 158) or 1 recipe Picadillo I (p. 148)*

2 *tomatoes, chopped*

2 *cups lettuce, shredded*

⅓ *cup feta cheese, finely grated (like Parmesan)*

Hot sauce

PUFFY TACOS

2 *cups Masa Harina or about*
     1 pound of masa *from a*
     tortilla factory
   Cooking oil for frying the
     tortillas
1 *recipe* Picadillo *II (p. 149)*
2 *tomatoes, chopped*
   Lettuce, shredded
   Hot sauce

Unfortunately, these magical little delights cannot be found often outside of south Texas, where they are made in homes and served at many Tex-Mex restaurants such as Henry's Puffy Taco in San Antonio.

Puffy Tacos are made with the same dough, or *masa*, as corn tortillas. After the dough is pressed into shape, instead of being cooked on an ungreased *comal* they are deep-fried. This causes them to puff into little crisp balloons. It takes a little practice to learn to make them, but once mastered they are easy.

Mix the Masa Harina according to the directions on the package and roll into 16 little balls. Usually this amount of *masa* would make about 12 6-inch tortillas, but Puffy Tacos are smaller than the usual variety.

Heat about ¾ inch oil in a small skillet until very hot but not quite smoking.

Form one of the balls into a very thin tortilla using a tortilla press. (See the directions for making corn tortillas on p. 99.)

This is the tricky part since making the taco shells takes but a few seconds so you have to move quickly. Carefully place the uncooked tortilla in the oil. Allow it to cook until it begins to puff, just a few seconds; then carefully turn it using tongs and a small spatula. The tortillas are delicate at this point, and the oil is very hot so be careful. Fry the tortilla for a few seconds then, using the tongs, fold it into a taco shell. Continue to cook it until the shell is just browned; then remove it to drain on absorbent towels. The result should be very puffy and light. Make the remaining shells in the same manner.

Stuff the shells with the *Picadillo* II, top with the lettuce and tomato, and serve with the hot sauce. *Serves 4.*

Tacos al Carbón
Charbroiled Tacos

In Mexican-American cooking *Tacos al carbón* are usually made with flour tortillas and filled with charbroiled meat or chicken. These delightful *antojitos* are one of the most popular aspects of the cooking of northern Mexico, the area where so many Mexican-Americans came from. However, it was not until the last ten years that *Tacos al carbón* were introduced in restaurants, bringing them out of the barrios and into the larger community.

The most important reason for this development was the discovery of *fajitas*. For years *fajitas* have shared with filet mignon the premier position on the menus of northern Mexico's steak houses, where they are called *arracheras*. Sometime in the late 1970s or early 1980s *fajitas* were introduced into south Texas restaurants. (There is now the usual Texas controversy about who invented them.)

Restaurateurs were quick to realize that *fajitas* was not the only thing they could cook on their newly installed mesquite broilers, so the same charbroiled specialties that Mexicans had been enjoying for many years were introduced to the rest of us. Unfortunately, these same restaurateurs felt compelled, for marketing reasons, to call them chicken, shrimp, pork, lamb, or whatever *fajitas*. Since *fajitas* refers specifically to the skirt steak it would be more correct to call these variations "*fajita* style."

Because *fajitas* are much more than just a filling for tacos the recipe for them is included under the entrée section. However, the best of the other *al carbón* fillings are included in this section.

One thing that *Tacos al carbón*, *fajitas* or otherwise, have in common is that they are charbroiled, preferably over mesquite coals. If mesquite wood is not available, real mesquite charcoal is the next best alternative. The next choice is to use petroleum-based briquettes, either those containing mesquite or the plain variety, in combination with mesquite chips, which are now widely available.

When cooking pork, lamb, or beef for these recipes, it is advisable to broil it the way the Mexicans do, slowly and at some dis-

tance from the coals for a fairly long time. This allows the fat to melt rather than burn off, which helps tenderize even the toughest cuts. The only exceptions to this are when cooking fish, shrimp, or chicken. With regard to tenderizing, I recommend that meats to be cooked *al carbón* be marinated, especially beef and chicken. However, I prefer natural tenderizers rather than the bottled variety, which usually contain way too much salt and/or garlic and onion powder that leave an artificial taste.

TACOS DE FAJITAS ESTILO CALIFORNIA
California-style Fajitas Tacos

2 *pounds* fajitas

12 *flour tortillas*

1 *recipe* Pico de gallo *(p. 112)*

1 *recipe Guacamole (p. 144)*

½ *cup sour cream*

½ *cup black California olives, sliced*

This is a dressed-up version of the Texas-style Fajitas Taco that is found in the instructions for *fajitas* in the entrée section (p. 271).

Broil the *fajitas* according to the directions in the section on "Entrées" (p. 271) and chop them into bite-size pieces.

Mix the *Pico de gallo*, Guacamole, sour cream, and olives together to make a thick sauce.

Soften the tortillas on a hot griddle and stuff them with the *fajitas*; then top them with a generous amount of the sauce and serve. *Serves 4.*

TACOS DE PESCADO AL CARBÓN

Charbroiled Fish Tacos

This California recipe makes a delectable meal and a colorful presentation suitable for nearly any occasion. Use whatever fish is freshest, but remember that the less fatty varieties such as cod tend to become quite dry when charbroiled. The filling, which is designed to be used with flour tortillas, is delicious.

Mix all the marinade ingredients together and marinate the fish for 1 to 3 hours; then charbroil it over medium-hot coals. When the fish is properly cooked, place it on a chopping block and cut it into bite-size pieces.

To prepare the tacos, first make the sauce/topping: melt the butter over medium heat, add the remaining ingredients except the tortillas, and sauté until the chiles and onions are just soft.

Then heat the tortillas briefly on a griddle over medium heat (see the chapter on "Tortillas and Bread," p. 97, for other options) and place 3 on each of 4 very large serving plates.

Finally, spread the sauce/topping over the chopped fish, spoon it onto the tortillas, and serve with Guacamole, *Pico de gallo*, and lime wedges. *Serves 4.*

THE FILLING:

2 *pounds fileted red snapper, salmon, or your favorite fish*

THE MARINADE:

6 *tablespoons olive oil*
1 *tablespoon lime juice*
½ *teaspoon chile powder*
¼ *teaspoon cayenne pepper*
¼ *teaspoon ground black pepper*
3 *cloves garlic, minced*
¼ *teaspoon salt*
½ *teaspoon Worcestershire sauce (optional)*

THE TACOS:

3 *tablespoons butter*
3 *cloves garlic, minced*
2 serrano *chiles, stemmed, seeded, and minced*
2 *green onions, minced*
    Pinch cayenne pepper
    Salt to taste
2 *tablespoons cilantro, minced (optional)*
12 *flour tortillas*
1 *recipe Guacamole (p. 144)*
1 *recipe* Pico de gallo *(p. 112)*
    Limes, cut in wedges

TACOS DE PESCADO EMPANIZADO

California-style Fried Fish Tacos

8 *pieces deep-fried, battered or breaded fish, about 4½ inches by 2 inches or any other size suitable for stuffing a folded corn tortilla*

8 *large corn tortillas*

½ *cup tartar sauce*

1 *recipe Guacamole (p. 144)*

1 *cup lettuce, shredded*

1 *cup tomato, chopped*

4 *limes, quartered*
  Salsa picante

These tacos are particularly popular at small, Mexican-American owned fast-food outlets. You can cook your own breaded or battered fish or use frozen.

Fry the fish, drain it, and keep it warm.

Toast the tortillas on an ungreased griddle, turning them frequently until they are beginning to get crisp.

Place a piece of fish in the center of each tortilla; then fold it in half into the typical taco shape. Top each piece of fish with some tartar sauce; then garnish it with some lettuce and tomato.

Serve the tacos with the lime quarters and salsa. *Makes 8 tacos to serve 4.*

TACOS DE CARNE DE RES AL CARBÓN

Charbroiled Beef Tacos

You can use any cut of meat for these tacos, but for an authentic taste stay away from the more expensive cuts such as sirloin and tenderloin. These will be dry and tough if cooked to more than medium rare. For the same reason avoid round steak.

To make the marinade, mix together all ingredients.

Marinate the meat, refrigerated, for at least 3 hours.

Meanwhile, build your fire. This meat should be cooked slowly at a fairly low temperature over mesquite, about 10 minutes on each side. At the end of the cooking time the meat should be slightly crisp but not at all burned.

If you are using the optional fried onion topping, prepare it while the meat is marinating.

While the meat is cooking either make or heat already made flour tortillas on an ungreased *comal* or griddle, and wrap them in a towel or place them in a tortilla warmer.

When the meat has finished cooking, cut it into ¼- to ½-inch pieces.

You can assemble the tacos for all diners, but even better, place the cut up meat, tortillas, garnishes, and sauces on the table and allow everyone to help themselves.

If you are using all the options, place some meat in a hot tortilla, top with some fried onions, some cheese, then the Guacamole, *Pico de gallo*, and hot sauce. *Serves 4.*

THE MARINADE:

½ *cup olive oil*

3 *tablespoons lime juice*

2 *cloves garlic, minced*

¼ *teaspoon cayenne pepper*

½ *tablespoon paprika*

½ *teaspoon ground black pepper*

½ *teaspoon salt*

½ *teaspoon Worcestershire sauce (optional)*

THE TACOS:

2 *pounds boneless chuck steak, cut ¼ inch thick*

2 *onions, sliced and fried in 2 tablespoons olive oil with 1 clove minced garlic and 2 minced serrano chiles until well browned (optional)*

12 *flour tortillas*

1 *pound Monterey Jack cheese, grated (optional)*

1 *recipe Guacamole (p. 144)*

1 *recipe Pico de gallo (p. 112)*

Your favorite hot sauces

TACOS DE POLLO AL CARBÓN
Charbroiled Chicken Tacos

2 *pounds boneless, skinned chicken breast*

1 *bunch green onions*

12 *flour tortillas*

1 *recipe Guacamole (p. 144)*

1 *cup sour cream*

Tomatillo Sauce (p. 116), Green Chile Sauce (p. 111), or another favorite sauce

Your favorite tomato-based hot sauce

For the marinade, see the marinade recipe for *Tacos de carne de res al carbón*, p. 195.

Build a fire in your barbecue. As mentioned in the discussion of "*Tacos al carbón*" (p. 191), when cooking chicken in this manner you want to have the coals very hot and close to the grill.

Marinate the chicken for at least 1 hour.

Place the chicken and green onions over the coals. You should cook the chicken only until it is done and no longer, or it will be tough and dry. This should take no more than 4 to 5 minutes. To make cooking the onions as easy as possible, wrap a thin strip of aluminum foil around them to hold them together.

Because the chicken will cook rather quickly you should make or heat the tortillas ahead of time and wrap them in a towel or place them in a tortilla warmer.

When the chicken is done and the onions are beginning to brown, remove them from the fire; then chop them into ¼- to ½-inch pieces, mix them together, and place them in a serving bowl.

As with *Tacos de carne de res al carbón* (p. 195) you can assemble the tacos yourself, but I prefer to put the cooked ingredients on the table and allow guests to help themselves.

To make the individual tacos, place some of the chicken-green onion mixture in a tortilla and top with Guacamole, sour cream, and both a green and a red hot sauce. *Serves 4.*

TACOS DE CAMARONES AL CARBÓN

Charbroiled Shrimp Tacos

These tacos can be served in either flour tortillas or corn tortillas which have been fried semicrisp (see instructions about tacos, p. 183).

Soak the skewers in water to keep them from burning during the cooking.

Build your fire. As with *Tacos de pollo al carbón* you want a very hot fire very close to the grill.

Marinate the shrimp for ½ to 1 hour; then thread them on the skewers.

Heat or cook the flour tortillas or fry the corn tortillas.

Cook the shrimp just until they are done, about 2 to 3 minutes total. If your fire is hot enough, they will be nicely browned on the outside but just cooked on the inside.

To assemble the tacos, place some shrimp in each tortilla, top with the Guacamole and the sauces, garnish with the lettuce or cabbage, and serve. *Serves 4.*

4 *Oriental-style wooden barbecue skewers*

Marinade (see marinade for Tacos de carne de res al carbón, *p. 195)*

1½ *pounds medium shrimp, peeled and deveined*

12 *flour tortillas, or 12 corn tortillas, fried semicrisp*

1 *recipe Guacamole (p. 144)*

1 *recipe Pico de gallo (p. 112)*

1 *recipe Salsa ranchera (p. 115)*

Shredded lettuce or shredded cabbage

TACOS PARA DESAYUNO

Breakfast Tacos

12 *flour tortillas*
 4 *pieces bacon, chopped*
 1 *recipe* Picadillo III *(p. 150)*
 4 *eggs, slightly beaten*
 1 *recipe Refried Beans*
     (p. 132) [optional]
 1 *cup mild cheddar or*
     Monterey Jack cheese,
     grated

The fact that nearly every fast-food chain is offering either breakfast tacos or breakfast burritos is no surprise to south Texans, who have been enjoying these items for years. You can use any desired filling to make breakfast tacos. The following filling is one of my favorites.

Either make the flour tortillas or soften already made tortillas on an ungreased *comal* or griddle.

Heat a skillet over moderate heat, add the bacon, and fry it until it is soft. Add the *Picadillo* III and cook until well browned.

Add the eggs and continue cooking, stirring constantly, until they are well incorporated and set.

To assemble the tacos, spoon filling on each tortilla, add some beans (if used), top with cheese, and serve with your favorite hot sauce. *Serves 4.*

TACOS DE CARNE GUISADA

Beef Stew Tacos

 1 *recipe* Carne guisada
     (p. 258)
12 *flour tortillas*

This is one of the favorite tacos served in south Texas, particularly in small Tex-Mex cafés. It is also one of the easiest to prepare.

Heat the *Carne guisada* and soften the tortillas on an ungreased *comal* or griddle.

Fill the tortillas with the *Carne guisada* and serve. *Serves 4.*

TACOS DE CAMARONES AL MOJO DE AJO

Shrimp Tacos wth Garlic Sauce

These are a California version of the tacos that are often sold from stands and in small restaurants in Baja California and along Mexico's west coast.

Heat about ¾ inch oil in a small skillet until it just begins to smoke, being careful not to allow it to catch fire.

Make semicrisp taco shells according to the directions in the introductory portion of this section (p. 183).

Fill the shells with the shrimp mixture, top with the avocado, and serve with the lime wedges. *Serves 4.*

12 *corn tortillas*
    Cooking oil for frying the tortillas

 1 *recipe* Camarones al mojo de ajo *(p. 289)*

 2 *avocados, skinned, seeded, and sliced into thin strips*

 2 *limes, cut into wedges*

INDIAN TACOS

2 tablespoons olive oil

1 pound ground beef

4 cloves garlic

½ teaspoon whole cumin

1 teaspoon oregano

2–3 tablespoons New Mexico chile powder

½ teaspoon salt

1 cup water

3 cups Frijoles de olla, drained (p. 130)

4 Indian Fry Breads (p. 104)

2 cups mild cheddar cheese, grated

2 cups shredded lettuce

2 tomatoes, chopped

Although not actually Mexican-American, Indian Tacos are so good and such an important part of New Mexico's cooking that I have included them. You rarely find these delicious tacos in ordinary New Mexican restaurants. I have no idea why this is except that, because of their size, the cost of producing them is rather high. (You will be surprised at the quantity of "filling" required.) These tacos are found mostly on the reservations and in nearby towns such as Farmington, New Mexico, where they are a staple of drive-ins.

In a heavy pot or Dutch oven heat the olive oil over medium heat; add the ground beef and cook until just browned.

Meanwhile, grind the garlic, cumin, and oregano to a paste in a *molcajete* or mortar and pestle.

Add the chile powder, garlic paste, and salt to the meat and cook about 1 minute. Next, add 1 cup water and stir to make certain the meat is well broken up.

Add the beans, bring the chile mixture to a simmer, and cook, uncovered, until most but not all the moisture has evaporated.

Place the fry breads on serving plates and ladle the chile over them. Top with the cheese, lettuce, and tomatoes, and serve. *Serves 4.*

TAQUITOS, FLAUTAS, AND CHIMIQUITOS

Taquitos, or "little tacos," and *flautas*, "flutes," are made by wrapping corn tortillas tightly around a filling, then frying them into crisp, golden brown cylinders. *Chimiquitos* are made exactly the same way but with thin flour tortillas. They resemble *chimichangas* except that the ends are left open as with *taquitos* and *flautas*. These tasty snacks are either eaten with the hands like tacos after being dipped in a sauce or guacamole, or, more formally, with a knife and fork after being covered with an avocado sauce and other garnishes.

The only difference between *taquitos* and *flautas* is their size. *Taquitos* are made with small tortillas and *flautas* either with large tortillas or 2 small ones placed together to form the long flute-like shape for which they are named.

To make Taquitos, Flautas, and Chimiquitos:

As with making enchiladas the tortillas must first be softened so that they can be rolled without cracking. This does not necessarily mean that they must be softened in oil. An easier, less messy method is to toast them on a *comal* or griddle placed over medium heat until they just become pliable. While this method always works with flour tortillas because of their fat content (flour tortillas should never be softened in oil), it is only possible with corn tortillas that are very fresh, which is not often the case with those found in most supermarkets. If the tortillas are the least bit dry, they will crack during the rolling process and should be softened briefly in hot oil and drained as they are for enchiladas.

After the tortillas have been made pliable, either through toasting or frying, place a small amount of filling in a line just off the tortilla's center; then roll it into a tight cylinder and secure it with a wooden toothpick (plastic toothpicks will melt during the cooking process).

After the *taquitos*, *flautas*, or *chimiquitos* have been formed, heat about 1 inch of oil in a medium-size skillet over medium-high heat until a drop of water sputters instantly. Using kitchen tongs place 2 to 4 cylinders in the oil and fry them, turning them once, until they are crisp and just beginning to brown. The entire process should take no more than a minute. Adjust the heat so that the tortillas do not brown too quickly since this gives them a slightly burned flavor.

12 *small (4–5 inch) corn tortillas*

1 *recipe* Picadillo I *(p. 148)*

8 *ounces mild cheddar or provolone cheese, cut into strips about 4 inches long, ½ inch wide, and ⅛ inch thick*

1 *recipe Guacamole (p. 144)*
 Radishes for garnish
 Hot sauce

TAQUITOS DE PICADILLO Y QUESO

Taquitos with Ground Beef and Cheese Filling

Soften the tortillas either by toasting them or briefly frying them as described on p. 205; then put a line of the *Picadillo* I just off center as described on p. 201. Place a strip of cheese on top of the filling, roll the tortilla, and fry the *taquito*.

Serve either topped with or accompanied by the Guacamole, radishes, and your favorite hot sauce. *Serves 4.*

FLAUTAS DE CARNE SECA

Flautas with Beef Jerky Filling

Soften the tortillas; then fill them with the *Machaca*, roll them as described on p. 201, and secure them with wooden toothpicks.

Make the sauce by beating the 4 ingredients together until smooth. This is easily done in a food processor using a steel blade.

Fry the *flautas* as described on pp. 201–02 and serve them topped with the sauce. *Serves 4.*

12 *large (6–7 inch or bigger) corn tortillas or 24 small tortillas*
1 *recipe* Machaca *(p. 156)*

AVOCADO SAUCE:

2 *avocados, chopped*
2 *tablespoons cilantro, minced*
2 *tablespoons juice from can or jar of pickled jalapeño chiles*
½ *cup sour cream*

CHIMIQUITOS

Soften the tortillas by toasting them briefly on a *comal* or griddle. Place a small line of *Machaca* just off center, roll the tortillas into tight cylinders, and secure them with wooden toothpicks.

Fry the *chimiquitos*, drain, and serve them topped with the Avocado Sauce. *Serves 4.*

12 *very thin 6–8 inch flour tortillas*
1 *recipe* Machaca *(p. 156)*
Avocado Sauce (p. 203)

ENCHILADAS

While the versatile taco may be the most widely recognized member of the Mexican food family, the enchilada is arguably the most popular. One restaurant owner after another has told me that enchiladas are their bestseller.

This section first describes the various types of enchiladas, then gives general directions for assembling the most common Mexican-American varieties. Following this are recipes for my favorite enchiladas.

TYPES OF ENCHILADAS

In Mexican-American cooking enchiladas nearly always consist of corn tortillas that have been dipped in hot oil and sometimes in sauce as well, and then either wrapped around a filling of meat, cheese, or occasionally seafood. However, in New Mexico the enchiladas are traditionally stacked like pancakes. The assembly is completed by topping the rolled or stacked enchiladas with sauce, grated cheese, and sometimes sour cream, and then heating them until the sauce is bubbling and the cheese is melted.

As noted in the "Introduction," enchiladas in Mexico are usually prepared without the final sauce and heating. The result is that they are often consumed barely warm rather than piping hot. This is explained by the fact that in addition to a shortage of ovens enchiladas are often sold by street vendors and eaten with the hands. This was also the case in early Mexican-American cooking, especially before modern ovens became prevalent. I have included a recipe for this type of enchilada, one that was a staple of vendors around San Antonio's market area in the early part of the century.

You will find two significant variations from the above descriptions in the following recipes for enchiladas. These include the Sonora-style enchilada, which is almost never found outside of southern Arizona, and the *encharito*. The former is made from a thick corn tortilla that is either baked on a griddle or fried before being topped with sauce and cheese and being passed under the broiler or heated in the oven. The latter, made from a flour tortilla, resembles an enchilada-style burrito and is an old California rancho recipe that is, inexplicably, almost never found in restaurants.

The details of making typical Mexican-American-style enchiladas are as follows:

Before doing anything decide how you are going to cook the enchiladas. Most ovens will hold a total of 4 serving plates on 2 different racks. So if you are serving 4 people or less, and if you have plates made to withstand baking temperatures, this is a convenient way of cooking the meal. The plates will be scalding hot just like in your favorite restaurant. If you are serving a crowd or lack ovenproof crockery, the enchiladas can be prepared using large casserole dishes, then placed on serving plates with a spatula. If this method is chosen, heat the serving plates in another oven or in a dishwasher set on the dry cycle. As you prepare the enchiladas according to the following instructions, place them either on the individual serving plates or in the casserole dishes. For purposes of simplicity the recipes that follow give instructions only for making the enchiladas on separate serving plates.

To Make Rolled or Stacked Enchiladas:

Soften the tortillas: To perform this task, immerse the tortillas in about an inch of hot oil heated until a drop of water sputters instantly; cook them just until they become pliable, then drain them on absorbent towels. In addition to making the tortillas supple enough so they can be rolled without cracking, the oil coating prevents the enchiladas from becoming soggy when the sauce is added.

Sauce the tortillas: Either dip the tortillas in the prepared sauce or spoon some on both sides. Although many restaurants skip

NUTRITION HINT: A much easier and less fattening way to soften tortillas for enchiladas (or any other purpose) is to spray the tortillas with a spray oil such as PAM, wrap them in a cotton towel, and microwave them, turning the package once, until they become pliable. This usually requires a total cooking time of 45 seconds to 1½ minutes.

this step, do not skip it if you want a really authentic enchilada. The difference in texture and flavor will be noticeable.

Fill or stack the enchiladas: If you are making rolled enchiladas, place a portion of the filling about 1 inch to either side of the tortilla's center and wrap it into a loose cylinder. The most common mistakes made by novice cooks when making their first enchiladas are to use too much filling and to wrap the enchiladas too tightly. Remember that in Mexican cooking less is often more and that many restaurants use no filling at all. They simply pour sauce and sprinkle cheese over loosely wrapped, softened tortillas. A rule of thumb when making cheese or meat enchiladas is to use about ¾ of an ounce of filling per tortilla.

If you are making New Mexico-style stacked enchiladas, use the same rule of thumb to determine the amount of filling. However, instead of rolling the sauced tortillas you place one flat on the plate, sprinkle on some filling, add another flat tortilla, and repeat the process. Two to 3 enchiladas per person is the normal serving size unless they are part of a combination plate, and then 1 or 2 is the standard.

A particularly endearing aspect of enchiladas is that the basic preparation outlined above, as well as the preparation of the sauce, can be done well in advance. This leaves only the final steps to be accomplished just prior to serving.

Final preparation: a) Cover the enchiladas with ½ cup or more of whatever sauce you have chosen. b) Add optional items such as minced onion and sour cream. c) Sprinkle the enchiladas with grated cheese.

Heating the enchiladas: Place the enchiladas in an oven preheated to 350 degrees and bake until the sauce bubbles and the cheese is melted, about 10 minutes.

Enfrijoladas are a type of enchilada made almost entirely with refried beans. To make *enfrijoladas,* soften the tortillas as for rolled or stacked enchiladas, then dip them in the beans, and fold

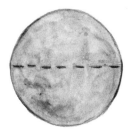

NUTRITION HINT: Because thinned refried beans are used in *enfrijoladas* both as filling and sauce they are very easy to make. And if you omit the frying and just puree the beans, you will have an extremely low-fat but still delicious and traditional dish.

them over twice as shown in the diagram. This allows you to skip the third, or "filling," step and proceed to the garnish and heating steps. Top the *enfrijoladas* with grated cheese.

Enchilada Fillings:

CHEESE

By far the most popular filling, cheese is easy to use, inexpensive, and except for grating, which is easily accomplished with a food processor, requires no further preparation. For specific cheeses see the chapter "Basics: Ingredients and Equipment" (p. 73), which discusses the alternatives, including mild cheddar, provolone, Monterey Jack, mozzarella, farmer cheese, and some of the Mexican types now available.

MEAT

Meats often used in enchiladas include beef, pork, chicken, and turkey. Beef and pork can either be ground or shredded, but chicken and turkey are almost always shredded. While the shredded versions are considered more authentic Mexican, the ground fillings are more typically Mexican-American. Sometimes these fillings are mixed with a little of the enchilada sauce before being rolled in, or stacked between, the tortillas, but usually they are not. For ground and shredded meat fillings, see the chapter "Basic Fillings" (p. 147).

Before attempting these recipes please read the introductory discussion of enchiladas (pp. 204–07).

THREE-COLOR MEXICAN FLAG ENCHILADAS

PREPARING THE ENCHILADAS:

12 *corn tortillas*
    Oil to soften the tortillas
    Filling I: 2 ounces Shredded Beef (p. 154) and 2 ounces cheddar cheese, grated
    Filling II: 2 ounces Monterey Jack cheese and 2 ounces provolone cheese, grated
    Filling III: 2 ounces cheddar cheese and 2 ounces Monterey Jack cheese, grated

ASSEMBLING AND COOKING THE ENCHILADAS:

¾ *cup All-purpose Enchilada Sauce (p. 172)*
1½ *cups Texas-style Mild Green Chile Enchilada Sauce with* Tomatillos *(p. 180)*
4 *ounces mild cheddar cheese, grated*
1 *cup sour cream*
2 *large or 4 small Anaheim or New Mexico chiles, seeded and peeled*
   Shredded lettuce, chopped tomatoes, and sliced black California olives for garnish

This recipe produces a dish similar to the one which is featured at Los Olivos restaurant in Scottsdale, Arizona. It combines three kinds of enchiladas, with different sauces, toppings, and fillings and makes a spectacular presentation resembling the red, white, and green of the Mexican flag. If you wish, you may simplify the preparation of fillings by using just one type of cheese.

Soften the tortillas as explained in the introductory section on enchiladas (pp. 205–07) and fill 4 with Filling I, 4 with Filling II, and the remaining 4 with Filling III.

Place the enchiladas on each of 4 ovenproof serving plates in the following order: the enchilada with Filling I at the left side, the one with Filling II in the middle, and the enchilada with Filling III to the right.

Pour an ample amount of All-purpose Enchilada Sauce over the enchiladas on the left side and Texas-style Mild Green Chile Enchilada Sauce with *Tomatillos* over the other two.

Sprinkle the cheddar cheese over the enchiladas.

Place a thick line of sour cream (a cake decorator helps) over the enchiladas in the middle and a slice of the green chile on the enchiladas on the right side.

Place the plates in an oven preheated to 350 degrees and heat for 10 minutes. Garnish the plate with the lettuce, tomatoes, and olives. *Serves 4.*

New Mexico Stacked Enchiladas

These are traditionally made with red chile sauce, but today they are often served with green chile sauce as well or with both red and green chile sauce. If you decide to try the recipe with both sauces, simply pour red chile sauce over half the stacked enchiladas and green chile sauce over the other half.

Heat the oil and, using kitchen tongs, soften the tortillas as described in the introductory section on enchiladas (p. 205) and remove them to paper towels to drain.

Warm the chile sauce and either dip each tortilla in it or spoon or brush sauce onto both sides of each tortilla.

Place a tortilla on each of 4 ovenproof serving plates, and sprinkle on ¾ of an ounce to an ounce of cheese. Top the cheese-covered tortilla with another tortilla and repeat the process so that each plate has 3 stacked enchiladas. Do not put any cheese on the final or third tortilla at this point.

Spoon the remainder of the chile sauce over the enchiladas so that it covers most of the plate, top with the remaining cheese, and place the plates in an oven preheated to 350 degrees for 10 minutes.

While the enchiladas are heating fry the eggs, if used, either sunny-side up or over easy. When the enchiladas are thoroughly heated, top the stacks with the eggs. Serve the enchiladas with New Mexico-style Refried Beans (p. 132), *Posole* (p. 317), or Spanish Rice (p. 128), or all three. *Serves 4.*

12 *blue corn tortillas, or substitute white or yellow corn tortillas*
Oil to soften the tortillas

1 *recipe Basic New Mexico Chile Sauce with Whole Chiles (p. 166), 1 recipe Basic New Mexico Chile Sauce with Chile Powder (p. 167), 1 recipe Basic New Mexico Chile Sauce with Pork (p. 168), 1 recipe New Mexico Green Chile Enchilada Sauce (p. 178), or both a red and green chile sauce*

1 *pound Monterey Jack cheese, grated*

4 *eggs (optional)*

ISABEL SALCIDO'S CALIFORNIA-STYLE STACKED ENCHILADAS

Oil to soften the tortillas

12 corn tortillas

2 recipes either All-purpose
    Enchilada Sauce (p.
    172), Basic New Mexico
    Chile Sauce with Whole
    Chiles (p. 166), or Basic
    New Mexico Chile
    Sauce with Chile
    Powder (p. 167)

1 pound mild cheddar
    cheese, grated

½ cup onions, minced

¾ cup black California
    olives, sliced or minced

½ cup sour cream (optional)

I have been told by more than one Mexican-American whose family was among the earliest California residents that their mothers often made stacked enchiladas. The obvious difference between these enchiladas and their more famous cousins in New Mexico is the fact that they were often stacked in one large tower instead of in individual portions and were then cut into wedges before serving. But the real differences relate to the cooking technique that allows the huge stack to be made without becoming soggy, and to the typically California use of olives and sour cream. To accomplish this, instead of being merely softened, the tortillas are cooked in oil until semicrisp. The addition of olives and lots of chopped onion as well as the frequent use of sour cream makes this dish truly distinctive.

The following version of this dish was the creation of Isabel Salcido. In the "Introduction" I mentioned that it was her son Ray who introduced my family to Mexican-American cooking. I am writing this recipe on the night of Ray's ninetieth birthday. When he arrived for dinner, I had all the ingredients carefully arranged. Ray supervised the preparation, with the patience of a cordon bleu chef teaching an eager apprentice, giving the incisive advice that reveals the critical subtleties.

This dish can be made with just one recipe of sauce, but it is easier to work with if the larger amount is used.

Heat the oil on one burner to soften the tortillas and keep the sauce warm on another. Using kitchen tongs, slide a tortilla into the hot oil, but instead of taking it out after a few seconds, allow it to cook until it is just barely semicrisp, that is, still pliable but becoming crunchy.

When the tortilla is the proper texture, remove it from the oil and place it in the warm sauce. Immediately place another tortilla into the oil to cook. When this second tortilla is almost crisp, remove the first tortilla from the sauce to a serving plate, sprinkle on some cheese, onions, and olives, then place the second tortilla in the sauce. Continue in this manner until all 12 tortillas have been added to the stack, as well as a final topping of cheese, olives, and onions.

After the final topping of sauce add a dollop of sour cream. Serve the enchiladas with Mexican Rice (p. 126) and/or Refried Beans (p. 132). Mexican-style coleslaw or shredded lettuce mixed with just a small amount of vinegar and oil also go well with this dish (see Shredded Cabbage or Lettuce Garnish, p. 145). *Serves 4.*

ENCHILADAS DE CALIFORNIA ANTIGUA
Old California Rolled Enchiladas

These enchiladas are reminiscent of those served in the days of the Spanish ranchos. Unfortunately, they are not part of the current Mexican-American restaurant fare.

Heat the oil, soften the tortillas, and drain them on absorbent towels (see p. 205 for instructions).

Coat the tortillas with some of the sauce. Then roll the chicken in the tortillas.

Meanwhile, preheat your oven to 350 degrees.

Place 3 rolled enchiladas on each of 4 ovenproof serving plates. Pour sauce over the enchiladas and top with the cheese. Heat in the oven for 10 minutes or until the cheese is melted and the sauce is bubbling. *Serves 4.*

12 *corn tortillas*
   Oil to soften the tortillas
1 *recipe Shredded Chicken*
   (p. 158)
1 *recipe Old-style California*
   Enchilada Sauce (p. 174)
¼ *pound Monterey Jack*
   cheese, grated

ENCHILADAS ESTILO TEX-MEX

Tex-Mex Enchiladas

12 *corn tortillas*
   Oil to soften the tortillas
1 *recipe Basic Tex-Mex
   Sauce (p. 170) or Tex-
   Mex Chile-Beef
   Enchilada Sauce (p.
   176)*
1 *pound mild cheddar
   cheese, grated*
1 *cup onion, minced
   (optional)*

This is the mainstay of the famous Tex-Mex combination plate and often the most popular item on the menus of restaurants specializing in this type of food.

Texans like controversy and love to argue about food, focusing on such questions as: who invented *fajitas* and who serves the best? Is ground meat appropriate for chile? About the only thing most Texans agree upon is that pinto beans should not be flavored with chile powder, but even that is occasionally contested. There is no agreement on the question of how much, if any, onion should be added to Tex-Mex Enchiladas. I favor just a little onion with the cheese filling and a little more sprinkled on with the sauce, but like most people in the Lone Star State suit yourself.

Using kitchen tongs soften the tortillas in oil as explained in the introductory remarks on enchiladas (p. 205); then place them on paper towels to drain. When they are cool enough to handle, either immerse them in the sauce, which should be warm, or spoon or brush some sauce on both sides of each tortilla.

Place an ounce or slightly less of the cheese and some onion, if used, just off center of each tortilla and either roll or fold the enchiladas. Rolling means to wrap them into fairly tight cylinders; folding means to roll them more loosely.

Place 3 enchiladas on each of 4 ovenproof serving plates. Top the rolled or folded enchiladas liberally with the sauce and add more cheese and onion, if used.

Place the plates in an oven preheated to 350 degrees for 10 minutes. Serve the enchiladas with Mexican Rice (p. 126) and Refried Beans (p. 132). Some cooks also garnish the beans with a little grated cheese and stick a tortilla chip or two in them. *Serves 4.*

ENCHILADAS VERDE CON CREMA

Green Chile Sour Cream Enchiladas

These enchiladas are good with either the Texas-style Mild Green Chile Enchilada Sauce with *Tomatillos* (p. 180)or the New Mexico Green Chile Enchilada Sauce (p. 178), which is at the other end of the chile heat spectrum.

Preheat your oven to 350 degrees.

Using kitchen tongs soften the tortillas in oil as explained in the basic enchilada instructions (p. 205). Either dip the coated tortillas in the sauce or spoon enough on them to coat both sides.

Place a small amount of chicken on each tortilla and roll it into an enchilada; then place 3 of the completed enchiladas on each of 4 ovenproof serving plates.

Top the enchiladas liberally with the sauce, top them with some sour cream (a cake decorator makes this easy and attractive), and then sprinkle them with the cheese.

Place the plates in the oven for 10 minutes or until the cheese is melted and the sauce is bubbling. Serve the enchiladas with Mexican Rice (p. 126) and/or Refried Beans (p. 132). *Serves 4.*

12 *corn tortillas*
   Oil to soften the tortillas
1 *recipe Texas-style Mild Green Chile Enchilada Sauce with* Tomatillos *or 1 recipe New Mexico Green Chile Enchilada Sauce (p. 178)*
2½ *cups Shredded Chicken (p. 158)*
¼ *pound Monterey Jack cheese, grated*
1 *cup sour cream*

ENCHARITOS DE CALIFORNIA
Early California Encharitos

2½ tablespoons olive oil

2 cloves garlic, minced

3 onions, chopped

1 cup black California olives, sliced

4 9-inch flour tortillas

1 recipe Basic New Mexico Chile Sauce with Whole Chiles (p. 166) or 1 recipe Basic New Mexico Chile Sauce wth Chile Powder (p. 167)

½ pound mild cheddar cheese, grated

½ pound Monterey Jack cheese, grated

Green portion of 2 green onions, minced

Shredded lettuce

Vinaigrette

Encharitos resemble burritos in that they are made with flour tortillas; but they are rolled, sauced, and otherwise prepared and served like enchiladas. The word *encharito* aptly expresses the hybrid quality of this dish. However, since to me it really is a cheese enchilada made with a flour tortilla, I included it in this section rather than in the section on burritos. Much like the early California *chilaquile*, the *encharito* combines the piquant bite of chile sauce with the sweetness of onions cooked to a golden brown and the earthy taste of olives.

Heat the olive oil in a skillet over moderate heat and sauté the garlic and onions, stirring often, until they are a rich golden brown. In order to get the onions properly brown (which brings out their natural sweetness), you will need to turn the heat to low at some point to keep them from scorching. The entire process should take 20 to 30 minutes. During the last 5 minutes of cooking, add ¾ cup of the olives to the onions and garlic.

Preheat your oven to 350 degrees.

If you are not making the tortillas fresh, soften those you are using on an ungreased griddle over medium heat. This will take about 10 to 15 seconds on each side.

Bring the chile sauce to barely a simmer and spoon some onto both sides of each tortilla. Spread the sauce so that both sides are well coated. This is important since it keeps the tortillas from drying and scorching during the cooking process.

Mix the cheeses and put ½ to ¾ cup on each tortilla, top with equal portions of the onion-olive mixture, and then roll the tortillas as for enchiladas. Place 1 *encharito* on each of 4 ovenproof serving plates.

Cover the *encharitos* with the sauce and top each with equal portions of the remaining cheese and the remaining olives; finally, sprinkle each portion with the minced green onions.

Bake the *encharitos* for 10 minutes or until the cheese is melted and the sauce is bubbling. Serve garnished with shredded lettuce in a mild vinaigrette. *Serves 4.*

ENCHILADAS DE TEJAS ANTIGUA
Old-style Texas Enchiladas

These enchiladas, served with fried potatoes, are reminiscent of those served by street vendors in the plazas of central Mexico and which found their way to south Texas in the late 1800s. They were particularly popular on the streets of San Antonio, where they were often prepared by the famous "chile queens." These often boisterous and flirtatious women, who set up their food stalls around Military Plaza and other areas, are a colorful part of the city's history. Unfortunately, around the 1930s their food stalls fell prey to enforcement of health regulations.

Enchiladas de Tejas antigua are made in the Mexican fashion, which means there is no final addition of sauce and no baking. They must be assembled all at once and quickly so that the tortillas will be hot enough from their immersion in the oil and the sauce to at least partially melt the cheese. Be careful not to burn yourself in the process. Because of this they are a little more hectic and messy to prepare than most enchiladas, but I urge you to try them as they have a unique taste and texture that really gives you the flavor of the old days. You, like me, will wonder why they are not still popular.

Oil for frying the potatoes
1 cup potatoes, peeled and cut into ¼-inch pieces
Oil for softening the tortillas
12 corn tortillas
1 recipe Old-style Texas Enchilada Sauce (p. 172)
¾ pound Monterey Jack cheese, grated
½ cup onion, minced
2 cups shredded lettuce
1 large tomato, chopped

Heat about ¼ inch oil in a skillet over medium to medium-high heat and fry the potatoes until they are brown and crisp. Drain and reserve the potatoes.

Add some oil to the pan, turn the heat to medium high, and when it is hot, soften the tortillas.

Dip the tortillas in the sauce; then wrap a small amount of cheese in them and place them on individual serving plates. Top the completed enchiladas with the potatoes, onion, lettuce, and tomato and serve immediately. *Serves 4.*

ENCHILADAS SONORENSES
Sonora-style Enchiladas

TO MAKE THE DOUGH:

1½   *cups Masa Harina*
½   *teaspoon baking powder*
½   *teaspoon salt*
3–4 *tablespoons beaten egg*
1   *cup water*
    Cooking oil or lard

FOR THE ENCHILADAS:

1   *recipe All-purpose*
    Enchilada Sauce
    (p. 172) or another of
    your favorites
3   *ounces grated, mild*
    cheddar cheese mixed
    with an equal amount
    of grated Monterey
    Jack cheese (6 ounces
    in all)
½   *cup green onion, minced*
½   *cup olives, minced or*
    sliced
1   *recipe Shredded Cabbage*
    or Lettuce Garnish
    (p. 145)
1   *recipe Mexican Rice*
    (p. 126)

The Sonora-influenced cooking of Arizona and California pro-duced the only flat or stacked enchiladas I have seen outside of New Mexico (see Isabel Salcido's California-style Stacked Enchi-ladas, p. 210). It also produced an even more unique enchilada. It is made by rolling specially prepared dough, or *masa*, into the shape of a large, thick pancake, which is then fried or baked on a *comal*. The result, which is rather like a very fat corn tortilla, is then covered with sauce, cheese, and garnish like an ordinary enchilada. In this country, the Sonora-style enchilada is rarely found outside of Arizona in either home or restaurant cooking.

This dish sounds simple because it is; but it is also very satisfy-ing, with a taste and texture that are different from any other enchilada. You can vary the result considerably, depending on how you make the *masa* and how you cook it. For example, the following recipe uses a small amount of egg in the dough, while others use only the same *masa* which is used to make corn tor-tillas. El Charro restaurant in Tucson, Arizona, does not use egg but does add a small quantity of both potato and cheese to the *masa*. Also, you can cook the *masa* cake in three basic ways: with no oil, in deep fat, or with just enough oil to grease the pan. My personal preference is the latter method.

Preheat your oven to 350 degrees.

Combine the dry ingredients in a bowl; then stir in the beaten egg, making sure it is well combined.

Add the water, a little at a time, until a medium dough is formed. It should not be particularly wet and should be worked no more than necessary.

NUTRITION HINT: If you bake the *masa* on a *comal* or griddle with no fat, use a sauce such as one of the green chile sauces, and minimize the amount of cheese, you will have an extremely low-fat and very satisfying meal.

Divide the dough into 4 equal portions and roll into balls. Place 1 ball between waxed paper and roll it out until it is about 5 to 6 inches in diameter and ¼ inch, or slightly less, thick. Repeat the process with the remaining balls of dough.

Either bake the formed dough on an ungreased *comal*, deep-fry it, or proceed as follows: Heat a skillet over moderate to moderately low heat. Add just enough oil to coat the bottom of the pan and pour off any excess. Cook the formed dough on one side until it is well browned, 2 to 4 minutes; then remove it. Add a little more oil to the skillet and cook on the other side until the *masa*-cake is just cooked through.

Place 1 completed *masa*-cake on each of 4 ovenproof serving plates. Top with the sauce, then the cheese, and garnish with the green onion and olives.

Heat the enchiladas in the oven until the cheese is melted and the sauce bubbles; then serve with Mexican Rice and Shredded Cabbage or Lettuce Garnish. *Serves 4.*

TAMALES

Tamales are one of the most unique aspects of Mexican cooking. Tacos, burritos, and enchiladas have been likened to sandwiches, crêpes, and manicotti, but it is difficult to find anything well known in another cuisine that is sufficiently tamale-like.

The tamale of today has changed little from the Indian original. Perhaps lard and pork have replaced armadillo fat and iguana in most places, but the form is virtually the same. First, corn is processed and ground into the same *nixtamal* that is used to make corn tortillas, and then fat, usually lard, is added to make a smooth, light dough. The dough, or *masa*, thus produced is then spread on a corn husk or, in southern Mexico, a banana leaf; a small amount of filling is added, either meat or sweetened fruit, and the husk or leaf is formed into a cylinder or rectangle which is then rolled or folded and tied to hold the package together. Finally, the tamales are steamed. The result is unwrapped at the table.

In Mexico tamales come in all sizes and types, from the giant Yucatán version, which can measure a foot or more, to the small *uchepos* of Michoacán. As noted above, in parts of Mexico, notably Oaxaca and Chiapas, tamales are made with banana leaves and often filled with chicken or pork *mole*. The Mexican-American tamale does not usually have these variations. It is virtually the same as the tamale found throughout northern Mexico. In the United States tamales vary in size from the fairly small, thin Tex-Mex version to the large variety often found in other states, particularly California. Except for sweet tamales the filling is usually pork or turkey, but sometimes venison seasoned with chile paste.

One other difference between Mexican-American tamales and those in southern Mexico is notable. Southern Mexicans seem to take tamale-making much more seriously than northerners. This is reflected in the purity of the *masa*. Southern cooks usually use white corn and spend hours ensuring that only perfect kernels go into their *masa* and that every bit of skin is removed from them, giving them a very white color and light taste. Northerners are not quite so picky, and consequently their tamales are usually less smooth and darker in color. I have found both versions in Mexican-American cooking, but the more casual northern attitude predominates.

The one and very significant exception to the above method of making tamales is the green corn tamale, which is found most often in Arizona. This is a tamale that is made from fresh corn or fresh corn with just a little corn flour *masa* rather than a *masa* made entirely from dried corn. The fresh kernels, preferably from white corn, are ground with lard and milk, some cheese and green chile is often added, and then they are wrapped and steamed like other tamales. As can be imagined, the taste has a sweetness that only comes from the use of fresh ingredients.

The tamale's only disadvantage, and it is a significant one, is that it requires a large amount of lard. Unfortunately, it is one of the few dishes that loses nearly all its character if shortening is substituted. I have tried many nonlard tamales and even some that have virtually no fat added, and would rather do without.

In Mexican-American households tamale-making is an important part of the Christmas tradition. Usually the lady of the house, aunts, and children will spend an entire day or more in the kitchen in mini-assembly lines turning out vast quantities of what they consider the best tamales ever made. Most will be given away, but enough will be frozen so that they can be enjoyed on special occasions throughout the year.

As is evident from the way tamales are traditionally made in Mexican-American households, tamale-making is ideal for large families since a lot of repetitive work is required. However, do not despair since the process can be accomplished by one or two people in a fairly short period of time. The best way to do this is to buy the *masa* already prepared from a *tortillería*. If tamale *masa* is not available, simply buy tortilla *masa* and add lard. If this is not an option, the next best bet is to make your own *masa* using either Masa Harina or MaSeca (see the chapter on "Tortillas and Bread," p. 97).

Don't worry if you can't find the traditional corn husks called

for in the recipe. Parchment paper or pieces of old white sheets make decent substitutes.

Sweet, or dessert, tamales are a particular treat, also defying comparison with any other dish of another cuisine. Usually sugar, fruit syrup, or jam is added to the *masa*, and the tamales are made without a filling, although sometimes a fruit filling is added.

MEAT-FILLED TAMALES

As mentioned above pork and turkey are the most common fillings for tamales. Turkey is particularly popular in California. However, in Texas venison tamales are considered a special delicacy. The filling is made from shredded meat that is mixed with chile paste and allowed to season, refrigerated, overnight.

Some cooks add chile powder or sauce to the dough for both flavoring and color as is often the custom in northern Mexico. For this reason I have included chile powder as an optional ingredient.

MEAT TAMALE DOUGH

4 *cups Masa Harina*
4 *teaspoons mild chile powder*
1½ *tablespoons salt*
1 *teaspoon baking powder*
4 *cups chicken or turkey broth*
1½ *cups lard, at room temperature*

As many people do not have access to a *tortillería* where fresh tamale dough, or *masa*, can be purchased, the following recipe is given for *masa* that is made with Masa Harina. If you are able to buy prepared *masa*, mix 1 pound with a little more than ¾ cup lard. Actually the best way to ensure that you have the right ratio of lard to *masa* is to use the time-honored float test. After you have whipped the lard to a light consistency, begin mixing it into the *masa*. Periodically place a small piece of the resulting mixture into a glass of water. As soon as the *masa* floats you have the correct mixture! Please note that the following recipe calls for the minimum amount of lard that is necessary to make good, light tamales. A perhaps more common recipe would bring the amount of lard up to 2 to 2¼ cups.

Mix the dry ingredients together; then add the broth to make the *masa*.

Either place the lard in an electric mixer and beat it until it is fluffy or perform this operation by hand. Then gradually beat the *masa* into the lard until it is completely incorporated and fluffy.

MEAT TAMALE FILLING

Soak the chiles in hot water for at least 15 minutes; then remove the stems, veins, and seeds, and place them in your blender. Add the garlic, oregano, salt, and about half the water. Blend the chile mixture, adding additional water but no more than is necessary to make a thick paste.

Place the shredded meat in a bowl and stir in the chile paste. Allow the meat to season overnight in your refrigerator.

This recipe makes enough to fill about 2 dozen tamales, or more if you skimp on the filling the way the commercial producers do.

Assembling the Tamales:

Dried corn husks are nearly always used to wrap Mexican-American tamales, except when making green corn tamales, where fresh husks are often used.

First, soak the husks in hot water for at least ½ hour; then remove them and dry them lightly with a towel.

Next, place enough dough on the husk to cover the area shown in the diagram. The amount you use will depend on the size of the husk and the size of the tamale you wish to make. For Tex-Mex-style tamales only about 2 to 3 tablespoons of dough is spread about ¼ inch thick while ½ cup of dough is spread ¾ inch thick or more for some California-style recipes. Also of consideration is how you will secure the tamale. If the husk is nearly completely filled, you may have to tie the ends with string, which is time consuming. On the other hand, if the husk is only partially filled, you may be able to simply fold both sides over, a much easier and quicker alternative.

2–4 ancho *chiles, depending on whether you want hot or mild tamales*

2 *cloves garlic*

½ *tablespoon oregano*

½ *teaspoon salt*

½ *cup water*

2 *cups shredded pork, turkey, or venison*

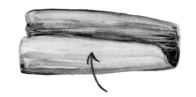

Once the dough is spread, roll the tamale up as indicated in the diagram and either fold the husks over to secure them or tie them as discussed above.

To cook the tamales, stack the tamales in a large steamer and steam for 1 to 2 hours (depending on the size of the tamales) or until the dough becomes firm and spongy and does not stick to the husks. *Makes 12 to 36 tamales, depending on their size.*

TAMALES DE ELOTE

Green Corn Tamales

Fresh or dried corn husks

2 cups fresh corn kernels, or substitute frozen corn

1¼ cups lard or shortening

¼ cup–½ cup Masa Harina

1 pound mild cheddar or Monterey Jack cheese, grated

½ tablespoon salt

2 green chiles

Green corn tamales are seldom found outside of Arizona. This Sonoran specialty is usually made exclusively from fresh corn kernels, hence its name. However, without a grain grinder it is difficult to get the corn ground to the proper consistency. Also, the corn must be fairly dry and have just the right starch content, which precludes the use of frozen corn. For these reasons this recipe includes a small quantity of Masa Harina. The result gives an authentic taste and is much easier to produce.

Although some cooks make the dough just with the corn, then fill the tamales with the chile and cheese as you would a regular tamale, I think the following version, which incorporates the chile and cheese in the dough, is much simpler and just as good.

This outstanding recipe was given to me by Catalina Gonzáles, owner of Tony's Jacal restaurant near Del Mar, California. It is delicious made with fresh rather than dried corn husks, and you should use them if available. If you do not have enough, use the dried variety.

If using dried corn husks, cover them with boiling water and leave them for ½ hour to soften.

Using a food processor grind the corn kernels into as fine a paste as possible. If your kernels are quite dry, you may need to add a little milk.

Melt the lard and add it along with ¼ cup of the Masa Harina and the other ingredients and continue processing into a firm paste. If the result is still too watery, add some more Masa Harina.

Spoon about 2 to 3 tablespoons of the dough onto a corn husk and roll it and tie it as called for in the general instructions on making tamales (pp. 218–20). If you are using fresh husks, you may need to use 2 or 3 overlapping each other.

Steam the tamales for 1 hour. *Makes approximately 1 dozen tamales, depending on their size.*

QUESADILLAS

Quesadillas are possibly the easiest of all the *antojitos* to prepare. These delightful snacks can be as simple and satisfying as a plain grilled cheese sandwich or as interesting as the French *croque monsieur*.

In Mexico *quesadillas* are made from either flour or corn tortillas or sometimes the raw *masa*, or dough, which is then fried. But in Mexican-American cooking the flour tortilla variety is the most common. After the tortilla is softened by toasting it quickly on a *comal* or griddle over medium heat, it is then topped with cheese, folded over (just like a turnover), and replaced on the *comal* to cook until the cheese is melted. You must turn the *quesadilla* at least once to ensure that both sides are lightly browned. Some cooks brush the folded *quesadilla* lightly with oil or butter before cooking, which creates a crisper texture and more complex flavor. Yet others make a sandwich with 2 tortillas so that the resulting *quesadilla* is round rather than turnover shaped. It is then cut into 4 pie-shaped wedges before serving.

QUESADILLA FILLINGS

12 *medium-size flour tortillas*
1 *pound mild cheddar, mozzarella, provolone, Monterey Jack, or a Mexican queso blanco, asadero, or Oaxaca cheese, or a combination of 2 or more, grated*

All *quesadillas* contain cheese (without which they could not be called *quesadillas*). The cheese, when melted, also keeps the *quesadilla* from falling apart. In the more elaborate versions a combination of cheeses can be used. Also, several other fillings are often added that transform the *quesadilla* from a simple snack into something much more elaborate and interesting as shown in the following variations. Simply follow the above directions and stuff with one or a combination of the cheeses plus any of the additional suggested items. Following the list of fillings is my favorite version.

To the basic cheese filling can be added 1 or a combination of the ingredients listed to the right.

In addition to the above, do not hesitate to add a dash of your favorite hot sauce and/or relish. For a festive look, garnish the *quesadillas* with shredded lettuce and tomato, minced green onion, and some chopped olives. *Serves 4.*

½ *pound grilled or smoked chicken (as prepared for* Tacos de pollo al carbón, *p. 196), chopped*

½ *pound grilled* Fajitas, *sliced very thin (pp. 271–72)*

½ *pound filling for* Tacos de carne de res al carbón *(p. 195)*

½ *pound* New Mexico-style Green Chile *(p. 262)*

½ *pound* New Mexico-style Chile con Carne *(p. 256)*

½ *pound* Picadillo II *(p. 149)*

½ *pound small shrimp sautéed in olive oil with a little garlic*

½ *pound boiled crab or imitation crabmeat*

3 *cups Refried Beans (p. 132)*

   Avocado slices

   Black California olives, sliced

QUESADILLAS DE FAJITAS

Fajita Quesadillas

1 tablespoon olive oil

1 onion, sliced thin

2 cloves garlic, minced

½ cup green chile, peeled, seeded, and chopped

½ teaspoon oregano

¼ teaspoon salt, or to taste

¼ teaspoon ground black pepper

¼ cup loosely packed, chopped cilantro

8 flour tortillas, 6–7 inches in diameter

¼ cup butter, melted

½ pound provolone cheese, grated

1 pound charbroiled Fajitas, sliced very thin (pp. 271–72)

These *quesadillas* are made from 2 unfolded flour tortillas, rather than from 1 folded into the shape of a turnover. The only tricky part is having your heat set so that the cheese melts and the tortilla reaches a nice golden brown at about the same time. The low setting works best for me.

Before making the *quesadillas* you first must prepare the chile and onion portion of the filling. To do this, place the olive oil in a skillet over medium heat; then add the onions and garlic. Cook, stirring often, until the onions are soft but not browned. Add the green chiles, oregano, salt, and pepper and continue cooking until the onions just begin to brown. Remove the skillet from the heat and stir in the cilantro.

To make the first *quesadilla*, brush one side of each of 2 tortillas with butter; then place them, buttered side down, on a griddle or skillet set over low heat.

Place enough cheese over each tortilla to cover it. Then spoon some of the onion and green chile filling on 1 tortilla; then add some of the *Fajitas* to the same tortilla.

When the cheese has melted and the bottom of the tortillas are a nice golden brown, place the tortilla that only has cheese on it on top of the filling on the other tortilla (cheese side down) to make a "sandwich." Cook a few more seconds, then remove from the heat to a serving plate. Before serving, cut the tortilla into 4 wedges (like a pizza) and garnish with a sprig of cilantro. Prepare the other *quesadillas* in the same manner. *Serves 4.*

CHEESE CRISPS AND MEXICAN PIZZAS

The humble but delicious cheese crisp, found mostly in Arizona, is nothing more than a flour tortilla topped with cheese and baked until the tortilla is crisp and the cheese is melted. The Mexican pizza, which is a cheese crisp with lots of other toppings, is also found primarily in Arizona. Although probably more an invention of Mexican-American restaurants than a dish derived from any cultural heritage, the Mexican pizza is a very popular item.

While both the cheese crisp and Mexican pizza can be made of corn tortillas, it is difficult to find them sufficiently large. Possibly for this reason flour tortillas are usually used. As many readers will not be able to readily obtain the large thin Sonora-style tortillas that are used in Arizona, I have given the amounts of cheese for various sizes of flour tortillas.

The following recipes are for appetizers. For a full meal simply double the amounts.

CHEESE CRISP

Preheat your oven to 375 degrees.

Place the tortilla in the preheated oven and bake it just until it starts to become crisp and a little brown, 2½ to 3½ minutes.

Remove the tortilla, sprinkle on the grated cheese, and top with the *jalapeño* chiles, if you are using them. Replace the tortilla in the oven and continue to cook it until the cheese is melted and bubbling. *Serves 4.*

MEXICAN PIZZA

To make this popular item, simply follow the directions for Cheese Crisp (above) through the addition of the cheese; then let your imagination run wild using the list of toppings at the right as a starting point. *Serves 4.*

---

1 *12–14-inch flour tortilla*

6½–8½ *ounces of mild cheddar or a mixture of mild cheddar and Monterey Jack cheeses, grated*

1 *9–10-inch flour tortilla*

3½–4½ *ounces of mild cheddar or a mixture of mild cheddar and Monterey Jack cheeses, grated*

2 *pickled* jalapeño *chiles, seeded and sliced (optional)*

Any of the taco fillings
Avocado, chopped
Bacon, cooked and crumbled
Black California olives, sliced
Chorizo, cooked
Green onion, minced
Salsa picante
Sour cream
Tomato, peeled, seeded, and chopped

TOSTADAS

There is often confusion about whether a *tostada* is the crisp appetizer chip used to dip hot sauce and guacamole or whether it is the flat, crisp whole corn tortilla topped with *picadillo*, guacamole, and a host of other items. In Mexico the latter is not served often except in restaurants catering to tourists. It is, in fact, more of a Mexican-American version of the *chalupa* or *gordita* than anything else. In restaurants I have found it safer to refer to the chips as chips or as *totopos* (as they are called in southern Mexico) and the more elaborate item as a *tostada*.

However, the best *tostada* I have had is different from either of the above. It is the *Tostada compuesta* served at Katy Meek's La Posta restaurant in Mesilla, New Mexico. Katy told me she invented the *Tostada compuesta* after a Middle Eastern acquaintance spoke lovingly of a dish his mother had made from dough, shaped like a bird's nest, cheese, and lettuce. She experimented and finally arrived at the *Tostada compuesta*, a corn tortilla fried into the shape of a small bowl, which is then filled with chile con carne and beans and garnished with lettuce, tomato, and grated cheese. Katy says that at La Posta this dish is second in popularity only to the enchiladas.

TOSTADAS

Oil for frying the tortillas
8 corn tortillas
1 *recipe* Picadillo II *(p. 149)*
   Shredded lettuce
2 avocados, peeled, seeded, and coarsely chopped
2 tomatoes, coarsely chopped
1 cup mild cheddar cheese, grated
   Hot sauce

This is my favorite version of the most common type of *tostada*.

Heat about 1 inch of cooking oil in a small skillet until it is very hot but not smoking. Fry the tortillas in the oil until crisp, keeping them as flat as possible.

Spoon some of the *Picadillo* II on each fried tortilla and garnish with the lettuce, avocados, tomatoes, and cheese.

Serve the *Tostadas* with the hot sauce. *Serves 4.*

TOSTADAS COMPUESTAS
Fixed-up Tostadas

The first step in this dish is to make the tortilla cup that distinguishes it from the usual flat *tostada*:

First preheat a deep fryer to 350 to 375 degrees.

Cut slits on each of 4 tortillas as shown in the diagram.

Put a tortilla in the deep fryer and, using a long-handled spoon or similar object (I use a soup ladle about 3 inches in diameter), press down on its center so that a cup shape is formed. Hold the tortilla in its new shape under the oil until it becomes crisp, then drain the shell on absorbent towels.

To make the *tostada*, first put about 2 tablespoons beans in each shell, add about 2 tablespoons New Mexico-style Chile con Carne, then top with some lettuce, tomato, and cheese. *Serves 4.*

8 *corn tortillas*

1½ *cups* Frijoles de olla
   (p. 130), drained

1½ *cups New Mexico-style
   Chile con Carne (p.
   156)*

2 *cups shredded lettuce*

4 *tomatoes, chopped*

1 *cup mild cheddar cheese,
   grated*

TOSTADAS DE QUESO
Cheese Tostadas

This *tostada* is a real hit with kids. It is something like a cheese crisp made with a fried corn tortilla.

Heat about 1 inch of cooking oil in a small skillet until it is very hot but not smoking. Fry the tortillas in the oil until crisp, keeping them as flat as possible.

Heat the *Chile con queso* over very low heat until it is fairly thick; then spoon it over the fried tortillas and serve. *Serves 4.*

Oil for frying the tortillas

8 *corn tortillas*

1 *recipe* Chile con queso
   (p. 121)

BURRITOS AND CHIMICHANGAS

Wrap a filling of beans and/or ground or shredded meat flavored with red or green chile in a giant, thin flour tortilla and you have a burrito. Deep-fry a burrito until golden brown and you have a *chimichanga*.

Until recently burritos and *chimichangas* were genuinely regional in nature. Just a few years ago they were rarely found outside of Arizona and California, whose cooking is based on that of Mexico's state of Sonora, home of these delicious items. Now, burritos are popular all over New Mexico and are even occasionally spotted in Texas.

Dave DeWitt, in his book *Foodlover's Handbook to the Southwest* presents several theories as to the origin of the word *chimichanga* as does Janet Mitchell in her article "Unwrapping the Truth about the Chimichanga" in a recent issue of *Tucson Guide Quarterly*. Some say that the word *chimichanga* is an expletive involving *changa*, which means female monkey in Spanish. Others contend that *chimichanga* is a nonsense word similar to *thingamajig*. Yet others see a relationship between the fact that *chimichanga* is sometimes spelled *chivichanga* and the fact that *chivo* means goat in Spanish. Also, at least three old-time Arizona restaurateurs claim to have invented the *chimichanga*. To add to the mystery, the *Diccionario de Mejicanismos* lists *chimichanga* as a variation of *chivichanga* and, loosely translated, defines it as "In Tabasco any bauble or trifle; a thing without importance whose role is unknown."

While I personally am not sure of the origin of the names for either burritos or *chimichangas*, thanks to Judy England, owner of the Santa Cruz Chili & Spice Co., located in Tumacacori, Arizona, near Tucson, I know why burritos became popular in Sonora. Judy, who lived for some time on a ranch in Sonora, explained that the cowboys would wrap some meat or beans in the giant, thin Sonora-style flour tortillas and place them in their saddlebags. She also explained that it was a mark of gentility to wrap an extra tortilla around the food, one that would be discarded before the burrito was consumed for reasons of hygiene.

Cooks being curious people it probably did not take long before someone tried immersing a burrito in hot lard, and advertised the results as being well worth the extra effort. Nobody really knows whether the *chimichanga* was invented in Arizona or Mexico, or in Arizona when it was part of Mexico. Actually, I tend to believe all the old-timers who lay claim to inventing the *chimichanga*. It is such an obvious thing to put a burrito in hot oil (the way a soft taco was put in oil and became a *taquito* or *flauta*) that the *chimichanga* was probably "invented" by many different cooks at different times. One thing I do know is that while *chimichangas* are found in Mexico, they are much more common in Arizona. Also, the Mexican variety is usually much smaller and rarely served enchilada style.

Both burritos and *chimichangas* are best made with the thinnest possible tortillas, so please consult the chapter "Tortillas and Bread" (p. 97) for appropriate instructions. Also, while both items were originally eaten with the hands like tacos (and still are), Mexican-American restaurants more often serve them "enchilada style," that is, covered with a chile sauce, cheese, and often sour cream and guacamole.

How to Make Burritos and Chimichangas:

Making burritos and *chimichangas* is easy once you know how. The proper technique is explained by means of the diagram on p. 232.

In Arizona burritos and *chimichangas* are made from paper-thin tortillas up to 18 inches in diameter. While they can be made with 9-inch tortillas, I don't recommend anything less than 12 inches, which is the most popular size except for the "minichimi" made from a tortilla about 7 inches in diameter. The only problem with this is that the average skillet is about 9 inches in diameter, and even large ones rarely exceed 11 inches. This makes it difficult to make the larger varieties. Also, outside of Arizona and California it is often difficult to find packaged flour tortillas over 9 inches in diameter. I suggest you use a large electric griddle to cook and soften the tortillas, if possible. But, in a pinch, use the easily purchased 9-inch variety.

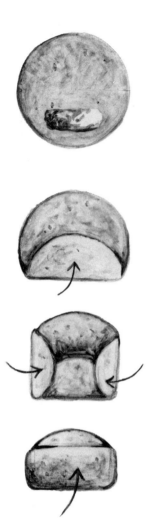

First, the tortilla must be softened so that it is pliable enough to fold without cracking. If you have a skillet or griddle large enough, heat it over medium; then, without using any grease, warm the tortilla for 15 to 20 seconds on each side or until it softens and begins to puff. As the tortillas are heated wrap them in a towel. This will keep them warm, and the steam will further soften them. Alternatively, wrap the tortillas in a towel and heat them in the microwave for 60 to 90 seconds, turning the package over about halfway through the process.

Next, lay a tortilla out flat on a work surface and place a portion of the filling you have chosen about halfway between the center of the tortilla and the edge nearest you. Because of the geometry of a circle the amount of filling varies a great deal depending on the size of the tortilla used. For example, a 9-inch tortilla has an area of about 64 square inches, while a 12-inch tortilla contains about 113 square inches. For a 12-inch tortilla you will need ½ cup or more of filling.

Fold the edge of the tortilla nearest you securely over the filling; then fold the sides to your right and left to close each end that was left open by the first fold. Finally, finish by rolling the tortilla away from you until it is completely closed.

If you are serving burritos, place them on plates with the seam side down. If you are making *chimichangas*, place completed burritos in a deep fryer heated to 350 degrees and fry them until golden brown. A good way to do this is to place a burrito, seam side down, in a fryer basket. Place another fryer basket on top to hold the burrito in place, and then lower it slowly into the fryer. If you do not have a second basket, hold the burrito down with long kitchen tongs to avoid being burned with any spattering oil.

Before making these recipes please review the above section on making burritos and *chimichangas*.

BURRITOS DE CHILE VERDE

Green Chile Burritos

This old-fashioned *burro* (or burrito) filled with a green chile stew is both a home-style and restaurant favorite, and rightly so. To me it is the essence of simple Sonoran cooking.

Heat the New Mexico Green Chile Enchilada Sauce and then the tortillas. Spread approximately ½ to ¾ cup of the sauce on each burrito and roll it up as directed above. Serve immediately. *Serves 4.*

1 *recipe New Mexico Green Chile Enchilada Sauce (p. 178)*
4 *flour tortillas, 12 inches in diameter*

BURRITOS DE CHILE VERDE ESTILO ENCHILADA

Green Chile Burritos, Enchilada Style

Make burritos as above and cover them with either of the green chile enchilada sauces; then add some grated Monterey Jack cheese. Place them on a rack about 4 to 6 inches under a broiler, and heat them until the sauce is bubbling and the cheese is melted, about 3 to 5 minutes. *Serves 4.*

BURRITOS DE CARNE ADOVADA

Carne Adovada Burritos

4 *flour tortillas, 12 inches in diameter*

1 *recipe* **Carne adovada de antes** *or* **Carne adovada de hoy** *(p. 246 or p. 247)*

1 *cup mild cheddar cheese, grated*

You can make these using either of the *carne adovada* recipes. They are also delicious with New Mexico-style Chile con Carne (p. 156).

Heat both the tortillas and the *carne adovada*. Place about ½ cup to ¾ cup of *carne adovada* on each tortilla, top it with ¼ cup of the cheese, and roll it up as instructed on p. 232. Serve immediately. *Serves 4.*

BURRITOS DE CARNE ADOVADA ESTILO ENCHILADA

Carne Adovada Burritos, Enchilada Style

Make *Burritos de carne adovada* as above and cover them with either the Basic New Mexico Chile Sauce with Whole Chiles (p. 166), Basic New Mexico Chile Sauce with Chile Powder (p. 167), or Basic New Mexico Chile Sauce with Pork (p. 168). For a really meaty version top them with New Mexico-style Chile con Carne (p. 156) and additional grated cheese, and place them 4 to 6 inches under your broiler. Cook them until the sauce is bubbling and the cheese is melted, about 3 to 5 minutes. *Serves 4.*

Burritos con Frijoles y Queso

Bean and Cheese Burritos

You can make this simple southwestern favorite using Refried Beans and cheese, but why not make it special by using the Black Bean Dip appetizer as a filling.

Heat the Refried Beans or Black Bean Dip.

Soften the tortillas and either spoon on some Refried Beans and cheddar cheese or an appropriate amount of the Black Bean Dip. Add some lettuce and tomato, roll, and serve. *Serves 4.*

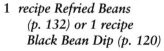

1 *recipe Refried Beans (p. 132) or 1 recipe Black Bean Dip (p. 120)*

4 *flour tortillas, 12 inches in diameter*

1½ *cups mild cheddar cheese, grated (if using Refried Beans)*

1½ *cups lettuce, shredded (optional)*

2 *tomatoes, chopped (optional)*

Burritos de Carne Guisada

Carne Guisada Burritos

Burritos are not very common in Tex-Mex cooking, but when you do find one it is usually this or a similar recipe.

Peel the potatoes, cut them into 1-inch pieces, and boil them until they are just soft.

Stir the potatoes into the *Carne guisada*, bring to a boil, and simmer for 5 minutes.

Soften the tortillas by heating them on an ungreased *comal* or griddle. Mound some of the *Carne guisada* and potato mixture onto the tortillas, wrap them, and serve. *Serves 4.*

2 *potatoes*

1 *recipe Carne guisada (p. 258)*

4 *flour tortillas, 12 inches in diameter*

BURRITOS PARA DESAYUNO

Breakfast Burritos

4 *flour tortillas, 12 inches in diameter*
4 *pieces bacon, chopped*
1 *large potato, chopped*
1 *recipe* Picadillo *III (p. 150)*
4 *eggs, lightly beaten*
1 *cup mild cheddar or Monterey Jack cheese, grated*
  Salsa

These make a terrific brunch entrée.

Soften the tortillas and wrap them in a towel to keep them hot.

Heat a large skillet over medium heat, add the bacon, and fry until most of the fat has been released. Add the potatoes and fry them until they are nearly tender. (You may have to add additional fat.)

Add the *Picadillo* III and cook, stirring constantly, until it is browned.

Add the eggs and cook, stirring constantly, until they are well set.

Place approximately ½ cup to ¾ cup of the filling in each tortilla and top with the cheese; then fold them as instructed on p. 232. Serve them immediately with your favorite salsa on the side. *Serves 4.*

FAVORITE CHIMICHANGAS

Any of the above burritos make fine *chimichangas*, especially when served enchilada style. However, in my opinion, the following recipe stands well above the rest.

CHIMICHANGAS DE MACHACA ESPECIAL

Deluxe Machaca Chimichangas

This is one of my favorite Mexican-American recipes and, for me, one of the chief treats of a visit to Tucson, Arizona.

Heat oil in a deep fryer to 350 degrees.

Soften the tortillas as instructed on p. 232.

Place approximately ½ to ¾ cup of the *Machaca* on each tortilla; then top each with ¼ cup cheese (reserve the remaining cup of cheese for the final topping), ¼ cup green chile, 1 tablespoon pickled *jalapeños,* and roll it up.

Meanwhile, bring the chile sauce to a simmer.

Fry the burritos one at a time until they are a crispy golden brown. Quickly drain the *chimichangas* and place them on individual serving plates.

Cover the *chimichangas* with the chile sauce, sprinkle with the remaining cheese, and then top each *chimichanga* with ¼ cup of sour cream. Garnish the plates with the lettuce and tomato and serve immediately. *Serves 4.*

4 *flour tortillas, 12 inches in diameter*

1 *recipe* Machaca *(p. 156)*

2 *cups mild cheddar cheese, grated*

1 *cup green chile, peeled, seeded, and chopped*

¼ *cup pickled* jalapeño *chiles, seeded and minced*

1 *recipe Basic New Mexico Chile Sauce with Whole Chiles (p. 166) or Basic New Mexico Chile Sauce with Chile Powder (p. 167)*

1 *cup sour cream*
  Shredded lettuce and chopped tomato for garnish

NOTE: If your deep fryer takes a long time to recover, you may want to place the first 2 or 3 *chimichangas* under the broiler for a few minutes to ensure they are hot after adding the sauce and cheese (but before adding the sour cream and garnish).

CHIMICHANGAS DE CARNE DE RES

Shredded Beef Chimichangas

4 *flour tortillas, 12 inches in diameter*

1 *recipe Shredded Beef (p. 154)*

4 *avocados, skinned and seeded*

1 *cup sour cream*

2 *pickled* jalapeño *chiles, seeded and minced*

2 *tablespoons vinegar from* jalapeño *can*

¼ *cup cilantro, minced*

Soften the tortillas as instructed on p. 232 and wrap them in a towel to keep them warm.

Place approximately ½ cup to ¾ cup of Shredded Beef on each tortilla.

Chop 2 of the avocados and apportion them equally on top of the Shredded Beef.

Fold the tortillas and fry them as directed in the preceding recipe (p. 237).

Meanwhile, mash the remaining 2 avocados; then stir in the remaining ingredients to make a thick, smooth sauce. A food processor makes quick work of this task.

Place the cooked *chimichangas* on individual serving plates and top them with the avocado sauce. *Serves 4.*

CHILES RELLENOS

In Mexico *Chiles rellenos* are made with large *poblano* chiles and filled with a sweet *picadillo* more often than with cheese. This recipe uses the Anaheim or New Mexico green chile, which is longer and narrower, and a cheese filling which is far more common in Mexican-American cooking. Because of its flatter, thinner shape this type of chile can be cooked with less oil, which simplifies the process and makes it less messy. In fact, these can be cooked with no more than a film of oil on the skillet if you complete the cooking process by baking the chiles. The result will not be as thickly covered with batter, but it will more resemble the home-style southwestern version of this Mexican favorite.

Chiles rellenos can be prepared several hours ahead and reheated in the oven. In fact, there is a lady in a small village in northern Mexico that I often visit who makes *Chiles rellenos* every Sunday morning. People stop by during the day, take them home, and reheat them. They are delicious!

To make the sauce, first blend the tomatoes to a thick puree. Then heat the olive oil in a saucepan over moderate heat, add the garlic, and fry for about 30 seconds; add the tomatoes and salt and cook until the sauce has thickened, about 15 to 20 minutes.

To prepare the chiles, first peel them (see instructions on peeling chiles, pp. 36–37). Be sure to leave the stems on and slit them on one side only to remove the seeds.

Put the cheese strips inside the chiles and fold them together. Dredge the filled chiles in flour and shake off the excess.

Beat the egg yolks for about 1 minute. Place the egg whites in a separate bowl, add the salt, and beat them until they hold stiff peaks. Fold the whites carefully into the yolks.

Heat a skillet over medium to medium-high heat and put in the cooking oil. If you are only going to add a film of oil, heat the pan over medium heat and preheat your oven to 350 degrees. If you are going to use more oil (½ inch is enough), use medium-high heat. The oil is the right temperature when a small drop of water sputters instantly, but a little trial and error is the best guide. When the oil is hot, dip the chiles in the batter and place them carefully in the pan. Fry the chiles, one at a time, until the bottoms are firm and brown. Turn the chiles and fry them on the other side.

Remove the chiles from the pan and drain on absorbent towels. If you used the lesser amount of oil, the batter will not be completely fried. Place them in the oven and bake them for 10 minutes. To serve, spoon some of the sauce on each of 4 serving plates and place the chiles on top of it. *Serves 4.*

THE SAUCE:

1¼ *pounds tomatoes, peeled, seeded, and chopped*
2 *tablespoons olive oil*
2 *cloves garlic, minced*
½ *teaspoon salt, or to taste*

THE CHILES:

8 *Anaheim or New Mexico green chiles*
8 *⅓-inch strips of Monterey Jack or mild cheddar cheese long enough to fit your chiles*
  Flour for dredging
3 *eggs, separated*
½ *teaspoon salt*
  Cooking oil

CHILAQUILES

Chilaquiles is one of the world's ultimate leftover dishes. Usually served at breakfast, but occasionally as a side dish with an entrée, *Chilaquiles* is made from leftover corn tortilla chips, cooked meats or poultry, and cheese.

If you have no leftover chips, simply make some by frying corn tortillas (the older and dryer the better) cut into strips about ½ inch by 2 inches, until crisp. Place the chips in a baking pan or medium-size ovenproof dish, pour a chile or enchilada sauce over them, and top with *picadillo*, shredded filling, ham or cooked bacon, and cheese. Heat the *Chilaquiles* by placing the dish in an oven preheated to 350 degrees until the cheese is melted and the sauce is bubbling, 10 to 15 minutes.

At breakfast *Chilaquiles* are often served with fried or scrambled eggs in the manner in which we serve hashed brown potatoes. They are also delicious as an accompaniment to broiled or fried meats and as part of a combination plate.

CHILAQUILES DE POLLO Y SALSA VERDE

Chilaquiles with Chicken and Tomatillo Sauce

12 *corn tortillas*
1 *recipe* Tomatillo *Sauce (p. 116), approximately 2 cups*
  Oil for deep-frying
1 *cup Shredded Chicken or Turkey (p. 158)*
½ *pound mild cheddar cheese, grated*
½ *cup sour cream*

This version of *chilaquiles* is one that is popular in both Mexican and Mexican-American cooking.

Cut the tortillas into strips about ½ inch by 2 inches and deep-fry them at 375 degrees until they are golden brown and crisp. Remove the fried tortillas to drain on absorbent towels.

Place the tortilla chips, the turkey or chicken, and the cheese in a bowl and mix well. Add and stir in the *Tomatillo* Sauce; then pour the contents of the bowl into a 9- or 10-inch iron skillet (one that can be placed in an oven) or a baking pan of similar size. Bake the *chilaquiles* in the oven for 10 to 15 minutes or until the sauce is bubbling and the cheese is melted.

Serve the *chilaquiles* for breakfast with refried beans or as part of a combination plate. *Serves 4.*

CHILAQUILES ESTILO CALIFORNIA

Chilaquiles California Style

This very simple and earthy dish was popular in early California as a ranch breakfast.

Cut the tortillas into strips about ½ inch by 2 inches and deep-fry them at 375 degrees until they are golden brown and crisp. Remove the fried tortillas to drain on absorbent towels.

Heat the lard or olive oil in a skillet over medium to medium-high heat, add the onions, and sauté them until they are quite brown but not burned.

Place the tortilla chips, the fried onion, olives, and cheese in a bowl and mix well. Add and stir in the red chile sauce; then pour the contents of the bowl into a 9- to 10-inch iron skillet (one that can be placed in an oven) or a baking pan of similar size.

Bake the *chilaquiles* in the oven for 10 to 15 minutes or until the sauce is bubbling and the cheese is melted.

For the feeling of a ranch breakfast, serve the *chilaquiles* by placing the skillet in which they were baked on the table using a trivet or other device to keep from scorching it. Add another skillet of Refried Beans (p. 132) and perhaps a bowl of rice, and allow the diners to help themselves. *Serves 4.*

12 *corn tortillas*
    Oil for deep-frying
2 *tablespoons lard or olive oil*
3 *cups onions, chopped*
1 *cup black California olives, minced*
½ *pound mild cheddar cheese, grated*
1 *recipe Basic New Mexico Chile Sauce with Whole Chiles (p. 166) or Basic New Mexico Chile Sauce with Chile Powder (p. 167), approximately 2 cups*

MISCELLANEOUS SNACKS

GORDITAS
Little Fat Ones

2 *cups Masa Harina*
½ *teaspoon salt*
¾ *teaspoon baking powder*
1⅓ *cups water*
   Cooking oil
1¾ *cups of your favorite*
   picadillo or shredded
   meat filling
   Shredded lettuce, grated
   cheddar cheese, and
   chopped tomato for
   garnish

Gorditas come in all sizes and are made from many types of dough, some containing flour as well as the *masa*, and others in which lard has been incorporated. Some are cooked on an ungreased *comal* and some are deep-fried. My favorite recipe for *Gorditas* employs both cooking methods. Choose your favorite filling from among the *picadillos* and shredded meats in the chapter on "Basic Fillings" (p. 147). And remember that, as with other fried foods, some experimentation is required to achieve the correct temperature and timing for making the best *Gorditas*, but they are worth the effort.

To make the dough, combine the Masa Harina, salt, and baking powder; then mix in the water. (A food processor fitted with a steel blade makes this task easier.) Form the dough into a firm ball; then allow it to rest, covered, for about 30 minutes. Divide the dough into 8 pieces; then using waxed paper as a work surface, pat each piece of dough into a circle about 3 to 3½ inches in diameter and about ¼ inch thick.

Heat a *comal* or heavy iron skillet over medium to medium-low heat. Also, heat about ⅓ inch oil in a small skillet until a drop of water spatters instantly.

Place the formed *Gorditas* on the *comal* or skillet and cook, turning once or twice, until they just begin to brown and the dough is nearly cooked through. Next, place the *Gorditas* in the hot oil and cook them until they are cooked through and slightly puffed; then remove them to drain on paper towels. When the *Gorditas* are cool enough to handle, split them like pita bread, stuff them with the filling, and garnish them with the shredded lettuce, grated cheddar cheese, and chopped tomato. *Makes 8 to serve 4.*

ATOLE

This Indian version of Cream of Wheat goes back to pre-Columbian times; yet it is still popular in Mexican-American households at breakfast time. Delicious and earthy when made the original way with water, this version with milk is even tastier. For the drink recipe see the chapter on "Drinks" (p. 95).

½ cup Masa Harina
2⅔ cups milk
¼ cup brown sugar
1 teaspoon cinnamon

Put the Masa Harina in a bowl and gradually whisk in the milk.

Pour the milk mixture into a pot, add the brown sugar and cinnamon, and bring to a boil. Turn down the heat and simmer the *Atole* for 5 minutes, stirring constantly. It will thicken to the consistency of Cream of Wheat. *Serves 4.*

STUFFED SOPAIPILLAS

This is New Mexico's answer to the enchilada-style burrito, and it is a good one. Hot *sopaipillas* are stuffed, then topped with chile sauce and cheese and served piping hot. My favorite filling is equal quantities of whole pinto beans prepared as for *Frijoles de olla* (p. 130), but drained of juice, Spanish Rice (p. 128), and *Picadillo* II (p. 149).

4 large sopaipillas, *freshly prepared* (p. 105)
2 cups of your favorite filling (see left or the chapter on "Basic Fillings," p. 147)
1 recipe of your favorite New Mexico red chile sauce (see the chapter on "Red Chile 'Master' Sauces," p. 159)
¾ cup cheddar cheese, grated

Preheat your oven to 350 degrees.

Cut a slit down one side of each *sopaipilla*, stuff them with some of the filling, and then place them on ovenproof serving plates. Top the *sopaipillas* with the chile sauce, sprinkle on some cheese, and then bake them at 350 degrees for 10 minutes or until the cheese is melted and the sauce is bubbling. *Serves 4.*

Platos Principales
ENTRÉES

In the past when most *norteamericanos* thought of Mexican food, it was usually the items that make up the Number 1 combination plate and other *antojitos* that came to mind. For most, that is probably still the case. However, as new urban restaurants are being established that specialize in interior Mexican dishes people are beginning to discover entrées such as *Mole poblano* and other aspects of this complex cuisine. Although many of these recipes carried over into Mexican-American cooking as did some of the more Spanish dishes such as *Bacalao*, they were not the staples of Mexican-American households. The cost, time required for preparation, and the difficulty of obtaining ingredients meant that such dishes were only cooked for special occasions when the extra time and expense could be justified. Also, greatly simplified versions of the grand Mexican and Spanish dishes were created based upon economic circumstances and the availability of ingredients.

Stews in particular epitomize Mexican-American home cooking. They are nutritious and easy to prepare in large quantities. Except for the more common chiles and *menudo*, these items are rarely served in restaurants. It is the same in Mexico, where many of the best dishes never make it to restaurant menus.

244

STEWS

CARNE ADOVADA

A specialty of New Mexico, *carne adovada* has changed considerably over the years. Originally used to preserve pork, the recipe is now a restaurant staple that is served as a filling for burritos as often as an entrée. Actually, the word *adovada* comes from the Spanish *adobada*, which means pickled. (Also based on *adobada* are the more familiar *adobo* sauces.) Although the sauce's original purpose was to preserve pork, in recent times *carne adovada* has evolved into a thick stew that is often difficult to distinguish from New Mexico-style Chile con Carne.

I am presenting two recipes for *carne adovada*; the first, *Carne adovada de antes*, re-creates the flavor and texture of the original dish, and the other, *Carne adovada de hoy*, presents an excellent example of the dish in its current incarnation. While *Carne adovada de antes* is fine as an entrée dish, it is even better as a filling for burritos or *chimichangas*.

NUTRITION HINT: *Carne adovada* is most often made with pork loin or pork shoulder, with the loin cuts being the least fatty. If fat is a significant dietary consideration, feel free to substitute pork tenderloin, which is nearly as low in fat as a boneless chicken breast. If you do this, I suggest you add a little olive oil and/or reduce the cooking times by about 25 percent in order to prevent dryness.

CARNE ADOVADA DE ANTES

Old-style Carne Adovada

This dish can be made using either whole New Mexico-style dried chiles or chile powder made from them. I think the chile powder version is somewhat better because the water necessary to emulsify the whole chiles makes the result a little too "steamy" and watery.

If you are using whole chiles, first rinse and toast them in an oven preheated to 275 degrees for 5 to 10 minutes, but do not allow them to burn. Next, remove the stems, seeds, and as many of the veins as possible; then cover the chiles with boiling water and soak them for at least 15 minutes.

Put all the ingredients in a blender and blend to a thick paste. The best way to do this is to blend first in short bursts, then for longer intervals, using the pulse feature, until the ingredients are well combined.

If you must add additional water, only use the minimum required to complete the mixture.

Combine the meat with the onion and chile paste and refrigerate, covered, for 2 to 3 days.

To cook, place the marinated pork in an oven preheated to 325 degrees, add ¼ cup water, and bake, covered, for 1 hour. Since the cooking pot should be as airtight as possible I suggest you use a layer of foil under its regular top.

Serve as a filling for burritos or tacos. *Serves 4.*

THE MARINADE:

3   dried New Mexico chiles or
    3 tablespoons New
    Mexico chile
    powder
½   cup onion, chopped
3   cloves garlic
½   teaspoon oregano
1   tablespoon vinegar
2   teaspoons honey or sugar
½   teaspoon salt
¼   teaspoon dried bay leaf,
    crumbled
½   cup water

THE MEAT:

2   pounds pork loin, cut into
    ¾–1-inch chunks
1   onion, chopped

CARNE ADOVADA DE HOY

"Modern" Carne Adovada

First, rinse and toast the chiles in an oven preheated to 275 degrees for 5 to 10 minutes, making sure not to allow the chiles to scorch. Next, remove the stems, seeds, and as many of the veins as possible and cover the chiles with boiling water for at least 15 minutes.

Place the chiles and remaining sauce ingredients in a blender and blend for 1 minute.

Toss the pork, onion, and bay leaves with the sauce and marinate, covered, in the refrigerator for 24 hours.

Place the pork mixture in an oven preheated to 300 degrees and cook, tightly covered (a secure layer of foil in addition to the cooking pot's top is recommended), for 3 hours and 15 minutes.

Serve with beans and/or *posole* or use as a filling for burritos. *Serves 4.*

FOR THE SAUCE:

- **15** *dried New Mexico chiles*
- **1** *cup onion, chopped*
- **4** *cloves garlic, minced*
- **2** *teaspoons oregano*
- **1½** *teaspoons salt*
- **2** *tablespoons vinegar*

THE MEAT:

- **2** *pounds pork loin, cut in ¾–1-inch pieces*
- **1** *onion, chopped*
- **2** *bay leaves*

POSOLE

Hominy

Posole, usually spelled *pozole* in Mexico, is nothing more than the dried corn kernel that has been cooked with unslaked lime. It is what we call hominy and what is ground to make tortillas.

While *posole* can be found throughout Mexican-American cooking, it is by far most popular and reaches its greatest heights in New Mexico. There it is served as everything from a side dish, with or in place of beans or rice, to a main entrée stew. The former has usually only enough meat in it for flavor, in the manner salt pork is used with beans, but the latter is often brimming with flavorful cuts of meat, simmering with spices and chiles. Pork is most often the choice, but in far northern New Mexico, particularly where Navajo cooking influenced the cuisine, lamb is the usual main ingredient. In Mexico *posole* is usually served as a rich soup. While I have had it in this form in New Mexico, most often their versions have a thicker, more stew-like consistency.

Posole, like New Mexico's tortillas, comes in white, yellow, and blue varieties. White *posole* is most often the choice for use in side dishes, probably because its color contrasts nicely with the red and green of the chile sauces. However, to me, the blue variety, especially when combined with lamb, epitomizes the earthy strength and individuality of northern New Mexican cooking.

While canned hominy can be used in place of the homemade variety, it is far from a perfect substitute. Although the flavor is fairly good, it lacks the texture of the real thing. Fortunately, dried *posole*, including the blue corn variety, can be easily obtained through mail-order sources (see the Appendix).

POSOLE CON CHILE COLORADO
Posole with Red Chile

This *posole* dish is cooked exactly like the dish on p. 250 except that 1) yellow or white *posole* is used in place of the blue *posole*, 2) pork shoulder or loin (without the flour coating) is used instead of the lamb, and 3) 2 to 4 dried New Mexico red chiles, broken or processed into very small pieces, are used instead of the green chiles. *Serves 4.*

CHICOS

While *posole* is made from corn that has been soaked in lime and peeled, *chicos* are made from corn that has been dried and steamed or roasted. Traditionally, the ears of corn are dried then roasted in the beehive-shaped *hornos* found behind northern New Mexican houses. Today, however, some manufacturers use ovens or a steam process to "roast" the *chicos*. I watched them made the old way at Rancho Casados farm outside of Española, New Mexico, and I can understand why shortcuts are taken. The process is somewhat long and tedious, but the resulting flavor from the smoke is worth it. *Chicos* have a slightly crunchier texture than *posole*, and the flavor, while subtle, is slightly nutty with just a hint of smoke.

The most traditional recipes combine *chicos* with pork and red chile so follow the recipe for *Posole* with Red Chile, substituting *chicos* for the *posole*. *Chicos* can also be substituted for *posole* in any of the other *posole* recipes.

ESTOFADO DE CORDERO Y POSOLE AZUL

Blue Corn Posole and Lamb Stew

1¼ *cups blue corn* posole

3 *tablespoons flour*

2 *pounds lean lamb stew meat, cut into 1-inch pieces*

½ *cup olive oil*

1 *cup onions, chopped*

2 *cups Anaheim or New Mexico chiles, peeled, seeded, and chopped*

4 *cloves garlic*

1 *teaspoon oregano*

½ *teaspoon whole cumin*

1 *teaspoon salt*

4½ *cups water*

This stew, full of the strong flavors of lamb and green chiles, was often the choice for holidays and special occasions when extra quantities of meat could be justified.

Soak the *posole* overnight. In the morning drain and discard the soaking water. Place the *posole* in a pot and cover it with water by about 3 inches. Bring the water to a boil, then simmer, partially covered, until the *posole* is tender, about 45 minutes to 1 hour. Remove the *posole* from the heat and reserve it and 1 cup of its cooking water.

Place the flour and lamb in a bag and shake it to coat the meat. Remove the meat and shake off any excess flour.

Heat a heavy pot or Dutch oven over medium-high heat. Add 6 tablespoons of the olive oil and when it is hot, add the dredged lamb. (You may wish to brown the lamb in 2 batches to ensure that the temperature of the oil remains high enough.) Cook the lamb, stirring continuously, until it is well browned; then remove it to drain, discarding any oil remaining in the pot.

Replace the pot on the stove and turn the heat to moderate. Add the remaining 2 tablespoons olive oil, then the onions. Cook the onions until they are just beginning to soften; then add the green chiles and continue to cook for 2 minutes.

Meanwhile, grind the garlic, oregano, and cumin to a paste in a *molcajete* or mortar and pestle and add to the pot with the salt.

Stir the ingredients briefly; then add the reserved *posole*, its cooking water, and the 4½ cups water. Bring the stew to a boil, then simmer, covered, for 45 minutes.

Remove the top of the pot and stir the stew. There should be quite a bit of liquid left. If not, add some additional water.

Turn the heat to medium high; then cook the stew at a rapid boil until the liquid is reduced to a medium-thick sauce. This rapid cooking not only causes the liquid to evaporate, but also causes the chiles and onions to fully combine with it, creating a natural thickening process.

Serve the stew, or better yet allow it to sit, refrigerated, overnight to allow the flavors to fully develop, then reheat it and serve it. *Serves 4.*

QUICK POSOLE

Despite the ease of this recipe's preparation and the fact that its ingredients include garlic and onion powders, it is very good. In fact, it is one of those recipes that defies the adage "no pain, no gain." More of a soup than a thickened stew, it makes a fine first course or light supper on a cold night when more elaborate dishes seem daunting.

Heat a pot over moderate heat, add the olive oil and the ground beef, and fry until the meat is browned.

Add the garlic powder, garlic salt, onion powder, oregano, and chile powder and stir to mix well into the meat.

Add the hominy and the broth or water, bring to a boil, and simmer for 15 minutes.

Serve in soup bowls. *Serves 4.*

1 *tablespoon olive oil*
½ *pound lean ground beef*
¼ *teaspoon garlic powder*
¼ *teaspoon garlic salt*
½ *teaspoon onion powder*
½ *teaspoon oregano*
2 *teaspoons hot New Mexico chile powder*
2 *16-ounce cans hominy, strained and rinsed*
5 *cups mild beef broth or water*

POSOLE Y FRIJOLES

Hominy and Beans

¼ cup lard or olive oil

2 cloves garlic, minced

1 teaspoon oregano

1½ cups Frijoles de olla
(p. 130) made with pink
beans, drained with
broth reserved

1½ cups cooked or canned
hominy

½ teaspoon salt, or to taste

In early California cooked beans and *posole* were often mixed and fried in the manner of refried beans.

Heat a skillet over moderate heat, add the lard or olive oil, and when it is hot add the garlic, oregano, beans, and hominy. Cook for 1 minute; then add the salt and enough of the reserved bean broth to make a soupy mixture. Continue to cook until the liquid has thickened. *Serves 4.*

GUISADO DE GARBANZOS

Garbanzo Bean Stew

1 cup garbanzo beans

2 tablespoons lard or olive
oil

¼ pound ham, cut into bite-
size pieces

¼ pound bulk chorizo

¼ pound bacon, chopped

2 cups onions, chopped

2 cloves garlic, minced

1 pound boneless pork loin,
cut into bite-size pieces

1 14½-ounce can tomatoes

½ tablespoon oregano

½ teaspoon ground pepper

½ teaspoon salt, or to taste

Garbanzo beans, or chickpeas as they are often called, are one of those items that are very popular in traditional Mexican-American home-style cooking but which have never made it to restaurant menus. This stew recipe is rich and delicious, a perfect foil for a cold winter's night beside a fireplace in a cozy adobe.

Soak the beans overnight. Rinse the beans, place them in a large pot or Dutch oven, cover with 3 inches of water, bring to a boil, and simmer for 30 minutes.

In a similar pot melt the lard or add the olive oil over medium heat. Add the ham, *chorizo*, bacon, onions, and garlic and cook, stirring often, until the meats are browned and the onion is soft.

Add the pork and continue cooking just until it is browned. Add the remaining ingredients, including the precooked beans with enough water to cover everything in the pot, and simmer, covered, for 45 minutes or until the beans are done and the pork is tender. *Serves 4.*

GUISO DE CHOCOLATE

Chocolate Stew

This dish is interesting not just because of its unique taste but also because it is a very simplified, Mexican-American version of a Mexican *mole*. Comparison with the more elaborate original shows how many of our favorite southwestern dishes evolved.

Heat a large stewpot or Dutch oven over medium-high heat. Add and heat the lard or olive oil; then add and brown the meat, stirring constantly.

Turn the heat to medium, add the garlic, chiles, and onion and continue cooking for 1 minute, stirring constantly.

Add enough water to cover the stew by 2 inches; then stir in the remaining ingredients except the chocolate. Bring the water to a boil, then cover and simmer the stew for 1¾ hours or until the meat is tender. Be sure and check the stew about every 15 minutes to make sure you have enough water to just barely cover the ingredients.

When the meat is tender, add the chocolate and continue simmering until most of the liquid has evaporated and the stew has thickened. Serve with rice and corn tortillas. *Serves 4.*

¼ *cup lard or olive oil*

2 *pounds lean stew meat, cut into ½–¾-inch pieces*

2 *cloves garlic, minced*

2 **ancho** *chiles, stemmed, seeded, and chopped*

½ *cup onion, chopped*

1 *cup canned tomatoes, drained, seeded, and chopped*

½ *teaspoon cinnamon*

¼ *teaspoon cloves*

2 *tablespoons sugar*

1 *teaspoon salt, or to taste*

½ *teaspoon ground pepper*

1 *ounce semisweet chocolate*

CHILE CON CARNE ESTILO TEX-MEX
Tex-Mex Chile

4 ancho *chiles or 4*
    tablespoons ancho
    chile powder

5 *cups water*

6 *cloves garlic, peeled*

1 *teaspoon oregano*

¼ *cup cooking oil*

12 *ounces chile-grind beef*

2½ *tablespoons ground*
    cumin

½ *cup tomato puree*

½ *teaspoon salt, or to taste*
    Roux made with 3
    tablespoons oil and ⅓
    cup flour

"Texas-style" chile is not the type of chile which has, in recent years, been popularized in a neverending string of chile cookoffs. Instead, it is the simple and probably original Texas chile that is still prepared in *tejano* households and restaurants in much of the state.

This dish is somewhere between a stew and a soup in consistency since the maximum amount of liquid is used to "stretch" the meat. But this is what gives the chile its special flavor and texture. Using more meat or less liquid changes the entire effect. It is properly made with chile-grind beef, which is a much coarser grind than regular ground beef. If this is not available, you can make it yourself by whirling lean stew meat cut into small pieces a few times in a food processor fitted with a steel blade. Other alternatives are to use the small pieces without the processing or, as a last resort, ordinary ground beef.

Gauging the amount of liquid in the dish without taking everything out of the pot and measuring it is difficult, but important to this recipe. Although a little unconventional, the simple method suggested works well.

First, prepare the chiles. If you are using whole chiles, remove their stems and seeds, then soak them in hot water for 15 minutes. Place the chiles in a blender. If you are using chile powder, place it in the blender. Add 1 cup of water, the garlic, and the oregano to the blender and blend for 1 minute. Add 2 more cups of water and blend a few seconds to mix well. If you used whole chiles, strain the mixture.

Heat a heavy pot or Dutch oven over medium-high heat, add the oil, and when it is hot add and brown the beef. It is best to do this in 2 batches. After the meat has been browned strain off the excess oil and return the meat to the pot.

Turn the heat to low and add the chile mixture from the blender; then add the cumin, tomato puree, and salt.

At this point you need to remember how high up the sides of the pot the liquid comes since you want to maintain this level throughout the cooking process. I usually measure the distance from the top of the pot to the liquid's surface with an old wooden chopstick and mark it at the appropriate place.

Simmer the chile, covered, for 1 hour and 40 minutes. Check the chile to make sure it is at the same level at which you started; then stir in about half the roux. Continue simmering the chile, uncovered, for an additional 20 minutes, stirring often to keep it from sticking as it thickens. It should be well thickened; if it isn't, add a little more of the roux.

Serve the chile in bowls topped with some grated cheddar cheese, over rice, or use it as an extra-thick enchilada sauce. *Serves 4.*

CHILE CON CARNE ESTILO NUEVO MÉXICO
New Mexico-style Chile con Carne

10–12   *mild New Mexico
          dried chiles, about
          3½–4 ounces*

5   *cups water*

8–10   *cloves garlic, peeled*

1   *tablespoon whole
      oregano*

¼   *cup olive oil*

2   *pounds very lean pork
      loin, cut into ½-inch
      pieces*

2   *tablespoons cider
      vinegar*

3   *bay leaves*

¾   *teaspoon salt, or to
      taste*

    *Roux made with 1
     tablespoon plus 1
     teaspoon oil and 2
     tablespoons flour*

1   *cup mild cheddar or
      Monterey Jack
      cheese, grated*

In old cookbooks chile con carne is often called *carne con chile*. I'm not exactly sure of the difference unless "chile with meat" means there is more chile than meat and "meat with chile" the opposite. Despite this, for both this recipe and the Texas chile recipes I've used the current, more familiar name.

By any name these dishes are the simplest and best of all the chile-based stews that have become part of southwestern culture. Try the Texas-style chile based upon beef and *ancho* chiles and the following New Mexican standby, which relies on pork and local New Mexico chiles. Whether one style or the other becomes your favorite or you create your own combining aspects of both, you will have learned a great deal about the region's cooking, not to mention having enjoyed some excellent, traditional meals.

This recipe is one of my all-time favorites. It evokes, as do some of the *posole* recipes, the crisp, cold, dry nights of northern New Mexico's winters.

Rinse the chiles; then toast them by placing them in an oven pre-heated to 275 degrees for about 5 minutes, making sure not to let them scorch. Remove the chiles, allow to them cool, and then remove the stems and most of the veins and seeds.

Place the chiles in a bowl, cover them with boiling water, and allow them to soak for at least 15 minutes. After soaking, place the chiles in a blender with 2½ cups of the soaking water and blend for 1 minute. Add the remaining 2½ cups water, blend briefly to mix, then strain into a bowl using a sieve or food mill.

Grind the garlic and oregano into a paste using a *molcajete* or mortar and pestle.

In a Dutch oven or other heavy pot, heat the olive oil over medium-high to high heat until it just begins to smoke. Add the meat and cook, stirring constantly, until it is well browned. To ensure that the meat is well browned, this should be done in 2 batches, unless you are using a very large pot.

Pour off any excess oil, add the chile puree, vinegar, bay leaves, garlic-oregano paste, and salt and bring to a boil. Cover the pot and simmer, checking every so often until the meat is very tender, about 45 minutes. This dish is easily ruined by scorching so check often and lower the heat, as necessary. If the sauce becomes too thick, add additional water.

Meanwhile, make the roux: Heat the oil in a small saucepan over medium-low heat, add the flour, and cook, stirring constantly, until the mixture just begins to brown and give off a nutty aroma. Do not allow it to burn.

When the meat is tender, remove the lid of the pot, take out the bay leaves, turn the heat up, and continue to simmer until the sauce begins to thicken, about 10 to 15 minutes. When the chile is properly cooked, you will notice a rich sheen form on the top as the oil is released. At this point you should add just enough of the roux to "bind" the dish and continue cooking for 5 minutes.

Serve the chile garnished with the cheese. This chile is often served with beans and rice, or alone with flour tortillas as is *Carne adovada de hoy* (p. 247), which it resembles.

I must confess that, untraditional as it is, my favorite way of serving this dish is over plain steamed rice, garnished with cheddar cheese. *Serves 4.*

NUTRITION HINT: If you make this dish with well-trimmed pork loin, one of the leanest cuts of meat, strain off all the excess oil, and omit the roux, it will be reasonably low in fat. Serve it with a low-fat cheese or none at all.

CARNE GUISADA
Beef Stew

2 *tablespoons cooking oil*

2 *pounds very lean beef stew meat, cut into 1-inch chunks*

½ *medium onion, diced*

½ *medium bell pepper, diced*

1 *medium tomato, diced*

1 *tablespoon garlic powder*

1 *teaspoon ground cumin*

2 *tablespoons tomato puree*

1 *bay leaf*

2 *tablespoons mild picante sauce*

Salt and pepper to taste

Roux, made with 1 tablespoon plus 1 teaspoon oil and 2 tablespoons flour

Carne guisada is the typical beef stew of Tex-Mex cooking and is found all over Texas. It is very much like the *guisada mexicana* or *cortadillo* found in Coahuila and Nuevo León. The principal difference is that the Mexican versions are usually hotter and are rarely thickened with flour. The following typical version of *Carne guisada* is from Carlos García, owner of San Antonio's El Chaparral restaurant.

Heat the oil over medium-high heat until it just begins to smoke; add the beef and stir constantly until it is well browned. (At this point the meat will start to release its juices.)

Add the onion and bell pepper, turn the heat to medium, and cook, stirring frequently, until the vegetables are just softened, 2 to 3 minutes. Then stir in the tomato and cook for 1 minute.

Add enough water to cover the meat; then add the remaining ingredients except the roux. Cover the stew and simmer until the meat is very tender. The exact timing will depend on the tenderness of your meat and could range from 1 hour to 1 hour and 45 minutes.

During the cooking, check the meat every 10 minutes and add additional water, if necessary. Bear in mind that when the dish is completed there should be just enough liquid to come about halfway up the meat, and it should be rather thick.

The final step is to add the roux. Add just enough, in 1 teaspoon batches, to give the sauce its final thickening and bind the ingredients together.

Remove the bay leaf and serve with Mexican Rice (p. 126) and Refried Beans (p. 132). *Serves* 4.

MENUDO

Tripe Stew

Menudo is one of the best-known entrée dishes and one of the few entrée dishes made of variety meats commonly served in Mexican-American restaurants. Reputed to be a fine hangover cure, *Menudo* is most often eaten as a late night or early morning meal, especially on weekends.

Menudo is traditionally cooked with a calf's or cow's foot, which helps thicken it rather like jellied consommé. They are usually found in the frozen food section of Hispanic grocery stores. If you cannot find one, feel free to omit it from the recipe. While most tripe sold in the United States has been cleaned, it is prudent to soak it in a vinegar solution to remove any off taste.

Place the tripe in a pottery or nonreactive container, cover it with water, add the vinegar, and soak it for 3 hours.

Remove the tripe and place it in a large pot, add the water, and the calf's foot, if used.

Grind the garlic, cumin, and oregano to a paste in a *molcajete* or mortar and pestle and add it to the mixture along with the chile powder.

Bring the liquid to a boil, partially cover, and simmer until the tripe is tender, 3½ to 4½ hours.

Add the salt and pepper and serve the tripe with its broth in large soup bowls, accompanied by the garnish. *Serves 4.*

2 *pounds tripe, cut into bite-size pieces*
3 *quarts water*
½ *cup vinegar*
1 *calf's foot (optional)*
6 *cloves garlic, minced*
1 *teaspoon cumin*
1 *tablespoon oregano*
2 *teaspoons chile powder*
   Salt and pepper to taste

THE GARNISH:

3 *green onions, minced*
2 *tablespoons dried* pequín *chiles, crumbled*
2 *tablespoons oregano*
½ *cup cilantro, minced*
½ *cup onion, minced*
2 *limes, quartered*

POLLO "CALIENTE"

Hot Chicken

½ cup lard, or substitute olive oil

1 pound potatoes, peeled and chopped into ½-inch pieces

1 bell pepper, chopped

1 jalapeño *chile, minced (optional)*

1 chicken, cut into serving pieces

4 cloves garlic

1 teaspoon cumin

2 cups water

½ teaspoon salt, or to taste

½ teaspoon ground pepper

Vernon Price, an acquaintance of mine, grew up in San Antonio's Mission District and learned to cook from his grandmother. Often showcasing his talents at local parties and weddings, Vernon specializes in game and home-style Mexican-American cooking. The following recipe is a fine example of the latter. The only change I have made to the original instructions is to reduce the total fat. As Vernon says, the food he learned to cook was meant to be inexpensive and filling, and a lot of lard suited both those purposes.

Heat the lard or olive oil in a large heavy pot or Dutch oven over medium to medium-high heat until it is very hot but not smoking. Add the potatoes, bell pepper, and *jalapeño*, if used, and fry the vegetables until they are soft but not browned.

Add the chicken pieces and cook, turning often, until browned.

Meanwhile, grind the garlic and cumin into a paste using a *molcajete* or mortar and pestle, and when the chicken is browned add them to the pot along with the water, salt, and pepper.

Cover the pot, simmer 30 minutes, and serve. *Serves 4.*

CHILE VERDE

Green Chile

Green Chile is popular in both Arizona and New Mexico. In Arizona the dish is usually made of beef and is most often used as a stuffing for burritos. New Mexico's *chiles verdes* are more often eaten as a main dish and are usually made with pork or a combination of beef and pork, but lamb is also often used. Some New Mexico cooks also add potatoes to the dish.

In *El Norte: The Cuisine of Northern Mexico* one of the green chile recipes is made with leftover charbroiled meat. I have since found that all green chiles are very good with meat that has been broiled or roasted. Not only does this seem to improve the flavor, but also greatly shortens the cooking time. If you wish to do this, weigh the meat before the initial broiling or roasting and use it in the following recipes. Where pork and beef are combined, these items can be added simultaneously and the cooking time reduced to about 30 minutes.

CHILE VERDE CON CARNE ESTILO NUEVO MÉXICO

New Mexico-style Green Chile

1   *tablespoon cooking oil*

⅔ *pound lean stew beef, cut into pieces measuring ½ inch or less*

1   *tablespoon olive oil*

1½ *cups onions, finely chopped*

1   *cup green chiles, stemmed, peeled, seeded, and finely chopped*

5   *cloves garlic*

1   *teaspoon oregano*

¼ *teaspoon cumin (optional)*

2½ *cups water*

2½ *tablespoons cooking oil*

1   *pound lean pork, cut into pieces ½ inch or less*

⅓ *pound lean ground lamb*

1   *cup potatoes, peeled and cut into pieces ½ inch or less (optional)*

¾ *teaspoon salt, or to taste*

Roux made with 1 tablespoon oil and 1 tablespoon plus 2 teaspoons flour

This is my favorite version of this recipe, which uses beef, lamb, and pork. If you do not like the flavor of lamb, simply substitute more pork or beef. While many New Mexico cooks do not use cumin, I think just a little adds to the dish.

Heat a large pot or Dutch oven over medium-high heat. Add the oil and when it just begins to smoke, add and brown the beef. Remove the beef and drain off the excess oil.

Turn the heat to medium, add the olive oil, and then cook the onions until they are soft but not browned. Add the green chiles and cook 1 additional minute.

Grind the garlic, oregano, and cumin, if used, to a paste in a *molcajete* or mortar and pestle and add them to the pot.

Return the beef to the pot and add the 2½ cups water. Bring to a boil, cover, and simmer for 45 minutes, checking occasionally to make sure there is enough water and adding more as necessary.

After the first 45 minutes brown the pork and lamb, in a separate pot with the cooking oil, in 2 batches; drain them and add them to the stew.

If you are using the potatoes, add them after rinsing. (The potatoes should be rinsed to remove the excess starch, which, if left on, will give an unpleasant, starchy flavor and texture to the stew.)

Add the salt and additional water to the pot, as necessary. (I usually add about ½ cup.) Bring the stew to a boil, cover, and simmer an additional 45 minutes. Check the stew occasionally to make sure there is enough liquid, adding more as necessary.

Uncover the pot and stir in about half of the roux. Continue to simmer the stew an additional 10 minutes or until it is well thickened, adding additional roux as necessary.

Green Chile, like most stews, is better if allowed to season overnight in the refrigerator, then reheated before serving. In any case, serve the Green Chile in bowls accompanied by flour tortillas or *sopaipillas*, or both. *Serves 4.*

CHILE VERDE ESTILO CALIFORNIA

California-style Green Chile

Almost any old Mexican-American recipe that combines raisins, olives, and often nuts with other ingredients probably originated in California, where these items were abundant. This is a fine dish with the raisins and olives combining with the green chiles to produce a result altogether different from the usual *chile verde.*

Heat the lard or olive oil in a large pot or Dutch oven over medium-high heat and, in 2 batches, brown the beef brisket.

Turn the heat to medium, add the onion, garlic, and green chiles and cook for 2 minutes, stirring constantly.

Add the remaining ingredients except the roux, plus enough water to cover everything in the pot by at least 1 inch.

Bring the liquid to a boil and simmer, covered, for 2 hours. Check the chile every 10 minutes or so and add water, if necessary. The ingredients should always be covered.

Add just a little of the roux and cook, stirring constantly, adding more roux as necessary to thicken the stew. *Serves 4.*

¼ *cup lard or olive oil*

2 *pounds beef brisket, cut into ¾-inch pieces*

1 *onion, chopped*

4 *cloves garlic, minced*

6 *green chiles, peeled, seeded, and chopped*

2 *tomatoes, chopped*

⅓ *cup raisins*

¾ *cup green pitted olives, sliced*

Water

2 *tablespoons vinegar*

½ *teaspoon oregano*

½ *teaspoon marjoram*

½ *teaspoon thyme*

1 *teaspoon salt, or to taste*

½ *teaspoon ground pepper*

Roux made of 1 tablespoon plus 1 teaspoon oil and 2 tablespoons flour

Doc Martin's Award-winning Green Chile

1 *tablespoon cooking oil*

½ *pound ground beef*

½ *pound ground pork*

½ *pound lean roasted beef,*
  cut into ¼-inch pieces

3 *tablespoons butter*

1 *medium onion, diced*

1 *clove garlic, minced*

⅓ *bunch cilantro, chopped*

2 *teaspoons Tabasco sauce*

1 *teaspoon oregano*

2 *teaspoons granulated*
  garlic

1 *teaspoon powdered onion*

2 *teaspoons powdered*
  cumin

1 *teaspoon dried parsley*

½ *teaspoon black pepper*

2 *tablespoons flour*

2 *cups beef stock, chicken*
  stock, or water

1 *Mexican beer*

1⅓ *cups green chiles, peeled,*
  seeded, and diced

1 *tomato, diced*

  Roux made with ¼ cup
  butter and ¼ cup flour

½ *cup Monterey Jack cheese,*
  grated

1 *cup lettuce, chopped*

1 *tomato, chopped*

8 *flour tortillas, heated*

1 *recipe* Sopaipillas *(p. 105)*
  Honey

Although by no means an authentic Mexican or Mexican-American recipe, the following Green Chile served at Doc Martin's, the restaurant at the famous Taos Inn, is simply delicious. When in Taos, New Mexico, I never miss a chance to sample this creation of chef Kathlyn Kolosvary.

I have edited the recipe given to me by the restaurant, mostly in regard to the amount of chile. The original recipe calls for twice as much as I use. In my testing I used Hatch medium-hot chiles, chiles grown in Hatch, New Mexico, which are very similar in heat to those available in most supermarkets. The amount specified here yields a result very similar to that at the restaurant.

Heat a large pot or Dutch oven over medium-high heat. Add the oil and when it just begins to smoke, add and brown the ground beef, ground pork, and roasted beef. Remove the meat and drain off the excess fat.

Turn the heat to medium, add the butter, and when it is melted add and sauté the onion and garlic until the onion is soft but not browned.

Remove the pot from the heat and add the cilantro, Tabasco sauce, oregano, granulated garlic, powdered onion, powdered cumin, parsley, pepper, and flour. Return the pot to the heat and cook, stirring constantly, for about 2 minutes.

Return the meat to the pot and add the stock or water, beer, chiles, and tomato. Bring the liquid to a boil; then add the roux. Simmer the chile, covered, for 45 minutes. Check and stir the chile about every 10 minutes. After 45 minutes remove the cover and continue to simmer, stirring often, for 15 minutes.

Serve the chile topped with the cheese, and with the lettuce, tomato, flour tortillas, *Sopaipillas*, and honey on the side. *Serves 4.*

REPOLLO FRITO

Fried Cabbage

This *Repollo frito* is another of my acquaintance Vernon Price's home-style recipes, and it contains much more than cabbage.

Heat a skillet over medium heat, add the bacon, and fry until it is soft and just beginning to brown.

Add the cabbage and fry it until it is soft, stirring often.

Add the round steak and continue to cook for 2 minutes.

Grind the garlic and cumin to a paste in a *molcajete* or mortar and pestle. Gradually add the can of tomatoes with green chiles to the *molcajete* and grind the mixture together with the garlic and cumin; then add the mixture to the skillet.

Mix the ingredients well, cover the skillet, and cook 20 minutes.

Serve with rice and flour tortillas or just the tortillas. *Serves 4.*

½ *pound bacon, chopped*

1 *head cabbage, cored and chopped*

1 *pound round steak that has been machine tenderized*

4 *cloves garlic*

1½ *teaspoons cumin*

1 *10-ounce can tomatoes with green chiles*

PUCHERO

Stew

1 *pound very lean beef stew meat, cut into ¾–1-inch pieces*
2 *tablespoons olive oil*
  Water
1 *bay leaf*
1 *onion, chopped*
3 *cloves garlic, minced*
2 *ancho chiles, seeded and coarsely chopped*
1 *teaspoon pepper*
1 *stewing chicken, skin removed and cut into serving pieces*
⅓ *pound kielbasa sausage, cut into ½-inch pieces*
2 *potatoes, peeled and chopped into 1½-inch pieces*
2 *carrots, peeled and sliced into ½-inch rounds*
1 *cup corn kernels*
1 *cup green beans, cut into 2-inch lengths*
2 *cups cabbage, chopped*
2 *zucchini, sliced into ½-inch rounds*
½ *teaspoon salt, or to taste*

Puchero, as noted in the quote by Father Juan Caballaria in the chapter "Mexican Food in the Southwest," was a dish often served on the Spanish ranchos of early California. There the cooking maintained closer ties to traditional Spanish cooking than in other regions. In fact, the addition of dried chiles is the only meaningful difference between this and several old Spanish recipes I have seen.

A staple designed to be both nourishing and delicious, *Puchero* was made either as a stew or soup, depending upon how much broth was added to the cooked vegetables and meats when served. With its large number of ingredients and inherent versatility, it is probably the granddaddy of the many different Mexican-American stews and *caldos* that are found in all parts of the Southwest today.

The following is my favorite version of this dish, but be assured that, at one time or another, every common ingredient (and some not so common) in the Southwest has been used in this stew in one combination or another. So almost any variation you create will probably be just as "traditional" as the one that follows.

In a large soup or stockpot brown the beef in the olive oil over medium-high heat. Cover the browned beef with water, bring to a boil, and simmer until the scum rises to the surface. Discard the water and again cover the beef with water and bring to a simmer.

Add the bay leaf, onion, garlic, chiles, pepper, and enough additional water to ensure that the ingredients are covered. Simmer the stew, covered, for 45 minutes or until the beef is just beginning to become tender, adding more water if necessary.

Add the chicken, sausage, and enough water to keep the ingredients covered and cook for another 15 minutes.

Add the remaining ingredients and continue cooking for a final 45 minutes, adding water as necessary.

Serve as a stew or a soup, accompanied by flour tortillas and your favorite table sauce. *Serves 4.*

QUESO Y JAMÓN

Cheese and "Ham"

This recipe is from Vernon Price, an acquaintance from San Antonio. The recipe was a family breakfast staple. Vernon's grandmother had fourteen to feed, and sometimes the chickens did not provide enough eggs, so this dish was designed to see the family through a good part of a day's hard work.

Heat a skillet over medium heat and fry the bacon until it has rendered much of its fat but has not browned.

Pour off all but 2 tablespoons of the bacon fat, add the onion and chiles, and continue cooking until the onion is soft but not browned.

Meanwhile, grind the garlic and cumin to a paste using a large *molcajete* or mortar and pestle. Gradually add the can of tomatoes with green chiles and grind into the garlic mixture.

Add the flour to the skillet and cook, stirring constantly, for 1 minute. Gradually add the tomato, garlic, and cumin mixture plus ⅓ cup of water. Bring the ingredients to a boil; then simmer for 5 minutes.

Remove the skillet from the burner and immediately add the cheese, stirring it until it is melted and combined with the other ingredients. Serve with hot tortillas. *Serves 4.*

½ *pound bacon, chopped*
1 *large onion, chopped*
4 serrano *chiles, seeded and minced*
4 *cloves garlic*
1 *teaspoon cumin*
1 *10-ounce can tomatoes with green chiles*
1 *tablespoon flour*
⅓ *cup water*
½ *pound cheddar cheese, grated*

BARBECUED, GRILLED, AND ROASTED MEATS

ABOUT MEXICAN-STYLE BARBECUE

Mexican-American barbecuing techniques, as with so many other aspects of their cooking, came largely from the native Indians with some significant contributions from the Spanish. Three basic techniques were used: pit-cooking, broiling over coals on a *parrilla* (grill), and spit-roasting. A fourth technique, *al pastor*, or roasting skewered meat on a vertical spit with the coals on one side, came originally from the Moors. While the latter style of cooking is still immensely popular throughout Mexico and sometimes used on south Texas ranches to prepare *cabrito*, for some reason it was not adopted in the United States to a meaningful degree.

Pit-cooking comes from the most basic Indian technique of building a fire in a hole lined with stones. When the wood has turned to glowing coals, the meat to be cooked, usually wrapped in leaves or gunnysack material, is placed on the fire (sometimes topped with heated rocks); then the hole is covered and sealed with damp earth. Twelve or more hours later the meat is uncovered and served. Early German settlers in Texas found a way to partially duplicate pit-cooking by placing the meat well to one side of the coals so that it was cooked by indirect heat and permeated with the fragrant smoke of the oak or mesquite used as fuel. This latter technique, used primarily in the preparation of beef brisket or "Texas-style" barbecue, produces an extremely tender and flavorful result after 12 to 18 hours. However, it lacks the steaming effect of the original pit method, which creates an even more succulent result, especially with tougher cuts. The best way for most of us to duplicate this cooking is with a water smoker. The meat will not be quite as tender as that from a real pit, but it will be tender enough and the flavor will be deliciously smoky.

Cooking with a grill, or *parrilla*, came from the Spanish. This style of cooking, in which a grill is placed a few inches over glowing coals, is the one most familiar to us and for which most of us will already have the equipment.

Spit-roasting probably began with a squirrel or rabbit being impaled on a stick and held over hot coals. Records indicate that this and the pit-cooking method were used by Indians from the earliest days. In Mexican-American cooking this method is often used for large cuts of meat. Fortunately, electric rotisseries which can be attached to charbroilers or barbecues can duplicate the effect with smaller cuts.

My research has shown that early Hispanic barbecue techniques were quite similar in Texas, New Mexico, and California. Perhaps the New Mexicans tended more to the use of vinegar or lemon juice and oil marinades and the *californios* to dry "rubs" of herbs and spices, but there are many more similarities than differences. While beef was a bit more common in California, goats and sheep were more often the entrée in New Mexico. *Cabrito*, or unweaned kid, could be called the unofficial national dish of southern Texas, but beef is also popular throughout the region.

Much more important to Mexican-American barbecuing than the actual cooking techniques and cuts of meat is how the meat is served. Traditionally, barbecues have been associated with weddings, births, and holidays and involve a communal effort. After all, the original purpose of these barbecues was to serve a great many people. While the meat is certainly the pièce de résistance, it is the side dishes of beans and *posole*, often cooked in caldrons, the huge quantities of special sauces, the steaming tamales and stacks of freshly cooked tortillas that make this type of barbecue memorable. And don't forget the strolling mariachis singing *corridos* of courage, love, and tragedy.

Fortunately, the Hispanic barbecue tradition lends itself to entertaining on even a small scale. My most successful dinner parties have been those fashioned after Mexican-style barbecues. In northern Mexico these affairs are often called *carnes asadas* after their main ingredient. Depending on the number of guests and how much trouble you wish to go to, barbecue one or more different kinds of meat; beef top sirloin, pork loin, leg of lamb, beef or pork ribs, or leg of kid are good choices.

No matter what cut of meat you decide on I suggest you marinate it. This not only makes the meat more tender it also makes it more flavorful. However, the last thing you want to do is use a marinade that intrudes on the meat with one flavor or another. It is amusing to find so-called authentic *fajita* recipes redolent of soy and Worcestershire sauces. Red wine vinegar is another ingredient that can overpower an otherwise subtle flavor combination. Marinades can range from a mixture of liquids, herbs, and spices in which the meat is immersed to a nearly dry "rub" of herbs and spices.

Whenever possible barbecued foods should be cooked over hardwood coals such as mesquite or oak. These items are now sold packaged throughout much of the United States. The next best fuel is real hardwood charcoal, and the least acceptable fuel is the more common petroleum-based briquettes.

When the meat is done, carve it into fairly small pieces and serve it with tamales (steamed or heated in the barbecue), *Frijoles de olla* (p. 130), Guacamole (p. 144), your favorite hot sauces (green chile sauce or *sarsa* was a mainstay at early California barbecues), tortilla chips, lots of corn and flour tortillas, and anything else you fancy.

FAJITAS
Skirt Steak

Since the early 1980s when Americans discovered *fajitas* this tasty dish has swept across the country leaving satisfied diners and some confusion in its wake.

Fajitas, which refers to skirt steak, came to us from Mexico (despite the claims of some overly nationalistic Texans). The skirt steak is very similar to the flank steak except it has much more fat. In Mexico where they are usually called *arracheras*, *fajitas* have long rated a place on the menus of restaurants right next to the vaunted filet mignon, and at about the same price. Ironically, during this same period United States butchers were using skirt steak to make hamburger! This is no longer the case since *fajitas* are probably served in more restaurants than not, including many with no other Mexican-style dishes. In any case, the popularity of *fajitas* has exposed this country to a style of Mexican cooking that predominates in northern Mexico.

How to Prepare and Cook Fajitas:

There are several factors that affect the success of *fajitas*, including how they are prepared and cooked and whether or not the *fajitas* are marinated.

As with other beef cuts *fajitas* can be broiled, charbroiled, pan-broiled, or smoked. Broiling *fajitas* in your oven will work, but it lacks the smoky taste that many consider important to the dish. The most traditional method is to broil the meat over mesquite coals. If mesquite is not available, use another hardwood like hickory or charcoal made exclusively with hardwood. Use petroleum-based briquettes only as a last resort.

If you decide to charbroil your *fajitas,* you then have a choice of whether to broil them quickly over very hot coals or for an extended period over less hot coals. Much of this decision depends on whether you have marinated the meat.

Fajitas are a relatively tough cut and need help to ensure that they are tender. They are tenderized in three basic ways. First, *fajitas* are often sold tenderized, that is, the meat has been run through a machine that chops the connective tissue (and everything else in the process) thereby rendering the meat tender. Unfortunately, this method also destroys the dish's texture.

Second, the meat can be tenderized with its own fat, with which it is amply endowed. Cooking the *fajitas* for an extended period over low coals melts the fat slowly and allows it to permeate and tenderize the meat. It also imparts a rich smoky flavor. This is how *fajitas* are usually cooked in northern Mexico, where the meat is put some distance from the coals and often cooked for 10 to 15 minutes or more on each side.

However, not everybody appreciates such a fatty entrée, at least not too often. If you trim the fat from the meat, you will lose much of the natural tenderizing effect. To compensate, you should use the third method of tenderizing, which is to marinate the meat. Some people use commercial meat tenderizer, but I do not like the artificial taste it leaves.

I do not pretend to be an expert on marinades. However, I do know that the agents that actually tenderize the meat as opposed to flavoring it are either acidic ingredients, such as vinegar, wine, and lime juice, or items containing strong enzymes, such as pineapple and papaya juice. These items weaken or dissolve connective tissue in a much less destructive fashion than does the mechanical tenderizing mentioned above. However, these tenderizing agents tend to affect only the outside portions of the meat. Probably for this reason some cooks cut *fajitas* in half lengthwise before marinating them. To do this effectively, you must place the meat in your freezer until it is stiff but not completely frozen. It will then be much easier to cut them, using a long, thin carving knife. Marinated *fajitas* can be broiled over much hotter coals than the more fatty version for 3 to 4 minutes on each side. This is important because quite often marinated meat cooked at lower temperatures does not develop the characteristic browned crispness on its exterior.

In Texas pan-broiling is probably the second most popular method of cooking *fajitas*. This technique, where a griddle is heated and very lightly oiled, works well if you are willing to forgo the smoky flavor of meat cooked over wood. An advantage of pan-broiling is that it gives the cook a much greater degree of control over the cooking temperature.

Fajitas can also be smoked. This takes the slow cooking method suggested above to its logical conclusion. It produces a marvelously tender, smoke-infused result that is quite similar to the famous Texas barbecued brisket. A water smoker or Texas-style smoker works well for this purpose.

How to Serve Fajitas:

Traditionally, *fajitas* are served with *Pico de gallo* (p. 112), a picante sauce, Guacamole (p. 144), and hot flour tortillas. The meat is usually sliced into bite-size pieces before being served. Several pieces of the meat are placed in a tortilla, topped with Guacamole, *Pico de gallo*, and hot sauce, and then folded into a taco before eating.

In their most striking presentation *fajitas* are served sizzling and steaming in an iron serving pan. You can buy one specially made for the purpose, or you can simply use an iron skillet or griddle. To create the sizzle, first heat the pan until it is very hot. After the meat has been cooked and sliced put it in a bowl and add about ¼ cup lime juice. Immediately empty the contents of the bowl into the hot skillet and remove it from the heat. As you take it to the table (being careful to keep from burning yourself), you will leave a trail of steam and smoke permeated by the rich smells of the dish.

The above is the basic way in which *fajitas* are usually served. However, there is one addition that I think greatly enhances the dish and that is to serve it *encebollada*, or covered with onions. To do this, cook 2 sliced onions in 3 tablespoons of oil with a little garlic and 3 or 4 whole *serrano* chiles until the onions are well browned. Add the onions and chiles to the bowl with the meat and lime juice and serve as directed above.

FAJITA MARINADES

As mentioned above I am not an expert on marinades, but after much trial and error I have found a few that work well. First, I should mention that personal prejudice precludes me from using marinades that leave either a strong wine vinegar flavor or those made with a lot of sweetened soy sauce. The former, to me, have an obvious rather than subtle flavor which is inappropriate, and the latter turn *fajitas* into beef teriyaki. (I include both soy sauce and Worcestershire sauce in a few recipes but only in very small amounts.) Below I provide recipes for three favorites, each with a different effect.

FAJITA MARINADE I

2 *pounds* fajitas
¾ *cup lime juice*
¼ *teaspoon Worcestershire sauce*
¼ *teaspoon soy sauce*
½ *teaspoon ground black pepper*
½ *teaspoon salt, or to taste*

This is the simplest marinade of all and one often used in Mexico. Made up nearly entirely of lime juice this marinade does not have quite the tenderizing effect of the one with pineapple juice (see p. 275), but it gives a fine, traditional flavor, especially when the *fajitas* are cooked over mesquite. This marinade is particularly effective with *fajitas* which have been halved lengthwise, making them especially thin. Because the action of the lime juice will cook the *fajitas* chemically as it does with *ceviche* they should be marinated no longer than 1 hour.

Mix the ingredients together, marinate the meat for 1 hour, and then either broil it over low coals or smoke. *Serves 4.*

FAJITA MARINADE II

2 *pounds* fajitas
¼ *cup lime juice*
2 *cloves garlic, minced*
1 *teaspoon paprika*
¼ *teaspoon cayenne pepper*
½ *teaspoon ground black pepper*
½ *teaspoon salt, or to taste*
½ *cup olive oil*
¼ *teaspoon soy sauce*
½ *teaspoon Worcestershire sauce*

This marinade, which is also called for in the *Carne asada III* recipe (p. 279), works well with meat that has been trimmed of fat. The meat should be left in the marinade for about 3 hours. As with the previous marinade the tenderizing effect is not extreme but should be adequate.

Mix the marinade ingredients together and marinate the meat for 3 hours; then broil it over hot coals. *Serves 4.*

FAJITA MARINADE III

The following marinade is excellent. The pineapple juice and *mescal* combine to create a smoky, tropical taste. It is also a very good tenderizer since the enzymes in pineapple juice are particularly effective for this purpose.

Blend together the garlic, lime juice, pineapple juice, and chiles; then strain the mixture into a bowl. Add the *mescal* or tequila, olive oil, and salt, marinate the *fajitas* for 1½ to 2 hours, and then broil them over very hot coals. *Serves 4.*

2 *pounds* fajitas
3 *cloves garlic, minced*
¼ *cup lime juice*
¼ *cup pineapple juice*
¼ *cup canned* chipotle *chiles*
3 *tablespoons* mescal, *or substitute tequila*
¼ *cup olive oil*
½ *teaspoon salt*

CARNE ASADA
Broiled Meat

As the title of this recipe indicates *carne asada* means simply broiled meat. To Mexican-Americans this can be anything from a rib eye or T-bone steak to a broiled piece of sirloin that has been chopped and mixed with sautéed onions, chiles, and spices. In California *carne asada* is often marinated while in other areas it usually is not. Because of the broad nature of this dish I have provided three different recipes that indicate the range of its possibilities. The directions for *fajitas,* which, by definition, are also *carne asada,* are included in previous recipes by themselves because of their singular popularity. *Carne asada,* much like *fajitas,* is usually served with *Frijoles de olla* (p. 130), Guacamole (p. 144), *Pico de gallo* (p. 112), salsas, and hot tortillas.

CARNE ASADA I
Broiled Rib Eye Encebollada

I was originally a little suspicious of this recipe because it uses an expensive cut of meat, a luxury not typical of most Mexican-American recipes. However, I soon realized that while this reaction made sense in an urban setting where meat must be purchased by the cut it did not make sense in rural areas where whole cows are butchered and the most expensive cuts are available along with the least expensive cuts.

Build a fire with mesquite, if possible, at least 4 inches from the grill and let it burn down to coals. Rib eye is a fatty cut of meat so if the fire is too hot, the fat will flame up as it melts, sometimes causing the meat to scorch.

After you begin the fire, heat a skillet over medium heat, add the 2 tablespoons olive oil, the garlic, and onions and fry until the onions are nicely browned, about 15 minutes. Remove the onions from the heat and reserve.

When the fire is ready, broil the steaks to the desired degree of doneness.

Top the steaks with the onions and serve with the Guacamole, beans, and/or rice, sauce, and tortillas. *Serves 4.*

2 *pounds rib eye steak, cut about ½ inch thick*
2 *tablespoons olive oil*
2 *cloves garlic, minced*
1 *very large or 2 medium-size onions, sliced*
1 *recipe Guacamole (p. 144)*
1 *recipe Mexican Rice or Spanish Rice (p. 126 and p. 128) and/or Frijoles de olla (p. 130)*
   Picante sauce
   Flour and/or corn tortillas

CARNE ASADA II

Marinated Broiled Flank Steak

THE MARINADE:

6   *cloves garlic*
½ *cup onion*
1   *teaspoon marjoram*
1   *teaspoon oregano*
½ *teaspoon sage*
1   *teaspoon thyme*
1   *teaspoon cracked black pepper*
1   *teaspoon chile powder*
1   *teaspoon salt*
2   *bay leaves, finely crumbled*
¼ *cup red wine*
¼ *cup white wine*
1½ *tablespoons red wine vinegar*
1½ *tablespoons cider vinegar*
2   *tablespoons lemon juice*
¼ *cup tomato juice*
⅓ *cup olive oil*

THE MEAT:

2   *pounds flank steak*
    Avocados, sliced
    Onions, roasted
    Salsa

This recipe is typical of the *carne asada* often made in California's Central Valley, where the meat is often marinated for days in crocks in small grocery stores.

The marinade for this dish is easily made in a food processor. Just drop the garlic through the feed tube while the machine is running. Stop the machine and add the onion and herbs and chop the onion coarsely. Finally, add the liquid ingredients and pulse just enough to mix well. Although all the quantities given for herbs refer to the dried variety, feel free to substitute a slightly greater amount of fresh herbs.

Mix together the marinade ingredients and marinate the meat in a nonreactive dish for at least 48 hours, refrigerated.

Charbroil the steaks over very hot coals. You will be amazed at how the steaks seem to increase in thickness during the cooking. Since the meat will be partially cooked by the marinade (as in *ceviche*) be careful not to overcook. This is why a hot fire is suggested, which will enable the meat to be well browned, even with a fairly short cooking period.

When the meat is done, top it with avocado slices, roasted onions, and your favorite salsa and serve it with Mexican Rice (p. 126) and hot flour tortillas. *Serves 4.*

NUTRITION HINT: Flank steak has many of the qualities of skirt steak, or *fajitas*, but is much lower in fat.

CARNE ASADA III

This recipe uses a good all-purpose marinade similar to the one called for in the preceding section on *fajitas*.

Mix the marinade ingredients together and marinate the meat for 3 hours. Broil the meat over a very hot wood or charcoal fire; then slice it diagonally and serve. *Serves 4.*

CARNE ASADA IV

Herbed Sirloin Roast

Read about barbecuing on pp. 268–70.

To make the rub, either grind the ingredients in a *molcajete* or mortar and pestle, or drop the garlic through the feed tube of a food processor, fitted with a steel blade, while it is turned on; then add the remaining ingredients.

Rub the herb mixture into the meat, wrap it in plastic wrap, and leave it in the refrigerator overnight. Before cooking allow the meat to come to room temperature.

This dish should be roasted over wood coals rather than grilled, which means it should be much further from the coals than the usual 2 to 6 inches. The best way to accomplish this without building a special barbecue for the purpose is by using a water smoker with the water dish removed. In any case, the coals should be 16 to 20 inches from the grill. Fill the charcoal container full of charcoal or heaping full with wood chunks. (Wood chunks burn down to a lesser volume than charcoal.) When the wood or charcoal has burned down to coals, roast the meat 10 minutes on the first side and 15 minutes on the other side for medium rare. Because this type of cooking is imprecise the above is just a guideline.

Serve the meat with beans or rice only or with the other ingredients of a typical Mexican barbecue described on pp. 269–70. *Serves 4.*

THE MARINADE:

- 2 *tablespoons lime juice*
- 2 *cloves garlic, minced*
- 1 *teaspoon paprika*
- ¼ *teaspoon cayenne pepper*
- ½ *teaspoon ground black pepper*
- ½ *teaspoon salt, or to taste*
- ½ *cup olive oil*

THE MEAT:

- 2 *pounds top sirloin steak, approximately ¾ inch thick*

THE RUB:

- 10 *cloves garlic, chopped*
- 1½ *tablespoons oregano*
- 1 *tablespoon thyme*
- 1 *tablespoon cracked black pepper*
- ½ *tablespoon dried marjoram*
- ½ *tablespoon red wine vinegar*
- 1 *tablespoon olive oil*

THE MEAT:

About 2½ pounds top sirloin, 2 inches thick

CORDERO ASADO

Roast Lamb

3 *New Mexico or ancho dried chiles, stemmed and seeded*

3 *cloves garlic, chopped*

2 *tablespoons cider vinegar Water*

3 *tablespoons cooking oil*

1 *leg of lamb, boned and tied for rotisserie roasting*

This recipe uses the same basting sauce that is used in the recipe for Roast Turkey (p. 283). If you do not have a rotisserie barbecue, cook it in a water smoker or bake it in the oven.

Soak the chiles in hot water for 15 to 20 minutes; then place them in the blender with the garlic and vinegar. Add enough water to make a total of ¾ cup and blend for 1 minute. Add the oil to the blender and pulse once or twice or just until it is mixed with the chiles.

Baste the lamb well with the chile sauce; then place it on the rotisserie over medium-hot coals and roast it until done. *Serves 4.*

BARBACOA

Barbecue

1½ *tablespoons canned chipotle chiles plus 1½ tablespoons adobo sauce from the can*

4 *cloves garlic*

½ *teaspoon oregano*

¼ *teaspoon salt*

2 *tablespoons melted lard, or substitute olive oil*

1⅓ *cups water*

2 *medium onions, peeled and cut into ¼-inch rings*

2½ *pounds well-trimmed beef brisket, cut into 2-inch pieces*

1 *recipe Guacamole (p. 144) Salsa*

While the word *barbacoa* is literally translated as barbecue, in Mexican cooking, especially in the north, where so many Mexican-Americans came from, it often refers to the head of a cow or pig which has been cooked overnight in a pit. The head is wrapped in gunnysack material then lowered into a pit in which wood, usually mesquite, has been burned to coals over rocks. Often some of the rocks and coals are shoveled on top of the wrapped head; then the pit is sealed by wetting and tamping the earth. After 12 hours or more the head is removed and the meat scraped out. *Barbacoa* is traditionally served on weekends with tortillas, beans, hot sauce, and often guacamole.

I realize that few North American readers will have much interest in the above recipe, either because of the main ingredient or because a pit is not available. Actually, in the United States few cooks still use the pit method, usually steaming the head, which produces an unsatisfactory result. The following recipe, utilizing a clay cooker and beef brisket, does an excellent job of simulating both the taste and the texture of *Barbacoa* without the disadvantages of either the main ingredient or the cooking method.

Soak a clay cooker with its lid in water for at least 15 minutes.

Place all the ingredients except the onions, brisket, Guacamole, and salsa in a blender and blend for 1 minute. (You can substitute olive oil for the lard, but you will lose the authentic flavor.)

Place half the onions on the bottom of the soaked clay cooker, add the brisket, and then top with the remaining onions. Pour the liquid from the blender over the meat.

Place the cooker in the oven, turn the temperature to 425 degrees, and bake for 2 hours and 15 minutes.

Remove the meat, which should be very tender, and shred it with the cooked onions by pulsing it in a food processor fitted with a plastic blade.

Serve the *Barbacoa* with hot tortillas, beans, Guacamole, and your favorite salsa. *Serves 4.*

—

NOTE: The *Barbacoa* will be extra special if you marinate the meat in the blended mixture overnight.

CABRITO AL PASTOR
Kid Shepherd Style

This is unweaned goat, or kid, cooked "shepherd style" that is served in Nuevo León and northern Tamaulipas. It is rarely found in restaurants in the United States but is often served on special occasions on ranches in south Texas. Usually the kid is strung whole onto a long, heavy spit and placed at about a 70-degree angle over fairly low mesquite coals. The position is changed about every 20 minutes until the meat is crusty on the outside and just done on the inside.

The *cabrito* for *Cabrito al pastor* is always butchered just before it is weaned (when it is not more than 30 days old) because once grass has been introduced into the diet the flavor and tenderness are compromised. Here lies the problem for those of us who do not raise goats or know someone who does. While *cabrito* is now available in south Texas supermarkets and often in Hispanic grocery stores, elsewhere it is usually older, tougher, and less flavorful. Such a product is fine for stewed *cabrito* but not for *Cabrito al pastor* or *Cabrito al horno* (Oven Baked Kid).

If you are fortunate enough to procure a kid that has been butchered at the proper time, the best way to simulate the *al pastor* cooking method is to cook it 1 to 2 feet from low mesquite coals, turning it about every 10 minutes until it is properly cooked. It can also be cooked in a water smoker or Texas-style barbecue. It also helps to marinate the meat in a marinade of ⅓ lemon juice to ⅔ olive oil for 3 hours.

Cabrito al pastor is traditionally served with Guacamole (p. 144), *Pico de gallo* (p. 112), picante sauce, and hot tortillas. *Serves 4.*

PAVO ASADO
Roast Turkey

This is a very old recipe. Both the simple chile basting sauce and the stuffing were used with all types of roast and barbecued meats, including lamb, pork, beef, and chicken.

Soak the chiles in hot water for 15 to 20 minutes; then place them in a blender with the garlic and vinegar. Add enough water to make a total of ¾ cup and blend for 1 minute. Add the oil to the blender and pulse once or twice or just until it is mixed with the chiles.

This is probably a winter version of the stuffing which could well have included fresh instead of dried fruits during the summer.

Put the oil in a skillet over moderate heat, add the onion and garlic, and cook until the onion is soft but not browned.

Add the pork and continue cooking, stirring constantly to break up the meat, until it is browned.

Add the tomatoes plus ¼ cup of the juice from the can; then add the remaining ingredients except the bread crumbs, butter, and salt. Cook, stirring frequently, until most of the juice has either evaporated or thickened, about 10 minutes.

Add the bread crumbs and butter, stirring vigorously to make sure they are completely incorporated into the dish; then add the salt.

The stuffing can either be cooked inside the turkey or baked, covered, at 350 degrees for 30 minutes or more.

Stuff the turkey with the stuffing; then baste it well with the sauce. Place the turkey in an oven preheated to 350° and roast until done, basting it every half hour.

THE BASTE:

3 *New Mexico or ancho dried chiles, stemmed and seeded*
3 *cloves garlic, chopped*
  Water
2 *tablespoons cider vinegar*
3 *tablespoons cooking oil*

THE STUFFING:

2 *tablespoons cooking oil*
½ *cup onions, minced*
2 *cloves garlic, minced*
¾ *pound ground pork*
1 *14½-ounce can tomatoes*
¼ *cup juice from can of tomatoes*
½ *cup pecan bits*
½ *cup dried pears*
½ *cup dried apricots*
½ *cup dried apples*
¼ *cup raisins*
1 *teaspoon thyme*
½ *teaspoon marjoram*
½ *teaspoon sage*
1½ *cups dried bread crumbs*
1 *stick butter, melted*
1 *teaspoon salt, or to taste*

THE TURKEY:

1 *turkey, whatever size you like*
  The stuffing
  The baste

SEAFOOD

BACALAO
Dried Codfish

1   *pound dried, salted codfish*

2   *medium potatoes, peeled and chopped into ¾-inch pieces*

¼   *cup olive oil*

2   *medium onions, chopped*

4   *cloves garlic, minced*

2   *cups tomato sauce*

1¾ *cups water*

2   *tablespoons chile powder*

½   *tablespoon oregano*

2   *tablespoons parsley, minced*

½   *teaspoon salt, or to taste*

½   *teaspoon ground pepper*

½   *cup black California olives, sliced*

⅓   *cup bread crumbs, sautéed with 1 clove of minced garlic in a little olive oil for 1–2 minutes*

Most of the Spanish Southwest was arid and far from the ocean. With the exception of those fortunate enough to live along California's bounteous coast there was not much seafood in the early Spanish settler's diet. Even in New Mexico, whose rivers and lakes spawned several varieties of trout, Indian religious taboos against eating fish made this exquisite dish slow to gain popularity. So, when fish was eaten it was often Spain's famous codfish, salted on board ship then dried, which was easily transported and stored.

While *Bacalao* was fairly common in the early settlements, it is difficult to find in Mexican-American family repertoires except in those with a long Spanish tradition, of which very few remain. In spite of this, I felt it was important to include the following recipe for *Bacalao* because of its historical significance and because it still remains a tradition in some families, especially in California and New Mexico, particularly at Christmas. While *Bacalao* is Old World in origin, like so many other dishes it has been improved with the addition of an important New World ingredient, chile.

Please note that although the appearance of codfish in its dried state may be amusing, it is neither overly strong nor fishy in taste as is often thought. By preparing *Bacalao* according to the following recipe, the reader will discover why it became an important tradition in Spain and Portugal and later among the Southwest's early Spanish families.

If possible, buy boneless codfish. A fine product is now being produced in Canada and sold in Hispanic specialty markets in the United States.

The object of this recipe is to turn what at first glance resembles a mummified road-kill into one of the world's most famous peasant dishes. Step one of this process requires no more effort than soaking the fish in several changes of cold water for about 24 hours. Afterwards the codfish will have been reconstituted and look a great deal more like something that might be good to eat. After soaking the fish for about 24 hours you should have about 1½ to 2 pounds reconstituted fish. If you could not find filets, now is the time to remove the bones and skin. In either case cut the fish into ½-inch pieces.

Preheat your oven to 350 degrees.

Rinse the potatoes in cold water; then leave them covered with water until they are ready to be added to the dish.

Heat a Dutch oven over medium heat, add the olive oil, and cook the onions until they are soft but not browned. Add the garlic and cook an additional 30 seconds.

Add the remaining ingredients except the fish, potatoes, and bread crumbs and bring them to a boil. Add the fish and potatoes and bring to a boil once more; then cover the pot, place it in the oven, and bake for 30 minutes.

Remove the top of the Dutch oven and continue baking for 15 minutes; then sprinkle the bread crumbs over the dish and continue baking for an additional 15 minutes.

Serve the *Bacalao* with Spanish Rice (p. 128) and/or flour tortillas. *Serves 4.*

TRUCHA FRITA
Fried Trout

4 *pan-size trout, either whole or fileted*

   Cornmeal or flour for dredging

½ *cup olive oil*

2 *tablespoons butter*

2 *tablespoons lemon or lime juice*

2 *tablespoons parsley, minced*

2–3 *lemons or limes, cut into wedges*

When one considers both the abundance of trout in New Mexico and the fact that it is one of the most delicious fish in the world, it is easy to assume that this delicacy has been part of the area's diet throughout history. However, because of religious strictures among the Indians, it was not until the coming of the Spaniards that trout became a major factor in the area's cuisine.

Then as now trout was prepared either fried or broiled without the addition of much more than a little butter and lemon or lime juice. Trout can be served either whole or fileted. Although cooking the entire fish is the easiest and most traditional way, to me fileted trout is much easier to eat. To filet the trout, simply slice off the filets, beginning at the tail, as close to the bones as possible. Next, place the filets, skin side down, on a work surface. Feel along the filets for the short line of bones toward the top; then remove them by making 2 cuts, one on each side of the bones, at an angle that will join the cuts together as they reach the skin.

Dredge the fish in either the cornmeal or flour.

Heat a large skillet over medium to medium-high heat. Add about half of the olive oil and when it is hot add the fish. Sauté the trout until well browned on each side, about 4 to 5 minutes in all; then remove it to serving plates. You may need to add additional olive oil, especially if you fry the trout in 2 batches.

Remove the pan from the heat, add the butter, lemon or lime juice, and parsley, and stir to loosen and incorporate the browned pieces of flour or cornmeal; then spoon the flavored butter over the fish.

Garnish with lemon or lime wedges and serve with rice and/or your favorite vegetable. *Serves 4.*

TRUCHA ASADA
Broiled Trout

In New Mexico outdoor grilling has never been as popular as in other parts of the Southwest, such as Texas, so this method of cooking trout is not as common as the pan-fried method. However, it is so delicious that if the opportunity presents itself, it makes a fine choice.

Barbecuing fish has been made very easy by the introduction of smooth, porcelain-coated grills. The addition of some PAM or another spray oil just before cooking pretty well eliminates the old bugaboo of sticking.

4 *pan-size trout, either whole or fileted*

2 *tablespoons butter*

1 *teaspoon lemon or lime juice*

½ *tablespoon parsley, minced*

2–3 *lemons or limes, cut into wedges*

Build a fire in a barbecue using hardwood or hardwood charcoal, if possible.

Make a flavored butter by combining the butter, lemon or lime juice, and parsley.

Broil the fish until it is well browned on both sides, 4 to 5 minutes in all.

Serve the trout topped with the flavored butter, accompanied by lemon or lime wedges, rice, and/or your favorite vegetable. *Serves 4.*

CAMARONES CON PANTALONES

Shrimp in Trousers

Egg batter

½ *cup pimientos, finely chopped*

½ *cup parsley, finely chopped*

5 *ounces fresh shrimp, cooked*

Flour for dredging

Salt

This recipe and the story behind it come from the *Early California and Mexico Cook Book* by Don Ricardo, a fascinating exposition of early California cooking:

> Señora Eulalit Pérez de Guillen, born in Loreto, Baja California, was *'Duena de las llaves'* or keeper of the keys at mission San Gabriel for Padre Junípero Serra—she was probably the oldest woman in the world at the time of her death—a most colorful character in the early history of the California missions. She was the great-grandmother of Doña María de Jesús de Marron—*que dios bendiga*—whose greatest delight in life was to prepare delicious meals for her large family. *Camarones con pantalones* was one of her favorite dishes.
>
> Add the pimientos and parsley to the egg batter and mix thoroughly. Dry the shrimp on a tea towel and roll them in flour. Drop the shrimp in the batter; then spoon them into a deep-fry of lard or peanut oil. Cook them until they are a nice golden color, then remove them and drain them on absorbent paper. Lightly dust them with salt and serve (p. 41). *Serves 4.*

CAMARONES AL MOJO DE AJO
Shrimp in Garlic Sauce

Mexican cooking is replete with recipes for shrimp with garlic sauce, many of which are basically Spanish in origin. The following California version, originally from Baja California and Mexico's west coast, is one of the best I have tried. It is much like a Chinese stir-fry dish in that the raw ingredients must all be prepared in advance because it cooks very quickly. Because of the advance preparation it makes a good dish for entertaining, especially small groups. This recipe also provides the filling for *Tacos de camarones al mojo de ajo* (p. 199).

Heat a large skillet over medium-high heat, add 6 tablespoons of the olive oil, and when it is very hot, sauté the shrimp until they become opaque, about 30 seconds.

Add the remaining 2 tablespoons olive oil, the garlic, onion, and *jalapeño* chiles and continue cooking for about 30 seconds.

Add the tomato puree, lime juice, thyme, salt, and pepper and continue cooking until the sauce thickens, 30 seconds to 1 minute.

Add the cabbage and cilantro and continue cooking for 1 minute.

Serve with Mexican Rice (p. 126) and lime wedges. *Serves 4.*

½ cup olive oil
2 pounds small shrimp, peeled and deveined
5 cloves garlic, finely chopped
½ cup onion, minced
2 jalapeño chiles, stemmed, seeded, and minced
⅔ cup tomato puree
¼ cup lime juice
½ teaspoon thyme
½ teaspoon salt
¼ teaspoon ground black pepper
1 cup cabbage, finely shredded
¼ cup cilantro
2 limes, cut into wedges

MISCELLANEOUS ENTRÉES

ARROZ CON POLLO
Rice with Chicken

2–4 *tablespoons olive oil*
  1 *frying chicken, cut up*
     with some fat and skin
     removed
     Water
2½ *tablespoons olive oil*
1½ *cups long grain rice*
  ⅓ *cup onion, minced*
  2 *cloves garlic, minced*
  1 *teaspoon chile powder*
  1 *teaspoon oregano*
  1 *teaspoon thyme*
  1 *teaspoon salt, or to taste*
  ½ *teaspoon ground pepper*
  2 *tablespoons parsley,*
     minced
  1 *bay leaf*
  1 *cup canned or cooked*
     garbanzo beans
  ½ *cup green pitted*
     pimiento-stuffed olives
     (optional)

Surely every population that was at one time touched by Spanish influence serves *Arroz con pollo*. It is a dish related to paella that can include whatever your imagination creates. Traditional recipes for *Arroz con pollo* incorporate saffron, but the Mexican-Americans that could afford this luxury were few and far between. In this version chile powder is substituted, creating a unique and excellent result.

Heat a deep skillet or Dutch oven over medium to medium-high heat, add some olive oil, and fry the chicken pieces until they are well browned; then drain off the excess fat.

Cover the chicken with water and barely simmer, covered, for 20 minutes. Reserve the liquid.

Heat another Dutch oven or pot over medium heat, add the 2½ tablespoons olive oil, then the rice, and cook the mixture over very low heat for 5 to 10 minutes or until the rice is beginning to brown. Add the remaining ingredients except the bay leaf, garbanzo beans, and olives and cook an additional 3 minutes, stirring often.

Add the bay leaf, garbanzo beans, and olives; then stir in 18 ounces of the liquid in which the chicken was cooked. Place the browned chicken pieces on top of the rice mixture; then bring the liquid to a boil. Cover the dish, then barely simmer it until virtually all the water has evaporated, about 20 minutes.

Remove the pot from the heat, stir the contents together, replace the lid, and allow to steam for an additional 5 minutes. *Serves 4.*

SALPICÓN

Meat Salad

Salpicón is a shredded beef salad unique to Mexican cooking. Why it has never become popular in Mexican-American restaurants, or any other restaurants in the United States for that matter, is a mystery. The flavors are well balanced, and the presentation is very attractive. In addition, *Salpicón* is inexpensive and can be prepared well in advance.

Combine the dressing ingredients and reserve.

Mix together all the salad ingredients except the lettuce leaves, the avocado, and the tortillas and toss with the dressing. Allow the salad to marinate, refrigerated, for 1 to 3 hours.

To serve, mound the salad onto beds of lettuce on each of 4 serving plates. Top the salads with the avocado and serve with hot tortillas. *Serves 4.*

THE DRESSING:

2 *tablespoons lime juice*
2 *tablespoons vinegar*
1 *tablespoon liquid from a jar of pickled* jalapeño *chiles*
2 *cloves garlic, minced*
   Pinch oregano
5 *tablespoons olive oil*

THE SALAD:

4 *cups Shredded Beef (p. 154)*
½ *cup cilantro, minced*
2 *green onions, minced*
¾ *cup Monterey Jack cheese, coarsely grated*
2 *tomatoes, chopped*
½ *cup green chiles, peeled, seeded, and chopped*
   Lettuce leaves
2 *medium avocados, skinned, seeded, and chopped*
12 *flour tortillas, heated*

NUTRITION HINT: *Salpicón* has very little fat, especially if turkey is substituted for the beef and the amounts of olive oil, cheese, and avocado are reduced.

FIDEO

Pasta

2 *tablespoons cooking oil*
1 *pound potatoes, diced*
1 *pound ground beef*
3 *cloves garlic*
¼ *teaspoon cumin*
½ *teaspoon oregano*
1 *pound* fideo, *broken into small pieces*
2 *8-ounce cans tomato sauce*
½ *teaspoon pepper*
　Salt to taste

Fideo is probably the most popular type of pasta in the Mexican-American community. The nests made of twisted very thin spaghetti cook very quickly. The following recipe was given to me by an old friend, Pauline Zamudio.

In a large pot or Dutch oven heat the oil over moderate heat, add the potatoes, and cook them until they are just beginning to soften, about 5 minutes.

Add the ground beef and stir, breaking it up, until it is just browned.

Crush the garlic, cumin, and oregano to a paste in a *molcajete* or mortar and pestle and add the mixture to the potatoes and meat; then add the remaining ingredients, stirring together until well mixed.

Bring the contents of the pot to a simmer and cook until the *Fideo* is soft, about 10 minutes. *Serves 4.*

RANCHO PASTA

1 *pound angel-hair pasta*
1 *recipe Old-style California Enchilada Sauce (p. 174), simmered until very thick*
½ *cup feta cheese, grated*

This dish, in addition to being a perfect use for leftover sauce, is so good and so timeless that it would be very appropriate on the menu of any restaurant specializing in new southwestern cuisine.

Cook the pasta until it is al dente, top it with the sauce, and then sprinkle on the cheese. *Serves 4.*

TAMALE PIE

Is there anyone who grew up in the Southwest who does not remember the tamale pie served in the school cafeteria, probably with less than fondness? This dish, usually the stuff of food box recipes, is truly a Mexican-American innovation. It is unfortunate that so many inferior versions of it have besmirched the name of what can be quite an interesting dish.

Tamale Pie is usually made with either the same dough as regular tamales or with cornmeal. The stuffing can be nearly any leftover or one of those listed on p. 294. Although I have never found Tamale Pie on a restaurant menu, it can really be very good, as the following recipes demonstrate. Of the two, the first, made with regular tamale dough is my favorite. However, the second is also attractive, especially because of its much lower fat content. Tamale Pie is delicious served with any of the red or green chile sauces. It also makes a nice accompaniment to eggs.

TAMALE PIE WITH TAMALE MASA

THE CRUST:

- **1** *teaspoon chile powder*
- ½ *teaspoon baking powder*
- ½ *teaspoon salt*
- **1** *cup chicken broth or water*
- ½ *cup lard*
- 1½ *cups Masa Harina*

THE FILLING:

- **2** *cups Shredded Chicken (p. 158)*
- **2** *tablespoons oil*
- ¾ *cup cream-style corn*
- ½ *teaspoon salt*
- ½ *teaspoon black pepper*
- ⅓ *cup green chiles, peeled, seeded, and chopped*
- ½ *cup black olives, sliced or minced*
- ½ *cup grated cheddar or Monterey Jack cheese or a combination of both*
- **2** *ounces grated cheddar or Monterey Jack cheese for garnish*

For the filling use 2 cups of very thick Tex-Mex Chile (p. 254) or 2 cups *Picadillo* II (p. 149) mixed with 1 cup cream-style corn or the filling recipe at the left.

Preheat your oven to 350 degrees.

To make the crust, mix the dry ingredients together, then combine them with the chicken broth or water. Next, beat the lard until fluffy; then beat the Masa Harina into it.

Line the bottom and 2 inches of the sides of a *well-greased* shallow casserole dish with between ⅛ and ¼ inch of the dough.

To make the filling, combine all the ingredients or use one of the already prepared alternatives.

To assemble the pie, spoon the filling over the dough; then spread a thin layer of dough on top. The best way to do this is to pat out manageable pieces of the dough and place them over the filling like a patchwork quilt.

Place the completed pie in the oven and bake it for 30 minutes. Five minutes before the pie is done sprinkle additional cheese on the top. *Serves 4.*

TAMALE PIE WITH CORNMEAL

This version of Tamale Pie is made open-faced, with just a little cornmeal sprinkled on the top before baking to provide a crunchy texture.

Preheat your oven to 350 degrees.

To make the crust, mix together all the ingredients except the butter. (A few whirls in a blender accomplishes this task.)

Quickly, before the cornmeal settles out of the solution, pour it into a large pot and set it over medium-high heat. Bring the liquid to a boil, then add the butter. Turn the heat to medium low and simmer, stirring constantly, for 10 minutes. The mixture should be very thick.

Without allowing the mixture to cool, spread it onto the bottom and sides of a *well-buttered* shallow casserole dish.

Add the filling, sprinkle on about 2 tablespoons of additional cornmeal, and bake it for 30 minutes. *Serves 4.*

THE CRUST:

1 *cup cornmeal*
1 *teaspoon chile powder*
1 *teaspoon salt*
2½ *cups chicken broth or water*
2 *tablespoons butter*

THE FILLING:

Use the same filling as in the preceding recipe (p. 294).

NUTRITION HINT: The above crust can be made with either cooking oil or no fat at all. When combined with a low-fat filling, such as the chicken filling in the preceding recipe (which can be made without the olive oil), this makes a very low-fat dish.

MIGAS

Leftovers

8 ounces stale or toasted bread

6–8 tablespoons olive oil

1½ cups onions, chopped

3 very thick slices bacon, diced

3 cloves garlic, minced

¾ cup black California olives, minced

½ teaspoon thyme

½ teaspoon oregano

½ teaspoon marjoram

¼ teaspoon sage

½ teaspoon salt

½ teaspoon ground black pepper

1 tablespoon chile powder

¼ cup blanched, slivered almonds, finely chopped

1–2 tablespoons goat milk cheese (optional)

1½ cups Monterey Jack cheese, grated

This is a very old home-style recipe that, because of the diversity of its ingredients and the uses to which it can be put, is difficult to classify. To me its best application is as a unique and interesting side dish to broiled meat and poultry, but it can also be served as an appetizer or snack, either by itself or spread on toast.

Tear the bread into small pieces and soak it in water for 1 minute. Remove the bread, squeeze as much of the water out as possible, and reserve.

In an iron skillet or similar pan that can be placed in the oven, heat the olive oil over medium heat. Add the onions, bacon, garlic, olives, thyme, oregano, marjoram, sage, salt, and pepper and cook, stirring often, until the onions are soft and the bacon is cooked.

Add the chile powder and almonds and cook 30 seconds longer.

Add the reserved bread and stir well into the dish. Continue to cook, stirring often, until the bread is well incorporated with the dish and just beginning to brown.

Stir in the goat milk cheese, if used, top with the Monterey Jack cheese, and bake in the oven until the cheese is melted, 5 to 10 minutes.

Serve the *Migas* with roast chicken, pork, or beef or as an appetizer spread on toast. *Serves 4.*

Carnes de Caza

GAME

game is a category of cooking virtually unknown to most of us in the United States, and in most parts of Mexico as well. Unless you or someone in your family is a hunter items such as venison and dove are almost never available. And even with the advent of farm-raised game products such as Axis deer, quail, and rabbit, this situation will probably continue. For while we are psychologically accustomed to eating domestic beef, pork, and poultry, subconscious barriers exist to the use of "wild" game animals.

However, game was an important part of frontier living and is still significant in some rural areas, especially among Mexican-Americans in Texas and New Mexico.

Some of the lack of popularity of game among the general population undoubtedly can be ascribed to the fact that many of the dishes are, well, "gamey," and are acquired tastes. On the other hand, some are delicious by any standard, and it is those I have tried to include in this section. Like many of the variety meat dishes these recipes may gradually disappear. If your attitude toward food is at all adventurous, I urge you to try these recipes. You and those to whom you serve them will be rewarded for the effort.

CONEJO FRITO

Fried Rabbit

2 *rabbits, cut into serving
    pieces*
1 *quart buttermilk*
1 *cup flour*
1 *teaspoon salt*
½ *teaspoon ground black
    pepper*
  Oil for deep-frying
  Hot sauce

This "chicken fried" method of preparing rabbit is a Texas ranch favorite.

Soak the rabbit pieces in the buttermilk for at least 1 hour.

Mix the flour, salt, and pepper together and dredge the rabbit pieces in it, shaking off the excess.

Meanwhile, heat oil to 350 degrees in a deep fryer. Deep-fry the rabbit until brown and crisp and serve it with your favorite hot sauce. *Serves 4.*

CONEJO EN SALSA DE TOMATILLO

Rabbit in Tomatillo Sauce

2 *rabbits, cut into serving
    pieces*
  Flour for dredging
¼ *cup lard or olive oil*
2 *recipes* Tomatillo *Sauce
    (p. 116)*

This and the next recipe are typical rabbit stews often found in south Texas.

Toss the rabbit pieces in the flour and shake off the excess.

Heat the lard or oil in a large pot or Dutch oven over medium-high heat; add the rabbit pieces and fry them until just browned.

Stir in the *Tomatillo* Sauce, cover the pot, and simmer for 20 minutes. Serve with rice and flour tortillas. *Serves 4.*

CONEJO EN CHILE COLORADO

Rabbit Cooked in Red Chile

This recipe is another ranch favorite from south Texas.

Toss the rabbit pieces in the flour and shake off the excess.

Heat the lard or olive oil in a large pot or Dutch oven over medium-high heat; add the rabbit pieces and fry them until just browned.

Turn the heat to medium, add the garlic, and cook an additional 45 seconds.

Add the chile powder and toss until well mixed with the rabbit. Then add the water, oregano, vinegar, and bay leaf and simmer, covered, for 20 minutes.

Stir about half the roux into the sauce and continue simmering, uncovered, for 5 minutes. The sauce should still be rather thin. If it has not thickened properly, add some more roux and cook another 5 minutes. *Serves 4.*

2 *rabbits, cut into serving pieces*
   Flour for dredging
¼ *cup lard or olive oil*
4 *cloves garlic, minced*
¼ *cup ancho or New Mexico chile powder*
1 *quart water*
1 *teaspoon oregano*
1 *tablespoon vinegar*
1 *bay leaf*
   Roux made with 1½ tablespoons oil and 2 tablespoons flour

VENADO

Venison

For obvious reasons venison has been a favorite American food since before the arrival of Europeans. The Indians hunted and trapped deer in many ways, but the most interesting technique was practiced by the Tarahumara Indians of Chihuahua. The Tarahumaras, or Raramuris as they are often called, are famed for their endurance and are able to run for hours, and sometimes days, with virtually no rest. For sport, they have been known to literally run down deer (probably using more calories in the process than they obtained from the low-fat meat).

Venison can be gamey and dry. To avoid these problems, the deer should be well cleaned, then washed with vinegar, and left overnight.

The best home-style venison I have had was prepared by Vernon Price, an acquaintance from San Antonio. He has two favorite methods; in both cases he first makes small slits in the venison, then inserts thin slices of garlic in them. He then sprinkles the meat with salt, pepper, paprika, and garlic salt. Then, if a large enough Texas-style (indirect heat) smoker is available, he barbecues the deer whole. If not, he cuts the deer into manageable portions and sears them over hot coals. He then tops the meat with sliced bell pepper and onion, wraps it in aluminum foil, and continues to roast the meat over the coals until done.

You can simulate the barbeque method by using a water smoker, or use the second method on a normal charcoal grill. In either case serve the vension with *Frijoles de olla* (p. 130), Guacamole (p. 144), picante sauce, and hot tortillas.

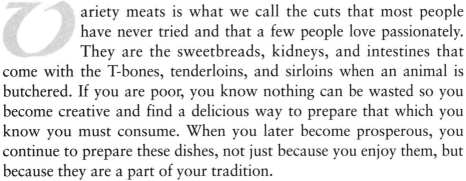

*V*ariety meats is what we call the cuts that most people have never tried and that a few people love passionately. They are the sweetbreads, kidneys, and intestines that come with the T-bones, tenderloins, and sirloins when an animal is butchered. If you are poor, you know nothing can be wasted so you become creative and find a delicious way to prepare that which you know you must consume. When you later become prosperous, you continue to prepare these dishes, not just because you enjoy them, but because they are a part of your tradition.

The main reasons many of us refrain from trying these items is that they sound objectionable and are quite different from what we are accustomed to eating. The fact is that, in most cases, variety cuts do take some getting used to, and, if one is not properly prepared for one's first experience, the results can preclude further experimentation. However, that so many who were raised on these items hold them is such great esteem is a testimony to the value of making the effort to appreciate their merits.

I am including some of the following recipes, not because I expect everyone to be enthusiastic about preparing them, but because their inclusion is important from a historical perspective. As the days of home butchering dwindle, these dishes are seldom found except on ranches and for special occasions. Soon they may be found only in the memories of old-timers.

HÍGADO CON CHILE VERDE

Liver with Green Chile

1½ pounds liver, thinly sliced
     Flour for dusting
¼   cup lard or olive oil
2   cups onions, chopped
1   clove garlic, minced
4   green chiles, stemmed,
     peeled, seeded, and
     chopped
1   15-ounce can tomatoes
     (not stewed)
1   tablespoon tomato puree
1   teaspoon oregano
3   tablespoons mild cider
     vinegar
½   teaspoon ground black
     pepper
½   teaspoon salt, or to taste

Dust the liver well with the flour; put the lard or olive oil in a skillet and sauté the liver over medium-high heat until it is well browned. Remove the liver to drain on absorbent towels.

Turn the heat to medium and cook the onions and garlic in the remaining lard or oil until the onions just begin to brown. Add the remaining ingredients and cook, stirring frequently, until the sauce is fairly thick.

Return the liver to the pan and cook until it is done, about 3 minutes. *Serves 4.*

MORCILLA

      Beef or pork parts that can
       include heart, liver,
       kidneys, intestines, and
       sweetbreads, as well as
       more ordinary cuts,
       totaling 2 to 3 pounds,
       cut into bite-size pieces
5   cloves garlic, minced
2   teaspoons oregano
1   tablespoon chile powder
½   tablespoon salt, or to taste
1   cup pig or cow blood
1   pork or beef stomach

Utilizing parts of the pig or beef that are normally ground into inexpensive sausage, *Morcilla* is one of the best examples of Mexican thriftiness. The meat is often wrapped in the *cuajo*, or stomach, from which rennet is made and steamed.

Mix together all the ingredients except the stomach; then fill the stomach with the mixture and tie it securely.

Steam the *Morcilla* for approximately 2 hours, or wrap it in damp gunnysack material and cook it overnight in a pit-barbecue. *Serves 4 to 6.*

MACHITOS
Wrapped Broiled Variety Meats

This is the dish you see cooking over mesquite coals next to *cabrito* in *cabrito* restaurants in the state of Nuevo León and in the border town of Nuevo Laredo. While almost never served in Tex-Mex restaurants, *Machitos* are an old-time *tejano* favorite. They look like giant irregular sausages threaded onto spits. A very old and traditional offering the dish arose from the basic need to use whatever food was available. The initial preparation is more involved in terms of locating the ingredients than most will want to tackle, but more and more prepared *Machitos* are turning up in Hispanic butcher shops throughout the Southwest.

1 *pound meat of kid or goat, boned and cut into 1-inch pieces*

1 *pound of goat or kid liver, kidney, and heart, cut into 1-inch pieces*

5 *cloves garlic*

½ *tablespoon oregano*

½ *teaspoon cumin*

¼ *cup mild vinegar*

1 *teaspoon salt*

2 *large sheets of the membrane from a kid or goat*

5–6 *feet of tripe or intestines*

Mix the kid or goat meat with the variety meats.

Grind together the garlic, oregano, and cumin in a *molcajete* or mortar and pestle and stir the mixture into the vinegar. Add the salt and toss the vinegar mixture with the meat.

Divide the seasoned meat into 2 batches and, using the membrane, roll each into a sausage-shaped package about 2 to 3 inches thick.

Wrap the tripe or intestines around the packages so that it completely covers them and secure with wood skewers.

Place the *Machitos* on skewers and roast over very slow mesquite coals until completely cooked, 30 to 45 minutes.

Serve with corn and/or flour tortillas, hot sauce, Guacamole (p. 144), and *Pico de gallo* (p. 112). *Serves 4.*

MOLLEJAS

Sweetbreads

1½ *pounds sweetbreads*
½ *cup lime juice*
¼ *cup olive oil*
  Salt to taste
½ *teaspoon* pequín *chiles, crushed*

Anyone who likes sweetbreads will appreciate this simple recipe.

Put the sweetbreads into a pot, cover them with water, bring them to a boil, and simmer them for 20 minutes. Remove the sweetbreads and place them in a marinade made by combining the lime juice, olive oil, salt, and crushed chiles for 1 hour.

Cook the sweetbreads over mesquite coals until done and serve with tortillas and Guacamole (p. 144). *Serves 4.*

RIÑONES

Kidneys

3 *tablespoons butter*
3 *tablespoons cooking oil*
4 *sheep or goat kidneys, sliced thin*
1 *cup onions, chopped*
¼ *cup green chiles, peeled, seeded, and chopped*
1 *15-ounce can tomatoes, drained, seeded, and chopped*
¼ *cup dry red wine*
¼ *cup tomato sauce*

This dish is popular with rural families that raise either sheep or goats.

Heat the butter and oil over medium-high heat in a large skillet.

Add and sauté the kidneys until browned; then remove them to a warm plate.

Add the onions and green chiles to the pan and cook them until soft and just beginning to brown.

Add the tomatoes, wine, and tomato sauce and stir well; then return the kidneys to the pan and simmer until the kidneys are cooked through, 5 to 10 minutes.

Serve the kidneys with Mexican Rice (p. 126) or Spanish Rice (p. 128). *Serves 4.*

Huevos
EGG DISHES

In Mexican-American home-style cooking egg dishes are among the cuisine's most prolific offerings. For this reason I have included only the most distinctive versions. Creative cooks have found uncountable ways to vary the preparation of this inexpensive source of protein. However, the vast majority are one version or another of eggs with a chile sauce, often combined with *chorizo*, ham, or bacon. When tomatoes are added, the dish becomes *Huevos rancheros*.

OJOS DE BUEY

Eyes of the Ox

14 *mild, dried New Mexico
    chiles*
2   *cloves garlic*
½   *tablespoon oregano
    Water*
2   *tablespoons olive oil*
½   *tablespoon vinegar*
1   *bay leaf*
½   *teaspoon salt, or to taste*

THE EGGS:

4   *corn tortillas
    Cooking oil*
8   *medium eggs*
1   *cup pitted black
    California olives, sliced*
2   *tablespoons parsley,
    minced*

In spite of its simplicity, Eyes of the Ox is one of the most evocative dishes from the early California ranchos. Eggs poached in a red chile sauce reminded the settlers of the solemn, unblinking eyes of their faithful workers and companions. Unpretentiously rustic but with a striking presentation, this dish is really special. I am surprised that I have not found it on restaurant menus. The dish was originally made in quantity in large skillets or clay *cazvelas*, but it can also be successfully cooked and served in individual shallow casserole dishes.

To make the sauce, first rinse the chiles and then place them in an oven preheated to 275 degrees and toast them for 5 to 10 minutes, or until just fragrant. Do not allow the chiles to burn or the dish will be ruined. Next, allow the chiles to cool and remove the stems, seeds, and as many of the veins as possible. Cover the chiles with boiling water and allow them to sit for 15 minutes.

Place the softened chiles in a blender with the garlic and oregano and 1¼ cups of the water in which the chiles were soaked. Blend the chiles for 1 minute. Add additional water to make a sauce somewhat thinner than a milk shake. There should be at least 4 cups in all.

Preheat your oven to 350 degrees.

Heat the olive oil in a large saucepan over moderate heat and add the blended chiles, vinegar, bay leaf, and salt. Simmer the sauce for 20 minutes at which point it should have the consistency of a medium-thick milk shake. If it is too thin, cook a while longer; if it is too thick, add some water. There should be about 3 cups sauce in all. When the sauce is done, remove the bay leaf.

Heat ⅓ to ½ inch of oil over medium-high heat in a small frying pan and "soften" the tortillas in the same manner as for enchiladas. They should be placed in the hot oil for just long enough to make them pliable, a few seconds at most if the oil is at the proper temperature. This can also be done by spraying the tortillas with PAM, wrapping them in a towel, and heating them in a microwave for 30 to 40 seconds.

If you are using individual serving plates or casserole dishes, place 1 tortilla in each of 4 of them and cover the tortillas with equal portions of the sauce. Break 2 eggs onto each plate or dish and place the dishes in the oven. The eggs should be properly set within 10 to 15 minutes.

The other alternative is to cook the eggs with the sauce in a large skillet. In this case the tortillas should be placed on the serving plates so that the eggs and sauce can be spooned onto them. With this method the eggs can be poached on top of the stove or in the oven. Using the stove top will be quicker, but it is a little more trouble since you have to keep the sauce warm enough to cook the eggs without allowing it to spatter them.

Garnish the plates with the olives and parsley and serve with Refried Beans (p. 132) and/or Mexican Rice (p. 126). *Serves 4.*

HUEVOS CON MACHACADO

Eggs with Beef Jerky

¼ *cup lard or olive oil*

½ *cup onion, chopped*

2 *cloves garlic, minced*

3 serrano *chiles, seeded and minced*

1 *tomato, seeded and chopped*

1½ *cups beef jerky, shredded, or 1 recipe* Machaca *(p. 156)*

8 *eggs, lightly beaten*

½ *teaspoon thyme*

½ *teaspoon ground black pepper*

1 *teaspoon salt, or to taste*

½ *cup cilantro, chopped*

This dish, which combines beef jerky or *Machaca* with eggs and chiles, is popular at all meals and in between. If you do not have access to a suitable beef jerky, use the recipe for *Machaca* in the chapter on "Basic Fillings."

Heat the lard or olive oil in a large frying pan over medium heat. Add and sauté the onion, garlic, and chiles until they are soft but not browned. Add the tomato and cook 1 additional minute.

Stir in the jerky; then add the eggs and the remaining ingredients and cook as for ordinary scrambled eggs.

Serve the eggs with flour tortillas, Refried Beans (p. 132), and your favorite hot sauce. *Serves 4.*

HUEVOS RANCHEROS

Ranch-style Eggs

This, the most famous Mexican egg dish on both sides of the border, is really only a generic name for fried eggs placed on a corn tortilla that has been cooked in a little oil until just medium crisp, then topped with a heated tomato sauce. Regional differences relate almost entirely to the type of sauce used. Of the three versions that follow the Texas-style version is the most common in Mexico and the Southwest, but, to me, the California version is the most interesting. Most recipes for *Huevos rancheros* do not call for cheese, but its addition adds an interesting dimension to the dish.

BASIC HUEVOS RANCHEROS

Heat the oil to a depth of about ⅓ inch in a small skillet over medium-high heat until it is very hot but not smoking. Using kitchen tongs place a tortilla in the oil and cook it for a few seconds on each side. The result should be just medium crisp, not crisp and hard like tortilla chips. Remove the tortilla to drain on absorbent towels. Cook each tortilla in the same manner. Then place the tortillas on each of 4 serving plates.

Remove most of the oil from the skillet and fry the eggs, 2 at a time. Because of the danger of salmonella the egg yolks should be well set and, better yet, cooked over easy.

Place the eggs on the tortillas and top them with the heated chile sauce and cheese. Serve with Refried Beans (p. 132), and/or Mexican Rice (p. 126) or Spanish Rice (p. 128). *Serves 4.*

Cooking oil
4 *corn tortillas*
8 *eggs*
Chile sauce (any of the red chile master sauces or red table sauces)
1 *cup Monterey Jack cheese, grated*

HUEVOS RANCHEROS ESTILO TEJAS
Texas-style Ranch Eggs

Make Basic *Huevos Rancheros* (p. 309) and top with 2 recipes of *Salsa ranchera* (p. 115) and cheese, if desired. *Serves 4.*

HUEVOS RANCHEROS ESTILO NUEVO MÉXICO
New Mexico-style Ranch Eggs

Make Basic *Huevos Rancheros* (p. 309) and top with 2 recipes of *Green Chile Sauce* (p. 111) and cheese, if desired. *Serves 4.*

HUEVOS RANCHEROS ESTILO CALIFORNIA
California-style Ranch Eggs

2 ancho *chiles, stems and seeds removed*

2 *14½-ounce cans tomatoes*

1¼ *cups juice from canned tomatoes*

2 *tablespoons olive oil*

½ *cup onions, thinly sliced*

2 *cloves garlic, minced*

1 *bell pepper, seeds and stems removed and thinly sliced*

½ *cup black California olives, pitted and sliced*

¼ *cup pimientos, chopped*

½ *tablespoon vinegar*

½ *teaspoon oregano*

½ *teaspoon salt, or to taste*

1 *cup Monterey Jack cheese, grated*

Make Basic *Huevos Rancheros* (p. 309) and top with the sauce at the left.

Soak the chiles in hot water for 15 minutes; then place them in a blender with 1 can of tomatoes and 1¼ cups of the tomato juice from the can. Blend the mixture for 1 minute, and then strain it into a bowl.

Remove the seeds from the tomatoes in the second can, chop the tomatoes, and add them to the chile-tomato mixture.

Heat a skillet over medium heat, add the oil, onions, garlic, and green pepper and cook until the onions are soft but not browned.

Add the reserved chile-tomato mixture and the remaining ingredients and continue to cook until the sauce is slightly thickened and the tomatoes are well cooked, about 5 to 10 minutes.

Spoon the sauce over the eggs and top with the cheese. *Serves 4.*

TORTILLA
Spanish-style Omelet

The reader may well ask why this dish is not in the section on tortillas? The easy answer is because it bears little resemblance to the thin bread which, in Mexican cooking, is called a tortilla. This recipe is for the early California version of the Spanish *Tortilla*, which is actually an unfolded omelet. The addition of green chile puts the New World stamp on this recipe, which was a supper favorite of the *californios*.

The recipe that follows is for 4 servings and calls for cooking all 4 portions together in 1 pan; however, it could be divided into 4 portions and cooked in smaller pans. It can also be prepared for 1 or 2 people by reducing the amounts of ingredients and size of the pan proportionately. If cooked in 1 pan, the finished omelet should be placed on a serving platter and cut into sections like a pizza.

In a medium-size skillet brown the *chorizo* in the olive oil over medium heat.

Add the potatoes, onion, and green chiles and continue cooking until the vegetables are soft but not browned.

When the vegetable mixture has cooled, remove it to a bowl and add the mixed eggs and salt and pepper.

Preheat your oven's broiler.

2 *tablespoons olive oil*

¼ *cup* chorizo, *crumbled*

4 *medium potatoes, sliced into ⅛-inch rounds and parboiled for 5 minutes or until just soft*

1 *medium onion, chopped*

½ *cup green New Mexico or Anaheim chiles, chopped*

8 *eggs, mixed together as for scrambled eggs*

Salt and pepper to taste

2½ *tablespoons olive oil*

½ *cup Monterey Jack cheese, grated*

1 *tablespoon parsley, minced*

In a very large skillet placed over medium heat, add the remaining 2½ tablespoons olive oil. When the oil is very hot but not quite smoking, add the egg and vegetable mixture, making sure it evenly covers the bottom of the pan. Turn the heat to between medium and low and continue to cook without touching the eggs until they are well set. The eggs should be browned on the bottom but not completely cooked on top. To finish them, place the skillet under the broiler until the top is just beginning to brown and the omelet is cooked through.

To serve, loosen the *Tortilla* from the pan with a spatula; then place a serving platter on top of the skillet. Invert the skillet so the platter is now on the bottom. This final move must be done quickly and firmly to keep the *Tortilla* flat. Immediately top with the cheese and parsley. *Serves 4.*

NUTRITION HINT: This dish can also be successfully prepared using egg substitutes, a little Parmesan cheese in place of the Monterey Jack, and by eliminating the *chorizo*—resulting in a very low-fat entrée.

Verduras
VEGETABLES

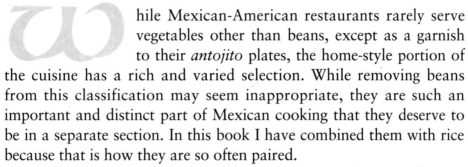

hile Mexican-American restaurants rarely serve vegetables other than beans, except as a garnish to their *antojito* plates, the home-style portion of the cuisine has a rich and varied selection. While removing beans from this classification may seem inappropriate, they are such an important and distinct part of Mexican cooking that they deserve to be in a separate section. In this book I have combined them with rice because that is how they are so often paired.

As in Mexican cooking, squash is the most popular ingredient in Mexican-American vegetable dishes, but there are many other vegetables used in simple but creative ways.

CALABACITAS OR COLACHE

Squash Stew

¾ *cup potatoes, chopped into*
⅓*-inch pieces*

2 *tablespoons olive oil*

¾ *cup onions, chopped*

2 *cloves garlic, minced*

¼ *cup New Mexico or*
Anaheim chiles, peeled,
seeded, and chopped, or
substitute 2–3 jalapeño
or serrano *chiles*

1 *large tomato, seeded and*
chopped

1 *tablespoon butter*

¾ *cup frozen or fresh corn*
kernels

3 *cups squash, chopped into*
⅓*-inch pieces*

½ *teaspoon salt, or to taste*

½ *teaspoon oregano*

4 *ounces Monterey Jack*
cheese, grated

¼ *cup cilantro, chopped*

Calabacitas, or "Little Squashes," is one of the most universally popular and versatile dishes in the Mexican-American repertoire. Incorporating the produce of carefully tended gardens, it can be as complicated or simple as the mood of the cook. Versions with a profusion of different ingredients really become vegetable stews, which were often called *Colache* in early California and other parts of the Southwest. The variety of chiles used denotes the dish's region with New Mexico and Anaheim predominant in New Mexico and *jalapeño* chiles or *serrano* chiles the rule in Texas. The type of squash used varies from region to region, but zucchini is a fine, usually available choice. The following all-vegetable version is a personal favorite. However, I encourage you to experiment with other ingredients or combinations since this is one of those dishes where the only rule is that it must contain *calabacita*.

Parboil the potatoes for 5 minutes or until they are barely soft.

Heat a skillet over medium-high heat, add the olive oil, and sauté the potatoes, onions, garlic, and *jalapeño* or *serrano* chiles (if used) until they are soft but not brown, about 5 minutes. Then add the tomato and continue cooking for 1 minute.

Turn the heat to medium, add the butter, then the corn, squash, and green chiles (if used), and oregano. Cook the vegetables, stirring often, until they are quite soft, about 15 minutes. Then add the salt.

Remove the skillet from the heat, add the cheese and cilantro, and stir just until the cheese is melted, then serve. *Serves 4.*

NUTRITION HINT: Traditionally, this dish is cooked until the vegetables are very soft. For reasons of nutrition or taste, you may prefer to serve them while still crisp. Because of the high moisture content of the squash and tomato this dish can be pre- pared with as little as a total of ½ tablespoon olive oil for those on restricted fat diets. The cheese can also be eliminated, or Parmesan or a smaller amount of feta cheese can be substituted.

NOPALITOS

Little Cacti

The nopal cactus is common throughout Mexico and in the southwestern United States. *Nopalitos* is a dish made from paddles of the nopal cactus from which the thorns have been removed and which have been cut into strips and cooked. Fresh nopal is widely available in southwestern grocery stores and in some Hispanic specialty markets elsewhere. It is also widely available canned.

Nopalitos are served either as a hot vegetable or as a salad. In both cases *Nopalitos* are boiled before being combined with the other ingredients. They are especially good with broiled chicken.

¾ *pound nopal cactus paddles*
2 *tablespoons olive oil*
1 jalapeño *chile, seeded and minced*
1 *medium onion*
3 *tomatoes, chopped*
½ *teaspoon salt, or to taste*
1 *tablespoon vinegar*

Remove the thorns from the cactus paddles and cut them into strips about 2 inches long by ¼ inch wide. Boil the cactus paddles until they are soft and the initial texture, which is unfortunately mucus-like, has disappeared and evolved into one much like that of cooked bell pepper.

Heat a medium-size saucepan over moderate heat, add the olive oil, *jalapeño* chile, and onion and cook until the onion is soft but not browned. Turn the heat to low, add the tomatoes, cooked cactus paddles, and salt and simmer, uncovered, for 30 minutes, adding the vinegar for the last 5 minutes of cooking. *Serves 4.*

QUELITES

Lamb's-Quarters

2 *tablespoons olive oil*

1 *onion, minced*

1 *clove garlic, minced*

¼ **pound** *chorizo (optional)*

2 *tomatoes, minced*

2 *pounds lamb's-quarters or*
   substitute spinach
   leaves, washed and the
   woody stems removed

¾ *cup water*

½ *teaspoon salt, or to taste*

¼ *teaspoon ground pepper, or*
   to taste

Early Hispanic settlers in the Southwest relied to a large extent on wild greens to satisfy their need for vegetables, particularly when traveling. *Quelites* (lamb's-quarters), wild mustard, and *verdolagas* (purslane) are but a few that were available, literally for the picking. Sometimes meat or *chorizo* was added to the vegetables.

Today, except in very rural areas, Mexican-Americans substitute spinach or something similar for the traditional wild greens. While the ingredients may have undergone change, the cooking method remains basically the same.

In a large pot or Dutch oven sauté the onion and garlic in the olive oil over moderate heat until the onion is soft but not browned.

Add the *chorizo*, if used, and brown, stirring to break up the meat.

Add the tomatoes and cook for 1 minute; then add the spinach and water. Cover and simmer for 5 minutes. Remove the top of the pot, add the salt and pepper, and continue cooking until the spinach reaches the desired consistency. *Serves 4.*

ELOTE CON CHILE VERDE

Corn with Green Chile

2 *tablespoons butter*

½ *cup onion, chopped*

½ *cup green chile, peeled,*
   seeded, and chopped

1½ *cups fresh corn, or*
    substitute frozen corn

1 *can creamed corn*

½ *teaspoon ground pepper*

½ *teaspoon salt, or to taste*

Melt the butter in a large saucepan over medium heat and sauté the onion until it is soft but not browned, about 5 minutes.

Add the green chile and cook for 2 more minutes. Add the remaining ingredients, bring to a boil, and simmer until the fresh or frozen corn kernels are soft. *Serves 4.*

POSOLE SIDE DISH

Posole is often served in place or even with rice and beans to accompany entrées and combination plates. When it is to be served as a side dish instead of as a stew, only enough meat is added during the cooking process to flavor the *posole*.

Soak the *posole* in water to cover overnight. The next day, drain and discard the soaking water. Place the *posole* in a pot and cover it with water by about 3 inches. Bring the water to a boil, add the remaining ingredients, then simmer, partially covered, until the *posole* is tender, about 45 minutes to 1 hour. Remove the lid from the pot and continue to cook until nearly all the liquid has evaporated.

Serve the *Posole* Side Dish with entrées or combination plates. *Serves 4.*

1¼ cups white or yellow
     posole
     Water
½ *cup onion, chopped*
2 *cloves garlic, minced*
1 *teaspoon oregano*
1 *bay leaf*
1 *teaspoon salt*
2 *ounces pork, diced*
½ *teaspoon ground black*
     pepper

MEXICAN-STYLE HASHED BROWN POTATOES

I first had this recipe on a ranch in Arizona and suggest you try it the next time you decide to prepare hashed brown potatoes of any sort. If you reduce the amount of potatoes by 1 cup and add 2 cups of diced squash, the dish becomes a fine accompaniment to broiled meats and poultry.

After you have peeled and chopped the potatoes, soak them in cold water for 10 to 15 minutes; then rinse them to remove the excess starch.

Heat a large frying pan over medium to medium-high heat, add the oil, and when it is very hot but not smoking, add all the ingredients. Cook, stirring often, until the potatoes are tender and well browned, about 10 to 15 minutes. *Serves 4.*

3¼ *cups potatoes, peeled and*
     chopped into ¼-*inch*
     pieces
¼ *cup cooking oil*
1 *cup onions, chopped*
1 *cup green chiles, seeded*
     and chopped
3 *cloves garlic, minced*
½ *teaspoon salt, or to taste*
½ *teaspoon ground black*
     pepper

TOSTONES

Fried Potatoes in Chile Sauce

1 recipe Basic New Mexico
    Chile Sauce with Whole
    Chiles (p. 166) or Basic
    New Mexico Chile
    Sauce with Chile
    Powder (p. 167)
4 potatoes, cut crosswise into
    ½-inch slices
    Oil for frying

This dish is a paragon of rustic simplicity. The rich flavors of the chile sauce marry well with the crisp fried potatoes to make an earthy accompaniment to roast meats.

Place the sauce in a large pot and heat it over low heat.

Meanwhile, place the cut potatoes in cold water for 10 minutes; then rinse them well to remove the excess starch.

Put the oil in a skillet to a depth of ¾ inch and heat over medium-high heat. When the oil is hot enough so that a drop of water sputters instantly, add and fry the potatoes to a golden brown in small batches.

Place the potatoes in the chile sauce and simmer for 3 minutes. *Serves 4.*

NUTRITION HINT: To drastically reduce the amount of fat without materially affecting the dish, roast the potatoes rather than frying them. To do this, first preheat your oven to 425 degrees; then toss the potatoes in 2 tablespoons olive oil and place them in 1 or 2 greased iron skillets (the potatoes should be flat in 1 layer). Add ½ cup water to the oil left after tossing the potatoes and pour it into the skillet(s). Add enough water to come halfway up the potatoes, and place the skillet(s) in the oven. Cook for ½ hour, then turn and continue to cook for 15 minutes. Remove the skillet(s) and allow to cool 3 to 5 minutes; then add the chile sauce and toss.

Postres y Dulces
DESSERTS AND SWEETS

exican-American desserts are based on Mexican favorites, which, in turn, are derived from a combination of Indian and Spanish cooking styles and ingredients, although unlike *antojitos*, Mexican-American desserts tend to be influenced more by the Spanish portion of the equation. This is particularly true with the flans, *natillas,* and other custards which are such an important part of the cuisine. This is not to say that there were not original contributions made to the Mexican-American dessert repertoire on this side of the border, but most of them relate to subtle nuances and to simplifications due to the need to substitute or do without certain ingredients. The frequent use of condensed milk is an example of this. Whatever the influences on these desserts may be, the results are nevertheless unique and delicious.

PANOCHA
Sprouted Wheat Flour Pudding

⅔ *cup brown sugar*

½ *cup water*

2 *cups (about 14 ounces)*
   panocha

⅓ *cup unbleached white*
   flour

½ *teaspoon cinnamon*

2 *tablespoons melted butter*

1⅓ *cups water*

The ingredients for this dish do not sound particularly promising, but I can assure you that the results are sensational, especially when served with vanilla ice cream, yogurt, or sweetened whipped cream.

Panocha is flour that is made from sprouted wheat, which has a naturally sweet, rich flavor. It is easily obtainable from Rancho Casados Farms by mail (see the Appendix).

Heat the brown sugar in a skillet over medium to low heat until it is just melted. Watch it carefully to make sure it does not scorch. When it is melted, add the ½ cup water and stir until the mixture is completely liquified.

Meanwhile, mix the *panocha*, white flour, and cinnamon. Add the butter and stir to make sure it is well mixed into the dry ingredients. Add the reserved sugar mixture and the 1⅓ cups water. The result will be a thin batter.

Preheat your oven to 350 degrees.

Place the pudding mixture in a baking dish, cover, and bake for 1 hour and 15 minutes to 1½ hours, stirring occasionally. The pudding is done when it is brown and well thickened.

Serve with vanilla ice cream, yogurt, or sweetened whipped cream. Irish cream liquor turns this into a really elegant dish. *Serves 4.*

BISCOCHITOS

Aniseed Cookies

Often spelled *Bizcochitos* these delicious cookies are a Christmas tradition in New Mexico. Although customarily made of lard, which gives them a flaky texture and rich rustic taste, I think the combination of shortening and butter called for in this recipe is just as rich while reducing the saturated fat. If you are a stickler for tradition and not concerned with the fat, use lard. In any case the result is very much like a combination of butter cookies and shortbread. *Biscochitos* can be made into any shape, from plain round to fancy cutouts.

¼ *cup shortening*
¼ *cup butter*
½ *cup sugar*
1 *egg*
¾ *teaspoon aniseed*
1 *tablespoon brandy*
1½ *cups flour*
1 *teaspoon baking powder*
¼ *teaspoon salt*
¼ *cup sugar*
½ *teaspoon cinnamon*

Preheat your oven to 350 degrees.

Cream together the shortening, butter, sugar, egg, aniseed, and brandy. The best way to do this is with an electric mixer or food processor fitted with a metal blade.

In a separate bowl mix together the flour, baking powder, and salt; then gradually add it to the sugar mixture. The resulting dough should be similar to pie crust.

Chill the dough for ½ hour; then roll it out to ¼ inch thick or a little thinner. The thinner they are the crunchier they will be. Cut the dough into whatever shapes you like and place them on an ungreased cookie sheet.

Mix together the remaining sugar and cinnamon and using about half of it, dust the top of the cookies.

Bake the cookies for 15 minutes or until they are firm to crisp and just beginning to brown.

Remove the cookie sheet and dust the cookies again with the remaining sugar-cinnamon mixture. Allow the cookies to cool and serve. *Makes 1 dozen or more, depending on the size.*

NATILLAS

Custard

4 *eggs, separated*

¼ *teaspoon salt*

5 *cups milk*

3 *tablespoons cornstarch*

½ *cup plus 2 tablespoons sugar*

¼ *teaspoon cinnamon*

½ *teaspoon vanilla*

This simple custard dish is very popular in New Mexico, where it is made two ways. Either the beaten egg whites are poached and the custard is placed on them like a French "floating island," or they are folded into the custard. To me the first alternative is the more interesting.

Traditionally, in the small villages of New Mexico condensed milk was used because of a shortage of fresh milk, but today that is not the case. In fact, some cooks will add whipping cream or half-and-half to the whole milk to make an even richer dessert. Also, most older recipes call for flour to assist the egg yolks in thickening the custard. However, cornstarch does a better job and does not impart a starchy taste to the dish.

If you intend to make the "floating island" alternative, beat the egg whites with the salt and just before they form stiff peaks add 2 tablespoons sugar. Continue beating until the mixture is stiff and glistens. If you intend to fold the whites into the custard, wait until after it has been made and cooled to beat the whites.

If you are making the "floating island" alternative, you must now poach the egg whites. Heat the milk in a skillet until it just barely simmers and add the beaten whites in large spoonfuls. The whites will puff up and be poached on one side in 1 or 2 minutes. Turn them and poach on the other side; then remove them to a plate to cool. Reserve 4 cups of the milk. If you plan to fold the whites into the custard, scald the milk. In either case allow the milk to cool.

In another bowl mix the cornstarch, sugar, and cinnamon; add the egg yolks and continue mixing. When the milk has cooled, beat it into the yolk mixture a little at a time until well incorporated.

You can cook the custard either in a saucepan or a double boiler. The danger here, as with all custards, is that the yolks will turn into scrambled eggs rather than thicken the sauce. The trade-off is that using a saucepan is faster, but the higher the heat, the more likely an unfortunate outcome. The double boiler method takes longer, but it is a much safer choice.

In either case heat the custard, stirring constantly, but do not let it boil. Continue cooking the custard until it is well thickened and easily coats a spoon. This should take 15 to 30 minutes.

When the custard is done, remove it from the heat and stir in the vanilla. Continue to stir the custard for 1 or 2 minutes since it will continue to cook. Allow the custard to cool, stirring occasionally.

When the custard has cooled, either pour it onto the poached egg whites or fold the beaten whites into it, depending on which method you chose. Chill the completed dish in the refrigerator for at least 3 hours before serving. *Serves 4.*

JIRICALLA

Custard Dessert

6 *eggs, separated*
3 *cups milk*
1 *cup sugar*
¼ *teaspoon cinnamon*
⅛ *teaspoon nutmeg*
⅔ *cup Masa Harina*
⅓ *cup confectioners' sugar*

This is a California version of cooked custard adapted from Ana M. Bégué de Packman's *Early California Hospitality*. It uses corn *masa* as the thickener. She says the name was invented by the *californios* and describes children, upon hearing that the dish was ready, yelling, "*Come y calla!*" ("Eat and shut up!")

Preheat your oven to 350 degrees.

Beat the egg yolks and add the milk, sugar, cinnamon, and nutmeg.

Beat the Masa Harina into the milk mixture.

Heat the milk and egg mixture over low heat, keeping it just below a boil and stirring constantly in order to keep the eggs from scrambling. Cook until the mixture thickens into a custard, about 10 minutes; then pour the mixture into a medium-size soufflé dish or loaf pan.

Beat the egg whites to soft peaks and spoon them on top of the custard. Sprinkle the custard with the confectioners' sugar and place it in the oven to set the egg whites into a meringue, about 20 to 25 minutes.

Allow the custard to cool and serve. *Serves 4.*

CAPIROTADA

Bread Pudding

Capirotada is a bread pudding that is served all over Mexico and in Mexican-American homes, particularly at Easter. This is by far the best version of this easily prepared dish I have ever tried.

Preheat your oven to 350 degrees.

Tear the bread into small pieces, place them on a baking sheet, and bake until toasted but not browned, about 3 to 5 minutes.

Place the white and brown sugar in a skillet and heat it over moderate heat. When the sugar begins to melt, turn the heat down and continue to cook until it is just melted.

Meanwhile, mix together the water, apple juice, brandy, melted butter, cinnamon, cloves, and salt.

When the sugar has melted, remove the skillet from the heat and slowly stir in the water mixture. If pieces of the sugar form lumps and do not dissolve, stop adding the liquid, replace the pan on low heat, and continue stirring until they do. Stir in the remaining liquid and set aside.

Place the bread in a baking dish just large enough to hold it in two layers. Put down one layer of bread, then sprinkle on half of the nuts and raisins. Add half of the apple slices, brush on half the sour cream, and sprinkle on half of the grated cheese. Repeat the process with the reserved ingredients.

Finally, pour the caramelized sugar mixture over all the ingredients, making sure it saturates everything in the dish. Bake, covered, for 30 minutes, remove the dish, and allow to cool slightly before serving. The dish can be made ahead and reheated. *Serves 4.*

8 ounces bread, crusts trimmed

½ cup white sugar

½ cup brown sugar

2 cups water

¼ cup apple juice

¼ cup brandy

2 tablespoons butter, melted

1 teaspoon cinnamon
  Pinch ground cloves

¼ teaspoon salt

½ cup pine nuts, or substitute pecans or blanched, slivered almonds

½ cup raisins

2 apples, peeled and sliced very thin

½ cup sour cream

1¼ cups Monterey Jack cheese, grated

PAN DULCE
Sweet Bread

DOUGH:

- ⅔ *cup milk*
- 2 *tablespoons lard or shortening*
- 2 *tablespoons butter*
- 2 *eggs, beaten*
- ⅓ *cup milk*
- 1 *package or approximately 2½ teaspoons dry yeast*
- ½ *teaspoon sugar*
- 4½ *cups flour*
- ½ *cup sugar*
- 2 *tablespoons brown sugar*
- ½ *teaspoon cinnamon*
- ½ *tablespoon salt*

TOPPING:

- ¾ *cup flour*
- 3 *tablespoons brown sugar*
- 3 *tablespoons sugar*
- ½ *teaspoon cinnamon*
- ¼ *cup butter*
- 2 *egg yolks*
- ¾ *teaspoon vanilla*

One version or another of *Pan dulce* is found in Mexican-American communities from California to Texas.

Heat the ⅔ cup milk just enough to melt the lard or shortening and butter; then allow the mixture to cool to room temperature. At this point stir in the beaten eggs.

Heat the ⅓ cup milk until it is just room temperature and stir in the yeast and ½ teaspoon sugar. Allow the mixture to sit until bubbles form on the surface, about 10 minutes; then stir it into the milk and egg mixture.

Meanwhile, mix together the flour, ½ cup sugar, 2 tablespoons brown sugar, the cinnamon, and the salt. Next, stir in the yeast and milk and egg mixture to make a medium dough, one that is not too damp or too dry, adding flour or water as needed.

Knead the dough for 5 to 10 minutes or process it in a food processor for 40 seconds. Lightly grease the dough, place it in a dish, cover it with a damp towel, and allow it to rise until doubled in size, about 1 to 1½ hours.

While the dough is rising cream together the topping ingredients.

After the dough has risen, divide it into 16 balls; then roll them into circles about 3 inches in diameter and place them on baking sheets. Brush each dough circle with a mixture of 1 egg white and 2 tablespoons water; then cover them with a thin layer of the topping. At this point you may leave the topping as is or cut designs such as parallel lines into it with a thin knife. Next, drape a damp towel over the rolls and allow them to rise until doubled in size, 30 to 40 minutes.

Bake the breads in an oven preheated to 375 degrees until done, about 20 minutes. *Makes 16 breads.*

ARROZ CON LECHE
Rice with Milk

This simple pudding is a clever way to make a lot of dessert at very little cost.

Bring the water to a boil in a large pot, add the rice, cover, and turn the heat to very low. Cook the rice for 20 minutes; then remove the top. If there is any water remaining in the pot, allow it to evaporate. Set the rice aside.

In a saucepan bring the evaporated milk and milk to a boil, stir in the sugar and cinnamon, and simmer for 5 minutes. Remove the pan from the heat, add the vanilla, and allow to cool for 15 minutes.

Preheat your oven to 350 degrees.

Place the egg yolks in a small bowl, and little by little beat in ½ cup of the milk mixture; then add and mix it into the rest of the milk-sugar combination.

Pour the milk mixture into the rice, add the raisins, and stir to mix well.

Pour the contents into a deep, buttered baking dish and place it in the oven. Bake for 1 hour to 1 hour and 15 minutes or until the liquid has been completely absorbed. Check the pudding fairly often during the last part of the baking since it can dry out and turn brown rather quickly. *Serves 4.*

4½ *cups water*
1 *cup rice*
1 *cup evaporated milk*
1 *cup milk*
⅔ *cup sugar*
⅛ *teaspoon cinnamon*
½ *teaspoon vanilla*
2 *egg yolks*
¼ *cup raisins*

BUÑUELOS

Spiced Fritters

THE DOUGH:

1 *cup flour*
¼ *teaspoon baking powder*
   Pinch salt
1 *egg*
1 *tablespoon butter, melted*
2 *tablespoons to ¼ cup water*
   Oil for frying

THE SYRUP:

1 *cup water*
1 *teaspoon aniseed*
½ *cup sugar*
½ *cup light brown sugar*
¼ *teaspoon cinnamon*

THE TOPPING:

2 *tablespoons sugar*
1 *teaspoon cinnamon*

Buñuelos are very much like Indian Fry Bread (p. 104) but more sophisticated. They puff like *Sopaipillas* (p. 105) and are served with a light syrup, dusted with sugar and cinnamon, or sometimes just the sugar and cinnamon without the syrup, particularly in Texas.

To make the dough, mix together the flour, baking powder, and salt; then beat in the egg, butter, and water until the dough holds together but is not sticky. A food processor performs this task easily. Allow the dough to rest for 15 minutes.

To make the syrup, bring the water to a boil with the aniseed, stir in the ½ cup sugar and ½ cup brown sugar, and cinnamon, and simmer for 5 minutes.

To form the *Buñuelos,* divide the dough into 6 equal portions and roll it into balls. Roll the balls out as thin as possible, as you would for flour tortillas.

To cook the *Buñuelos,* heat oil in a deep fryer to 375 degrees; then carefully place a piece of shaped dough in the deep fryer. It will puff immediately like a *sopaipilla* or fry bread. Allow it to cook until browned on one side, then turn and brown on the other side. Remove it to drain on absorbent towels.

When all the *Buñuelos* have been fried, spoon some of the syrup over them, dust with the sugar-cinnamon mixture, and serve immediately. *Serves 6.*

TAMALES DULCES

Sweet Tamales

Sweet Tamales can be made with any combination of fruits or jams that you like; and some cooks add nuts. They make a very nice snack at tea or supper time.

Place the corn husks in a pot, cover them with boiling water, and allow them to steep, covered, for ½ hour.

Mix the dry ingredients together; then add the water to make the dough. The dough should not be quite as damp as that used in meat tamales because you will be adding the preserves.

Beat the lard with an electric mixer until it is light and fluffy, 2 to 3 minutes.

Beat in the dough, a little at a time; then beat in the strawberry preserves.

Spread 2 to 3 tablespoons of the dough on a corn husk and then roll it up. If the husk is large and pliable enough, you may be able to fold over each end to seal it; if it isn't, tie the ends with string.

Steam the tamales for 1½ hours or until the dough is set and does not stick to the husks. *Serves 4.*

Dried corn husks
4 *cups Masa Harina*
½ *tablespoon salt*
1 *teaspoon baking powder*
½ *cup sugar*
1½ *cups water*
1½ *cups lard*
1½ *cups strawberry preserves*

EMPANADAS

Turnovers

THE DOUGH:

4 *cups flour*
½ *tablespoon salt*
1 *tablespoon sugar*
¾ *cup shortening*
¼ *cup lard*
¼ *cup butter*
  Ice water

Empanadas are pastry turnovers filled with a variety of items ranging from meat to fruit. When *Empanadas* are made without a sweet filling, they are more of a snack or entrée than a dessert. This type of turnover seems to be more common in Mexico than in Mexican-American cooking. Small *Empanadas* are called *Empanaditas,* which are often deep-fried instead of being baked.

Mix the flour, salt, and sugar together; then cut in the shortening, lard, and butter until the ingredients become a coarse-grained mixture. A food processor fitted with a steel blade performs this job well—just be sure not to overprocess.

Add only enough ice water to make a moist dough; then wrap it in plastic wrap and chill it in the refrigerator for 20 to 30 minutes.

When you are ready to make the *Empanadas*, remove the dough, divide it into 2 pieces, and roll it between ⅛ inch and ¼ inch thick. Cut the dough into circles 5 to 6 inches in diameter.

FILLINGS:

The most popular commercial filling for *Empanadas* is probably pumpkin pie filling. Other traditional fillings include mixtures of fresh or dried fruits and nuts. To fill the above dough recipe, you will need about 2 cups or slightly less of one of the following:

Pumpkin pie filling.

Dried fruits, including apples, apricots, raisins, dates, figs, peaches, and pears mixed with either pine nuts or almonds. Plump the fruits by soaking them for 15 minutes in hot water, or, if you feel extravagant, substitute brandy. Add some cinnamon and cloves to taste.

Fresh fruit such as apples, peaches, and pears mixed with nuts and raisins, plus some cinnamon and cloves.

Apple pie filling.

Picadillo II (p. 149) with some dried fruit and nuts added.

Place about 2 tablespoons of filling in the center of each circle, moisten the edges with water, and fold the circles together to create the turnovers. To seal the edges, press them together with the tines of a fork. The dough should produce about 1 dozen turnovers.

To make *Empanaditas,* cut the dough into circles 3 to 5 inches in diameter.

To cook the *Empanadas*, place them on a lightly greased baking sheet and bake them in an oven preheated to 375 degrees for 20 to 25 minutes or just until they are lightly browned.

If you want to fry the *Empanadas* or *Empanaditas*, heat the oil in a deep fryer to 375 degrees and fry them until brown and crisp. *Makes about 1 dozen.*

FLAN

Caramel Custard

CARAMEL SAUCE:

⅔ *cup sugar*
¼ *cup water*

CUSTARD:

4 *eggs plus 2 additional yolks*
½ *cup sugar*
2 *cups heavy or whipping cream*
½ *teaspoon vanilla*

This most famous of Spanish desserts deserves a place in any book on Mexican cooking. Over the years, I have tried many recipes for flan but have not found one any better than the recipe I used in my book *El Norte: The Cuisine of Northern Mexico*, so I am repeating it. It is especially good if you are able to use eggs from range-fed chickens since they are far richer than the super-market variety.

To make the caramel sauce, melt the sugar in a medium-size skillet over moderate heat; then add the water, a little at a time, stirring constantly. Be careful since the water will spatter when it hits the sugar. Cook the mixture for a few minutes until it turns a deep caramel color. Pour the mixture into a flan or pie pan and swirl it to coat the bottom until it begins to set, about 2 minutes.

To make the custard, beat the eggs and sugar together until well combined. Meanwhile, heat the cream until it is hot but not quite boiling. Allow it to cool for a few minutes, beat it into the egg mixture a little at a time, and then add the vanilla.

Pour the custard mixture into the caramelized pan and place it in a larger pan filled with enough warm water to come halfway up the side. Place both pans in an oven preheated to 350 degrees.

Bake for 45 minutes or until the custard is set, lightly browned, and a knife, when inserted, comes out clean. Remove the flan from the oven and allow to cool. Refrigerate for at least 4 hours or overnight.

To unmold, loosen the custard by passing a knife around the edges of the pan, then carefully invert onto a serving platter. *Serves 4.*

APPENDIX
Mail-Order Sources for Ingredients

Penderey's Spices
304 E. Belknap
Fort Worth, TX 76102
(800) 533-1870

Los Chileros
P.O. Box 6215
Santa Fe, NM 87502
(505) 471-6967

The Chile Shop
109 E. Water
Santa Fe, NM 87501
(505) 983-6080

Santa Cruz Chili & Spice Co.
P.O. Box 177
Tumacacori, AZ 85640
(602) 398-2591

Casados Farms
P.O. Box 1269
San Juan Pueblo, NM
87566
(505) 852-2433

GLOSSARY

Achiote: Seed from the annatto tree, most often used in Yucatán-style cooking.

Adobo: A chile-based marinade or sauce.

Agave: Agave Americana. Botanical name for the maguey cactus from which tequila, *mescal,* and *pulque* are made.

Ajo: Garlic.

Albóndiga: Meatball.

Al carbón: Charbroiling, cooking with charcoal.

Al horno: Oven baked.

Al pastor: Cooking on a verticle spit, or "shepherd style."

Anaheim: In Mexican cooking this refers to the Anaheim pepper, now more accurately called New Mexican.

Ancho: The dried *poblano* chile.

Anejo: This can refer to either certain types of aged liquor or to a dry, crumbly cheese much like a cross between feta and Parmesan.

Annato: This refers to the tree (Bixa orellana) from which achiote, its seed, used extensively in the Yucatán, is taken.

Antojito: A snack.

Antojitos mexicanos: Corn- or tortilla-based Mexican specialties, including tacos, enchiladas, and tamales.

Arracheras: The word used in Mexico for skirt steak, or *fajitas.*

Arroz: Rice.

Asadero: A typical Mexican cooked cheese made from equal portions of fresh and sour milk.

Asar: To broil or roast.

Atole: Gruel made from cornmeal.

Bacalao: Dried codfish.

Barbacoa: Barbecued or pit-cooked meat; often refers to the head of a cow, sheep, or goat that has been cooked in this manner.

Bebidas: Drinks.

Biscochitos: Aniseed cookies.

Borracho: Drunk; cooked with liquor, wine, or beer.

Buñuelo: Fried thin bread; fritter.

Burrito: A filling wrapped in a large flour tortilla.

Burro: Short for burrito.

Cabrito: Unweaned goat, or kid.

Calabacita: Squash.

Calabaza: Pumpkin, gourd.

Caldo: Soup or broth.

Californios: California's original Spanish settlers.

Camarón: Shrimp.

Capirotada: Bread pudding usually served during Easter week.

Carne: Meat.

Carne adobada or **adovada:** Meat marinated or pickled in chile sauce.

Carne asada: Usually refers to broiled meat, but in the north of Mexico also alludes to a picnic or cookout where meat is broiled.

Carne de res: Beef.

Carne seca: Dried beef. See also *machaca*.

Cebolla: Onion.

Cerveza: Beer.

Ceviche: Fish cooked (chemically) by marinating in lime juice.

Chalupa: Boat or canoe; flat tortilla with toppings.

Chaquehue: *Atole* made from blue rather than white or yellow corn.

Chicharrones: Deep-fried pork rinds, which have recently become very popular in the United States.

Chicos: Similar to *posole* but made from dried corn that has been roasted and steamed in a *horno* rather than being treated with lime.

Chilaquiles: Tortilla chips heated with sauce, meat, and/or cheese.

Chile colorado: Red chile. Usually refers to *ancho* or New Mexico dried chiles or the stew made with them.

Chile rellenos: Green chile, stuffed, battered, and deep-fried.

Chile verde: Green chile or stew made from it.

Chilhuacle: The chile found almost exclusively in Oaxaca that is a principal ingredient of the region's renowned *mole negro*. It may be the world's most expensive chile.

Chimichanga: Fried burrito.

Chimiquito: Stuffed and fried flour tortilla. Rolled like a *flauta* or *taquito* rather than being wrapped like a burrito or *chimichanga*.

Chipotle: This refers to the *chile chipotle*, a *jalapeño* chile which has been smoked until dry. First made by pre-Hispanic Indians, it comes canned in *adobo* sauce or dried. Very hot, it has a distinctive smoky flavor.

Chorizo: Sausage made with pork, chile, and vinegar.

Cilantro: Coriander, or Chinese parsley.

Colache: A stew made of squash and other vegetables.

Comal: Iron griddle.

De árbol: This refers to the *chile de árbol*, a small, thin, very hot dried chile.

Dolomitic lime: *Cal* in Spanish, this is the mineral added to corn when making *nixtamal masa* to loosen the kernel's skin.

Ejote: String bean.

Elote: Fresh corn on cob.

Empanada: Baked turnover.

Empanadita: Small *empanada*.

Encebollada: A dish, often meat, covered with cooked onions.

Encharito: A huge enchilada made with a flour tortilla; a cross between an enchilada and a burrito.

Enchilada: Corn tortilla wrapped around a filling, sauced and usually garnished with cheese and baked in Mexican-American cooking.

Enfrijolada: A type of enchilada made with corn tortillas, refried beans, and cheese.

Ensalada: Salad.

Escabeche: Pickled. Often refers to meat or poultry stewed with vegetables and vinegar. Popular in the Yucatán.

Estofado: Stew.

Fajita: Skirt steak, called *arracheras* in Mexico's interior. Refers to the cut of meat not the way it is served.

Fideo: Nest of thin pasta.

Flan: Baked caramel custard.

Flauta: One large or two small corn tortillas, filled, rolled, and fried.

Frijoles: Beans.

Fritada: A stew, usually made with goat meat, which always contains some animal blood.

Fry bread: Indian fried bread usually found in New Mexico.

Garbanzo bean: Chickpea.

Gordita: An *antojito* made from the same dough as corn tortillas and shaped to about the size of a small pancake. They are usually cooked on a griddle but are sometimes deep-fried.

Guacamole: Mashed avocado.

Guajolote: Turkey.

Harina: Flour. Usually refers to wheat flour as in *tortillas de harina*.

Harina de maíz: Flour made from dried corn. Masa Harina is the brand name of the product made by Quaker.

Harina enraizado: Flour made from sprouted wheat; also called *panocha*.

Horchata: A soft drink usually made with melon and/or rice.

Horno: Oven. A type of beehive-shaped adobe oven found throughout New Mexico.

Huevo: Egg.

Jalapeño: Refers to the *jalapeño* chile.

Jamón: Ham.

Javelina: This refers to the collared peccary, a small wild pig found in the Southwest.

Jícama: Root plant with a texture and taste similar to a cross between an apple and a water chestnut.

Jitomate: Word for tomato most commonly used in Mexico's interior.

Kielbasa: A type of Polish sausage.

Leche: Milk.

Lima: Lime. In Mexico the word *limón* is usually used.

Limón: Literally lemon, but in Mexico where lemons are rarely found it almost always refers to the small tart Mexican lime.

Machaca: From the verb *machacar*, which means to pound or break something into small pieces; refers to the dried, shredded meat that is typical of Sonoran cooking. See also *carne seca*.

Maguey: The cactus plant (Agave Americana) from which tequila and *mescal* are made.

Maíz: Dried corn.

Mano: Implement used to grind corn and chiles on a *metate*.

Manteca: Lard.

Mariscos: Seafood.

Masa: Dough; usually refers to ground *nixtamal*, which is used to make tortillas and, with the addition of lard and broth, tamales.

Menudo: A soup or stew made from tripe and a cow's foot.

Mescal: A liquor distilled from the fermented juice of the maguey cactus.

Mesquite: The hardwood tree from which the Southwest's most popular cooking fuel comes.

Metate: Volcanic rock on which corn and chiles are ground.

Molcajete: Mortar made from volcanic rock.

Mole: Stew. Usually refers to sauce with chiles and chocolate.

Mole negro: The best known of Oaxaca's famous "seven *moles*."

Mollejas: Sweetbreads.

Morcilla: Pork mixed with the pig's blood and spices and steamed within the animal's stomach.

Mulato: In Mexican cooking parlance this refers to the *chile mulato*, a dark chile most famous for its use in *Mole poblano*.

Nachos: Tortilla chips that are heated after being topped with cheese, chiles, and other items.

Natillas: Custard.

Nixtamal: Hominy; corn soaked in lime. Used to make *posole* or ground into *masa*, or dough, to make tortillas.

Nopal: Leaf or paddle of the nopal cactus.

Nopalitos: Cactus paddles cut into small pieces.

Olla: Pot.

Olla podrida: Stew.

Pan: Bread.

Panocha: Sprouted wheat flour; a dessert made from it.

Parrilla: Can refer to a griddle, like a *comal,* but usually refers to a grill used for charbroiling.

Pasilla: Refers to the *chile pasilla*, a long, thin, and very dark chile. Often confused in California with the *chile ancho.*

Pequín: Refers to the *chile pequín,* a tiny oblong-shaped chile that is extremely hot.

Picadillo: Hash; ground meat filling.

Picante: Hot; spicy.

Pico de gallo: A relish made of *jalapeño* or *serrano* chiles, onion, tomato, and cilantro, which is a traditional accompaniment to *fajitas.*

Piloncillo: Cone made of raw sugar.

Piñon nuts: Pine nuts.

Pipián: Indian stew or fricassee thickened by its ingredients rather than by flour.

Plátano: Plantain. A banana with a heavy skin and texture common throughout Mexico and Latin America.

Poblano: Large fresh green chile originally from Puebla. The chile which, when dried, is called the *ancho* chile.

Pollo: Chicken.

Posole: Dish made from hominy.

Postre: Dessert.

Puchero: Stew.

Puerco: Pork.

Pulque: A type of beer made by fermenting the juice from the maguey cactus.

Quelites: Lamb's-quarters (greens).

Quesadilla: Corn or flour tortilla grilled with cheese.

Queso: Cheese.

Queso blanco: A fresh white cheese, often called *queso fresco*.

Queso fresco: See *queso blanco*.

Relleno: Stuffed.

Requesón: A fresh curd cheese often called *queso fresco* or *queso blanco*.

Ristra: String of dried chiles.

Sal: Salt.

Salsa: Sauce.

Sangría: Fruit and wine or liquor punch.

Sangrita: A drink made with orange juice and/or tomato juice and chiles. Usually drunk with tequila.

Sarsa: The old California name for *salsa picante*.

Serrano: Refers to the *chile serrano*.

Sopa: Soup.

Sopaipilla: New Mexico-style fried bread.

Taco: Corn or flour tortilla wrapped around a filling.

Tamal or tamale: Corn dough with lard steamed with a filling in a corn husk.

Taquito: "Little taco" made by deep-frying a corn tortilla that has been wrapped around a filling.

Té: Tea. Usually refers to an herbal tea.

Tejano: Texan. Often refers to the early Mexican settlers in Texas.

Tejolote: Refers to the pestel used to grind items in a *molcajete*.

Tepín: Refers to the *chile tepín*, which is similar to the *chile pequín*, except that it is round rather than oblong in shape.

Tequila: Liquor made with distilled juice from the maguey cactus.

Tomate: Tomato. Commonly used in northern Mexico rather than the word *jitomate*.

Tomatillo: A small green tomato-like plant related to the gooseberry. Sometimes called *tomate verde*.

Tortilla: Flat unleavened bread made with a dough of corn or wheat.

Tortillería: An establishment where tortillas are made and sold.

Tostada: Fried corn tortilla chips; fried corn tortilla with toppings.

Tostado: Fried corn tortilla with toppings.

Totopo: Southern Mexican term for tortilla chips.

Verdolagas: Purslane (greens).

BIBLIOGRAPHY

Abreau, Margaret. *Food of the Conquerors: Native Dishes of New Mexico.* Santa Fe, N.M.: Rudal Press, 1954.

Bégué de Packman, Ana M. *Early California Hospitality.* Fresno, Calif.: Academy Library Guild, 1952.

Castelló Yturbide, Teresa. *Presencia de la comida prehispanica.* Mexico City: Fomento Cultural Banamex, 1987.

Cortés, Hernán. *Hernán Cortés: Letters from Mexico.* Translated and edited by Anthony Pagden. New Haven, Conn.: Yale University Press, 1986.

De Barrios, Virginia B. *A Guide to Tequila, Mezcal and Pulque.* Mexico City: Editorial Minutiae Mexicana, 1988.

De Benitez, Ana M. *Cocina prehispanica.* Mexico: Ediciones Euroamericanas Klaus Thiele.

De León, Arnoldo. *The Tejano Community 1836–1900.* Albuquerque, N.M.: University of New Mexico Press, 1982.

Del Castillo, Richard Griswald. *The Los Angeles Barrio 1850–1890: A Social History.* Berkeley, Calif.: University of California Press, 1979.

Dent, Huntly. *The Feast of Santa Fe.* New York: Simon and Schuster, 1985.

Dewitt, Dave. *Foodlover's Handbook to the Southwest.* Rocklin, Calif.: Prima Publishing, 1992.

Dewitt, Dave, and Nancy Gerlach. *The Whole Chile Pepper Book.* Boston: Little, Brown and Company, 1990.

Dobie, J. Frank, ed. "In the Shadow of History." *Publications of the Texas Folklore Society* 15(1966): 137–141.

Farga, Amando. *Historia de la Comida en México.* 2d. ed. Mexico City: Litográfica México, 1980.

Fergusson, Erna. *Mexican Cookbook.* Albuquerque, N.M.: University of New Mexico Press, 1934.

Flores, Carlotta Dunn, with Susan Lyons Anderson. *Favorite Recipes: El Charro Cafe and the Story of Its Colorful Past.* Tucson, Ariz.: El Charro Cafe, 1989.

Graham, Joe S. "Mexican-American Traditional Foodways at La Junta De Los Rios." *The Journal of Big Bend Studies* 2(January 1990): 1–27.

Griggs, Josephine C., and E. N. Smith. *A Family Affair: A Few Favorite Recipes of Mrs. Griggs.* Las Cruces, N.M.: Bronson Printing, 1968.

Hardwick, William. *Authentic Indian-Mexican Recipes.* 1965. Reprint. Ft. Stockton, Tex.: William Hardwick, 1972.

Heizer, Robert F., and Alan F. Almquist. *The Other Californians: Prejudice and Discrimination under Spain, Mexico, and the United States to 1920.* Berkeley, Calif.: University of California Press, 1971.

Hughes, Phyllis. *Pueblo Indian Cookbook.* 2nd ed. Santa Fe, N.M.: Museum of New Mexico Press, 1977.

Keegan, Marcia. *Southwest Indian Cookbook.* Santa Fe., N.M.: Clear Light Publishers, 1987.

Lappé, Frances Moore. *Diet for a Small Planet.* New York: Ballantine Books, 1985.

McCall, George A. *Letters from the Frontier*. Philadelphia: J. B. Lippencott, 1868.

McGee, Harold. *On Food and Cooking: The Science and Lore of the Kitchen*. New York: Macmillan Publishing Company, 1984.

McMahan, Jacqueline Higuera. *California Rancho Cooking*. Lake Hughes, Calif.: The Olive Press, 1983.

Meek, Katy Comuñez. *The Authentic La Posta Cookbook*. Las Cruces, N.M.: Katy Comuñez Meek, 1971.

Miller, S. G. *Sixty Years in the Nueces Valley*. San Antonio, Tex.: Naylor Printing Co., 1930.

Mitchell, Janet. "Unwrapping the Truth about the Chimichanga." *Tucson Guide Quarterly* (Winter 1992): 156–158.

Moore, Joan, and Harry Pachon. *Mexican Americans*. 2d. ed. Englewood Cliffs, N.J.: Prentice-Hall, Inc., 1976.

Novo, Salvador. *Cocina Mexicana o Historia Gastronomica de la Ciudad de México*. 5th ed. Mexico City: Editorial Porrúa, 1979.

Officer, James E. *Hispanic Arizona, 1536–1856*. Tucson, Ariz.: University of Arizona Press, 1987.

Orozco, Fernando L. *La Conquista de México*. Mexico City: Panorama Editorial, 1983.

Parr, Leslie, ed. *Mexican California: An Original Anthology*. New York: Arno Press, 1976.

Peterson, Frederick A. *Ancient Mexico*. New York: The Putnam Publishing Group, 1959.

Peyton, James. *El Norte: The Cuisine of Northern Mexico*. Santa Fe, N.M.: Red Crane Books, 1990.

Pitt, Leonard. *The Decline of the Californios: A Social History of the Spanish-Speaking Californians, 1846–1890*. Berkeley, Calif.: University of California Press, 1970.

Recinos, Adrain, ed. *Popol Vuh: Las Antiguas Historias del Quiche*. Mexico: Cultura Economica, 1952.

Ricardo, Don. *Early California and Mexico Cook Book*. Alhambra, Calif.: Borden Publishing Company, 1968.

Rivas, Heriberto García. *Cocina prehispanica mexicana*. Mexico City: Panorama Editorial, 1991.

Sahagún, Bernardino de. *Historia General de las Cosas de Nueva España*. Mexico City: Editorial Porrúa, 1956.

Santamaria, Francisco. *Diccionario de Mejicanismos*. Mexico City: Editorial Porrúa, 1992.

Southworth, May E. *One Hundred & One Mexican Dishes*. San Francisco and New York: Paul Elder and Company, 1906.

Sowell, Thomas. *Ethnic America: A History*. New York: Basic Books, 1981.

Strehl, Dan, ed. and trans. *The Spanish Cook: Selected Recipes from El Cocinero Español by Encarnacion Pinedo*. San Francisco: Weather Bird Press, 1992.

Taylor, Paul Schuster. *An American-Mexican Frontier, Nueces County, Texas*. 1934. Reprint. New York: Russell & Russell, 1971.

Verti, Sebastián. *Tradiciones mexicanas*. Mexico: Editorial Diana, 1991.

Weatherford, Jack. *Indian Givers*. New York: Fawcett Columbine, 1988.

Williams, Carey. *North from Mexico*. Philadelphia: J. B. Lippincott Company, 1949.

INDEX

Recipe citations are in **bold**.